A History of England
in 100 Places

Also by John Julius Norwich

Mount Athos (with Reresby Sitwell, 1966)
The Normans in the South (1967)
Sahara (1968)
The Kingdom in the Sun (1970)
A History of Venice: The Rise to Empire (1977)
A History of Venice: The Greatness and the Fall (1981)
Fifty Years of Glyndebourne (1985)
A Taste for Travel (1985)
The Architecture of Southern England (1985)
A History of Byzantium: The Early Centuries (1988)
Venice: A Traveller's Companion (1990)
A History of Byzantium: The Apogee (1991)
A History of Byzantium: The Decline and Fall (1995)
A Short History of Byzantium (1997)
The Twelve Days of Christmas (with illustrations by
Quentin Blake, 1998)
Shakespeare's Kings (1999)
Paradise of Cities: Venice in the Nineteenth Century (2003)
The Middle Sea: A History of the Mediterranean (2006)
Trying to Please (2008)
The Popes: A History (2011)

Edited by John Julius Norwich

Great Architecture of the World (1975)
The Italian World (1983)
Britain's Heritage (1983)
The New Shell Guides to Great Britain (1987–90)
The Oxford Illustrated Encyclopaedia of Art (1990)
The Treasures of Britain (2002)
The Duff Cooper Diaries (2005)
The Great Cities in History (2010)

A History of England in 100 Places

FROM
Stonehenge to the Gherkin

JOHN JULIUS NORWICH

JOHN MURRAY

First published in Great Britain in 2011 by John Murray (Publishers)
An Hachette UK Company

1

Text © John Julius Norwich 2011
Illustrations © Ed Kluz 2011

The right of John Julius Norwich to be identified as the Author of the Work has been asserted by
him in accordance with the Copyright, Designs and Patents Act 1988.

Illustrations by Ed Kluz

Maps drawn by Rosie Collins

Poem 'Ode to Electricity' by Hilaire Belloc reprinted by permission of Peters Fraser & Dunlop
(www.pfd.co.uk) on behalf of the Estate of Hilaire Belloc.

A CIP catalogue record for this title is available from the British Library

Hardback ISBN 978–1–84854–606–6
Trade paperback ISBN 978–1–84854–607–3
Ebook ISBN 978–1–84854–608–0

Typeset in Adobe Caslon by Servis Filmsetting Ltd, Stockport, Cheshire

Printed and bound by Clays Ltd, St Ives plc

John Murray policy is to use papers that are natural, renewable and recyclable products and made
from wood grown in sustainable forests. The logging and manufacturing processes are expected
to conform to the environmental regulations of the country of origin.

John Murray (Publishers)
338 Euston Road
London NW1 3BH

www.johnmurray.co.uk

For my grandchildren again –
in the hope that they will get as much fun
out of history as I have

Contents

Contents

Contents

Contents

TWENTIETH-CENTURY ENGLAND

Preface

I have spent the last half-century writing history of one kind or another, but although I once, many years ago, wrote a book about English architecture I have always somehow shied away from tackling the country itself. One reason, I suspect, was the amount of competition in the field. There are a thousand histories of England, ranging from the scholarly to the popular, the impartial to the tendentious, the consistently riveting to the utterly unreadable. The English furrow, in short, has been thoroughly ploughed already; how could I hope, with my own rather pathetic metal-detector, to find any further buried treasure?

Only, perhaps, by finding a completely different way to dig; and nothing but this prospect of a new approach could have finally persuaded me to conquer my fears and try my luck. The idea has been to choose 100 different sites, distributed as widely and as equally as possible throughout the country, each of which will serve as a milestone, marking or somehow symbolizing a great event; and the hope has been that a vaguely coherent history – fragmentary perhaps, episodic certainly, but a history none the less – will emerge.

But English history is long – particularly if you go back to Stonehenge – and 100, in this connection, seems a very small number. It was clear, then, that I could not attempt to cover the whole of Great Britain, but must limit myself strictly to England. It was sad indeed to have to give up Caernarfon Castle and the battlefields of Culloden and the Boyne, to name but three; but there was little choice. All I can do is gaze wistfully over our two immediate neighbours from Hadrian's Wall and Offa's Dyke, and shed a tear for all the lovely locations that got away.

Even with this limitation, the choice of sites has not been easy. Some were self-evident: Runnymede for example, and HMS *Victory* and the Tower of London; others – a Saxon church, or a village war memorial – were selected from any number of other candidates, perhaps for their relative unfamiliarity, or perhaps simply for their geographical location, since I have been at pains to spread the net as widely and evenly as I can. Despite my best efforts, I am fully aware that there are a disproportionate number in and around London, but this I fear is inevitable. I am also aware that by no means all the sites are in themselves particularly spectacular – this is in no sense a guidebook; each, however, tells its own story, and makes, I hope, its own contribution to the final picture.

And that picture is by no means exclusively political. History is also written in our landscape and our culture, in our science and our religion. I have tried to cover – insofar as the available space allows – all these, and also to trace the main changes over the centuries in our social and economic life. Have I found any of that buried treasure? I doubt it. Have I been absurdly over-ambitious? Very probably; but I have no regrets. The challenge has taught me a lot, and has been hugely enjoyable into the bargain. If my readers get half as much pleasure out of reading this book as I have had in writing it, I shall be more than adequately rewarded.

John Julius Norwich
Castle Combe, April 2011

List of Counties

NORTHUMBERLAND
Cragside
Fort of Housesteads, Hadrian's
Wall
Lindisfarne

NOTTINGHAMSHIRE
War Memorial, Lowdham

OXFORDSHIRE
Blenheim Palace
Great Coxwell Tithe Barn
Merton College, Oxford

SHROPSHIRE
Ironbridge

STAFFORDSHIRE
Etruria Hall, Stoke-on-Trent
Wightwick Manor,
Wolverhampton

SUFFOLK
Martyrs' Memorial, Bury St
Edmunds
Sutton Hoo
Wool Hall, Lavenham

SURREY
Hampton Court
Kew Palace
Runnymede

Sir Richard Burton's Tomb,
Mortlake
Tattenham Corner, Epsom Downs
Racecourse

TYNE AND WEAR
Jarrow Crusade Memorial

WARWICKSHIRE
Coughton Court

WEST MIDLANDS
Coventry Cathedral
Soho House, Birmingham

WILTSHIRE
Box Tunnel
Caen Hill Locks, Devizes
Old Sarum
Stonehenge

WORCESTERSHIRE
Church of St Lawrence, Evesham

YORKSHIRE
Captain Cook Memorial Museum,
Whitby
Fountains Abbey
Merchant Adventurers' Hall, York
Newby Hall
Towton Cross
Wilberforce House Museum, Hul

1. Stonehenge, Wiltshire
2. Flag Fen, Cambridgeshire
3. Colchester, Essex
4. Chedworth Roman Villa, Gloucestershire
5. Hadrian's Wall, Northumberland
6. Sutton Hoo, Suffolk
7. Lindisfarne, Northumberland
8. Bradwell-juxta-Mare, Essex
9. Offa's Dyke, Herefordshire
10. Battle Abbey, East Sussex
11. Hemingford Grey, Cambridgeshire
12. Appleby Castle, Cumbria
13. Canterbury Cathedral, Kent
14. Runnymede, Surrey
15. Merton College, Oxford
16. Church of St Lawrence, Evesham, Worcestershire
17. Middle Temple, London
18. Great Coxwell Tithe Barn, Oxfordshire
19. Ightham Mote, Kent
20. Merchant Adventurers' Hall, York
21. Fobbing, Essex
22. Eton College, Berkshire
23. Bodiam Castle, East Sussex
24. Wool Hall, Lavenham, Suffolk
25. Courthouse, Long Crendon, Buckinghamshire
26. Towton Cross, Yorkshire
27. Tower of London
28. Hampton Court, Surrey
29. Fountains Abbey, Yorkshire
30. Launceston Castle, Cornwall
31. Martyr's Memorial, Bury St Edmunds, Suffolk
32. Wingfield Manor, Derbyshire
33. Buckland Abbey, Devon
34. Globe Theatre, London
35. Raleigh Monument, East Budleigh, Devon
36. Coughton Court, Warwickshire
37. Battlefield of Naseby, Northamptonshire
38. Banqueting House, London
39. St Bartholomew's Hospital, London
40. Oliver Cromwell's House, Ely, Cambridgeshire
41. Eyam, Derbyshire
42. Milton's Cottage, Chalfont St Giles, Buckinghamshire
43. Woolsthorpe Manor, Lincolnshire
44. St Paul's Cathedral, London
45. Prime Meridian, Greenwich
46. Taunton Castle, Devon
47. Brixham Quay, Devon
48. Blenheim Palace, Oxfordshire
49. Pump Room, Bath
50. Ironbridge, Shropshire
51. Houghton Hall, Norfolk
52. New Room, Bristol
53. Brick Lane Mosque, London
54. Newby Hall, Yorkshire
55. Etruria Hall, Stoke-on-Trent, Staffordshire
56. Captain Cook Memorial Museum, Whitby, Yorkshire
57. Soho House, Birmingham
58. Cromford Mill, Derbyshire
59. Temple of Vaccinia, Gloucestershire
60. Caen Hill Locks, Devizes, Wiltshire
61. Kew Palace, Surrey
62. Coke Monument, Holkham, Norfolk
63. Dove Cottage, Grasmere, Cumbria
64. HMS *Victory*, Portsmouth, Hampshire
65. Wilberforce House Museum, Hull, Yorkshire
66. Peterloo Plaque, Manchester
67. Brighton Pavilion, Sussex
68. Old Sarum, Wiltshire
69. Tolpuddle Martyrs' Tree, Tolpuddle, Dorset
70. Copenhagen's Grave, Stratfield Saye House, Hampshire
71. Box Tunnel, Wiltshire
72. Albert Memorial, London
73. Deene Park, Northamptonshire
74. Mary Seacole Plaque, London
75. Down House, Kent
76. HMS *Warrior*, Portsmouth, Hampshire
77. Cragside, Northumberland
78. Stanley Grove School, Manchester
79. North Pier, Blackpool
80. Osborne House, Isle of Wight
81. Wightwick Manor, Wolverhampton
82. Sir Richard Burton's Tomb, Mortlake, Surrey
83. Lizard Marconi Wireless Station, Cornwall
84. Bateman's, East Sussex
85. British Motor Museum, Beaulieu, Hampshire
86. Epsom Downs Racecourse, Surrey
87. Lowdham, Nottinghamshire
88. Jarrow Crusade Memorial, Tyne and Wear
89. Fort Belvedere, Windsor, Berkshire
90. Heston, Middlesex
91. Churchill War Rooms, London
92. Coventry Cathedral
93. Bletchley Park, Buckinghamshire
94. Watford Gap Motorway Service Area, Northamptonshire
95. 20 Forthlin Road and 251 Menlove Avenue, Liverpool
96. Thatcher Plaque, Grantham, Lincolnshire
97. Greenham Common, Berkshire
98. National Theatre, London
99. The Mouth of the Channel Tunnel, Folkestone, Kent
100. The Gherkin, London

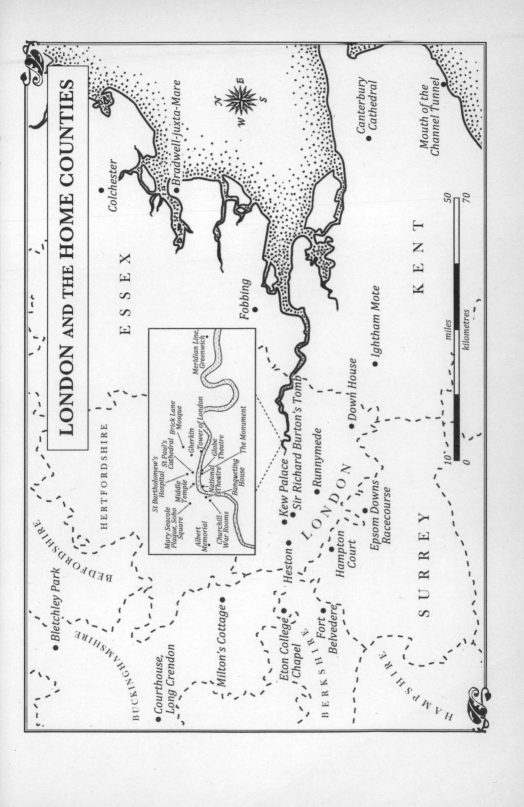

LONDON AND THE HOME COUNTIES

Prehistoric England

Introduction

*A*lthough this first section of our history is short, consisting of only two places, it covers by far the longest
period of time – some thirty centuries, from the Neolithic
Age of perhaps 3000 BC to the coming of the Romans. Over
such a period, and considering the paucity of our knowledge,
it is impossible to do more than generalize. Progress was inevitably made – in agriculture, in pottery, in carpentry and rough
metalwork – but it would have been painfully slow; our present
civilization probably advances in a week further than prehistoric man advanced in a millennium.

Geographically speaking, England was already much as it
is today, although most of it was thickly forested; a squirrel
could have travelled from the Severn to the Humber without
once touching the ground. As to the size of the population
we can only guess, but it is unlikely to have been more than a
million or so and perhaps substantially smaller. In the early
centuries they would all have been hunter-gatherers, semi-
nomadic and living in caves or primitive shelters in the forest.
Then, very gradually, they would discover the secrets of agriculture, and for the first time indulge in the luxury of a settled
habitation. The next step was a village, and so finally to a
town, though there were no towns worthy of the name until
long after the Roman invasion.

And what did these people leave behind? Not a lot. Apart from Stonehenge itself and other stone circles like it – the neighbouring one at Avebury and Stanton Drew in Somerset are the most important – and a number of long barrows and tumuli, mostly to be found in Wiltshire and Dorset, there is far too little to enable us to form a clear picture of these early inhabitants of our island. We should love to know more, for example, about their religions. On the Druids and their pre-occupation with oak trees and mistletoe we have the evidence of the Elder Pliny, who offers us a few unsubstantiated lines, and that's about all. With so few communications between the various settlements – though England's oldest road, the Ridgeway, ran between the Dorset coast and the River Thames – there would almost certainly have been countless other cults and beliefs, but we have no means of telling.

Where the selection of sites is concerned, Stonehenge was of course a foregone conclusion. Flag Fen we chose because it is as different as can be and is – to me at any rate – quite extraordinarily full of interest. It is also some two millennia later, belonging as it does to the Bronze Age rather then the Neolithic. Unlike Stonehenge, too, it is relatively little known, having been discovered less than thirty years ago. These two sites alone give, I know, hopelessly inadequate coverage of the earliest and most extensive period in our history, but there: we are limited to 100 altogether, and given the range and richness of what is to come, we simply can't afford any more.

I

Stonehenge
WILTSHIRE

Τhere are about 1,000 stone circles and henges – a *henge* simply means a Neolithic earthwork, normally without stones – in the British Isles; but none is so dramatic or impressive as Stonehenge, England's most revered ancient monument, which stands on a gentle hilltop just outside Amesbury in Wiltshire. There is in fact far more of it than meets the eye: the huge stone circle is only part of a massive ceremonial site encompassing most of the immediately surrounding land; traces of a second stone circle were discovered as recently as 2009. Not surprisingly, it is impossible to give it a precise date; the best scientific opinion puts it at 3000–2500 BC (though people went on fiddling with it for another 1,000 years after that), which makes it about the same date as the Great Pyramid. Admittedly, the pyramid has lasted longer; it still looks much as it did when it was first built – or would if you could eliminate the thousands of tourists – while Stonehenge (which also has tourists, and how) lacks about half its great stones. One of the countless enigmas that surround the site is what has happened to those that are missing; many of them seem to have disappeared completely. Could it be that after all that time a-building, the great monument was left unfinished?

And if so, why? It's possible, I suppose, that the missing

monoliths could have been removed, in order to be used for other purposes; but to dislodge and then to transport a four-ton hunk of rock is no easy task. And that leads us to another mystery, the one that always comes up in any conversation on the subject: how did those immense stones get there in the first place? In prehistoric times before there were roads, the only way to move them – having first freed them from the earth, presumably by levers – was to put them on huge rafts and float them down rivers; that was easy enough for the pyramid builders because they had the Nile almost on the doorstep, and anyway their stone mostly came from quarries close by. But the nearest river to Stonehenge is the Avon, nearly two miles away, and the huge bluestones that form the inner circle have been proved to originate in the Preseli Hills in Pembrokeshire, some 160 miles distant. Could they really have been loaded on to rafts on the coast of South Wales, sailed up the Bristol Channel, then floated *up* the comparatively narrow Rivers Wylie and Avon, with a difficult land crossing in between? Geoffrey of Monmouth, writing in the twelfth century, ascribes it all to Merlin, the wizard at the court of King Arthur – a theory that I sometimes think I prefer.

There was, of course, plenty of stone available much closer at hand – which makes this almost unbelievably difficult journey seem even more improbable. That is presumably why some geologists have come up with a new theory: that the stones are things called glacial erratics, which do not belong to the area in which they are found, having been transported there naturally by glaciers. In this case they would owe their present position to a terrifying phenomenon known as the Irish Sea Glacier, roughly fifty miles across, which swept down from the north millions – perhaps billions – of years ago.

And what was it all for? Here is yet another mystery. Forget all that stuff about Druids and mistletoe – the short answer is that we really don't know; and as the civilization that built the monument left no written records, we have to resort to guess-work. There is perhaps some clue in a stone known as the Heelstone, which stands away to the north-east, unfortunately almost touching the A344. To those standing inside the circle on Midsummer Day, the sun rises immediately above it. This, on the other hand, may easily be coincidental. One fact that seems moderately certain is that Stonehenge was, perhaps among other things, a burial ground: as recently as 2008, cremated bodies were found that could be dated to around 3000 BC, and burials seem to have continued for many centuries afterwards. Nor were they all of local people; isotope analysis has found the remains of one young boy of Mediterranean origin, while a metal-worker who died around 2300 BC (and has been nicknamed 'the Amesbury Archer') apparently hailed from what is now Bavaria.

Although it may not look like it, Stonehenge has been heavily restored on a number of occasions. We have only to compare the monument as it looks today with the innumerable eighteenth- and nineteenth-century watercolours to see how much work has been done. During the twentieth century, stones that had fallen over were re-erected, and several of the lintels – those that were meant to lie horizontally, supported by two uprights – have been replaced in their original positions, not without the help of generous quantities of cement. And there have been other 'improvements' too. When I first went there at the age of eight on a baking August day in 1938, my mother dressed me in a tiny pair of leopard-skin pants and I remember climbing all over the stones while she filmed me with what was then known as a ciné-camera. Alas, those days are over. The whole site was given a *cordon sanitaire* in 1977, and now the public is kept at a discreet distance away from the stones themselves, although you can still walk all the way round the circle. Even then, the fact that it nestles in the fork of two major roads is hardly conducive to your enjoyment.

No matter: Stonehenge still has its magic. Stay there a little while and let the atmosphere sink in; then, if you have time, go on to the great stone circle at Avebury, some twenty miles across Salisbury Plain to the north. It is thought to be even a little older than its more celebrated neighbour, and there is not really so much to see; but the surroundings are a good deal more salubrious and – since they include a rather pretty village – there is an admirable pub nearby with which to reward yourself when the day is over.

2

Flag Fen
CAMBRIDGESHIRE

Stonehenge, as its name implies, belongs to the Stone Age. Flag Fen, on the other hand, represents the Age of Bronze, which in England roughly covers the years 2100 to 750 BC. It must have been a worrying age to live in, particularly for a people principally engaged in agriculture and the rearing of livestock: the weather, which in Neolithic days had been comparatively warm and dry, was now deteriorating, all the time getting colder and with a steadily increasing rainfall. This would have been unpleasant wherever you lived; but in the fen country of East Anglia, where the ground is low, absolutely flat and in some places little more than a marsh, the increasing quantity of floods made it potentially disastrous.

It was also an age of change. Vast numbers of migrants were pouring in from mainland Europe, and recent research on the tooth enamel of bodies found in early Bronze Age graves has established the fact that a good many of them came from what is now Switzerland. (After the Alps, the Fens must have struck them as something of a contrast.) They brought with them what is now known to archaeologists as the *Glockenbeckerkultur*, because of the small bell-shaped beakers of pottery that they introduced; but they were also responsible for remarkable advances in metal-working techniques as well as for several new social customs, including the practice of individual burials rather than mass graves – as, for example, at Stonehenge – making them infinitely more informative from the archaeological point of view.

The settlement at Flag Fen was discovered as recently as 1982, largely because there was next to nothing to be seen on the surface. On investigation, however, the archaeologists found, perfectly preserved in the wetland, about a quarter of a million ancient timbers, all of them worked and shaped with tools, arranged horizontally in five very long rows. Together with another 60,000 verticals, they formed a causeway a kilo- metre or so long between Peterborough and the little town of Whittlesey. It is hard to date; but perhaps if we said around 1200 BC we should not be too wide of the mark.

What was this causeway for? Once again, it is difficult to say. It may have been a sort of defensive line, a border between the territory of one tribe and another; it may have been a means of getting herds of cattle across the fen; it may even have been both. About halfway across, however, it broadens out into an artificial island roughly the size of Wembley Stadium; and this island, it is believed, may have had some religious connotation. A large quantity of what seem to be votive offerings has been discovered. They include a gold ring, the more exciting because only one other of its period is known to exist; a scabbard decorated with what may be the earliest known example of Celtic art; and a superb collection of Bronze Age swords and daggers, many of them deliberately broken. One theory is that these were intended to assuage the obvious anger of whatever gods the fen people worshipped, in the hopes of being granted warmer and drier weather; but the jury is still out. And there have been plenty of other finds too, less valuable perhaps, but every bit as significant: also embed- ded in the mud were a set of shears in their original wooden case; a whole selection of metal-working tools; and the oldest wheel in England.

Fortunately, the swampy mud of the Fens is almost devoid of oxygen, which means that the timbers beneath it do not rot away as we might normally expect. The difficulty is that as soon as they are exposed to the air the rotting process begins; and on no account must they be allowed to dry out too quickly. This explains why, in the Preservation Hall, we can see some of the newly retrieved logs only through a thin and mist-like spray. Another effective method of timber conservation, also in use here, is that of so-called freeze drying: essentially freezing the wood so that all the moisture inside turns to ice, and then suddenly heating it so that the ice turns directly to steam, without passing through the water stage en route.

But the Preservation Hall is by no means the only interesting building at Flag Fen. Apart from the Visitor Centre near the entrance there is an admirable little museum at the far end of the site; a fascinating reconstruction of two Iron Age roundhouses, with interior linings of reeds and thatched roofs that descend to within a few inches of the ground; a fen bog garden and a Roman herb garden – to say nothing of a recreated but extensive Bronze Age settlement. The whole island has been carefully landscaped, and planted with trees and shrubs that would have been there at that time. It also seems to be an extraordinary – if unofficial – nature reserve, with some fifty different birds and heaven knows how many species of dragonfly.

But there is also its atmosphere. On one of the internet websites it is, rather surprisingly, compared to the Abbey Road crossing made famous by the Beatles; for my part I find it far more reminiscent of one of the smaller, uninhabited islands in the Venetian Lagoon, the surroundings of which are, in many areas and in many respects, strangely similar to the Fens. Both, I feel, are haunted, though their ghosts are benign; and both, in any weather but above all on clear summer days, are quite astonishingly beautiful.

Roman England

Introduction

F orget Julius Caesar. It has been suggested that his invasions of Britain in 55 and 54 BC marked the dividing line between prehistory and history, and perhaps they did; but he made no lasting impact on the island. The great moment – which changed it for ever – came almost exactly a century later in AD 43, when the legions of the Emperor Claudius overran the south-east and established the province of Britannia. At first they stopped at the Fosse Way, which linked two of their most important military bases, Exeter and Lincoln. Later, around AD 60, they had little trouble mopping up the south-west; but after that the advance became more difficult. Manpower was in short supply, lines of communication and supply were lengthening. Northern England and Wales were conquered but were never wholly reliable, and though there were plenty of military bases – Chester being the most important – there was always a slight feeling of insecurity. Few Romans built their villas in the north. In the last years of the century one or two intrepid legions pressed on as far into the wilds as Aberdeenshire; but Scotland was soon abandoned, and when Hadrian arrived in 122 he made the decision final. His superb wall – the most impressive military construction to be found anywhere within the Roman Empire – was the clearest possible demarcation of his northern frontier.

There was also a very considerable non-military immigration. Roman administrators, engineers, justiciars, builders of roads and bridges had followed the armies – when they had not accompanied them – and they had been joined over the years by merchants, tradesmen and manufacturers. The result was the appearance of Britain's first genuine towns. Roman town planning was not, it has to be said, an immediate success: three of their most promising attempts – Colchester, St Albans and London – were burned to the ground by Queen Boudicca (or, as I prefer to call her, Boadicea) and her Iceni tribesmen in AD 60–1. After that, however, things went a good deal better; by the end of the Roman occupation there were to be no fewer than twenty administrative centres (*civitates*) and perhaps another 100-odd communities describable as towns. Of course they were tiny by today's standards – London, the biggest, probably had a population of around 30,000 – but few cities north of the Alps could boast many more.

And then there were the villas. They start appearing in the south of England as early as the second century; but as time passed and prosperity increased, so too did their sophistication. Their greatest flowering came in the third and fourth centuries – long after most of the towns had stopped growing. This is the age of Chedworth and Fishbourne, of Rockbourne in Hampshire and of Lullingstone in Kent and of many others, some of which are lying still undiscovered, still awaiting the archaeologist's spade. But by this time the Pax Romana, which had made so much of this development possible, was beginning to crumble as new invasions threatened. More and more towns threw up defensive walls; from the later third century dates that magnificent series of defences around the south-east coast generally known as the Forts of the Saxon Shore. Finally in 367 came the 'Barbarian

Conspiracy', when Rome's three main enemies – the Picts, the Scots and the Saxons – launched a combined attack on the province. They were beaten back, but the writing was on the wall. The beginning of the fifth century saw a steady *dégringolade*: Gaul was overrun by Germanic tribes and much of the Roman army was transferred to deal with the situation (which it totally failed to do). Soon afterwards the army left in Britain mutinied; three leaders followed in swift succession; more troops were withdrawn; and in 410 the Emperor Honorius informed his British subjects that in future they would have to look after themselves.

The Roman occupation of Britain had ended on a note of anticlimax. A sadder, darker age was about to begin.

3

Roman Walls of Colchester
ESSEX

Dorchester, Winchester, Rochester, Manchester – in all these, including Chester itself, the 'chester' stands for *castra*, which means a Roman camp. Of them all, however, from the Roman point of view, the oldest and the most important is Colchester. It is prodigiously rich in Roman remains. Most of its magnificent walls still stand, marking the boundary of the ancient city, and despite their age look formidably strong, as does the great gate to the west, now known as Balkerne Gate, which is also mostly Roman work. Colchester has claimed to be the oldest community in England. In fact it isn't – Thatcham in Berkshire and Abingdon in Oxfordshire were both settlements in prehistoric times – but it is certainly the oldest *recorded* town. Under its Roman name of Camulodunum, it is mentioned by Pliny the Elder (who died in AD 79); but even before the Roman Conquest of Britain in AD 43 it was the centre of power for Cunobelin, the British King of the Catuvellauni tribe, better known to us – and to Shakespeare – as Cymbeline.

In early Roman days Colchester was the capital of Britain. After the administrative centre was transferred to London, it continued to do duty as a vitally important military base. As such it boasted a magnificent temple dedicated to the Divine Claudius – every Roman emperor, you may remember, was automatically deified after his death – on the ruins of which, about 1,000 years later, the Normans were to build Colchester Castle, that tremendous keep – in fact the largest they ever built – that still exists today. For a time all went well; but then, in AD 60–1, there came the great rebellion against Roman rule in East Anglia by the Iceni tribe under their terrifying Queen Boudicca (or Boadicea). (She is the subject of a somewhat alarming statue in cast aluminium erected in Colchester in 2009 – not a patch on Thomas Thornycroft's superb one at the end of Westminster Bridge.) In the course of this uprising, Colchester was sacked and burned until barely one stone was left on another. The entire population – said to have numbered some 30,000 – sought refuge in the Temple; they all perished when the flames took hold. London and St Albans fared very little better. It was four years afterwards, as part of the general process of reconstruction, that the massive 3,000-yard town walls were built – a little late, one feels – together with the great Roman Circus, designed for chariot racing and other less savoury performances, which was unearthed by local archaeologists beneath the headquarters of the Military Garrison as recently as 2004.

What was life like for a Roman legionary in Britain in the later first century AD and the early second? The first thing to remember is that he was intensely proud of his calling. He was a member of the greatest and the best trained army in the world, for which there was always a waiting list. Often acceptance depended on influence; it helped, too, if his father had been a legionary before him. He had to be a Roman citizen, over eighteen years old and above average height; and – though this was not spelt out in writing – he had to be superbly healthy and strong. Daily drills, punishing physical exercise and forced marches with heavy equipment, all under the army's tight and unremitting discipline, would either toughen a man or break him; and many were the recruits who, after a month or two of this treatment, would limp sadly away. In return for all this his salary would be good, but not princely; a portion of it was always deducted at source for his food, lodging and weaponry. Marriage was forbidden – though a good many had girlfriends in the neighbouring town or village – largely because he was expected to be ready to leave at a moment's notice for anywhere in the empire, a vast area extending, in its heyday, from the Pillars of Hercules (the modern Gibraltar) to Mesopotamia. The normal period of service was fixed at twenty-five years, after which each man was given a generous discharge bonus equivalent to thirteen years' salary.

Of course, the army was not exclusively composed of legionaries. There was a secondary army of much the same size – including many who were locally employed – founded by the Emperor Augustus and known as the *auxilia*. This existed primarily to accommodate those who were not imperial citizens and provided most of the specialist services:

road-makers and bridge-designers, architects and builders, archers and – rather surprisingly – most of the cavalry, both heavy and light. There was almost complete freedom of worship, both for legionaries and auxiliaries; coming as they did from every corner of the empire, they represented any number of different beliefs. The official religion was still that of Ancient Rome, based on the gods of Olympus – Jupiter, Juno, Minerva, Apollo and the rest; but soldiers were at liberty to bow their heads to whatever deities they pleased; as we know, in the later centuries the originally Persian god Mithras became increasingly popular. The only religion that was prohibited at the time of which we are speaking was Christianity, which by now was considered a serious threat to the Roman tradition.

The Colchester Castle Museum is well worth visiting. The rest of the town, alas, has been largely ruined by post-war planners; but nobody should miss the magnificent remains of St Botolph's, the first Augustinian priory in England which, despite its bombardment in 1648 during the Civil War, is still hugely impressive. Finally, just outside the town, try Bourne Mill, an enchanting little conceit built by Sir Thomas Lucas in 1591 as a fishing lodge. The outsize gables, with their joyfully irresponsible finials and curlicues, suggest the hand of the Dutch Protestant refugees who had established a community in Colchester. It is owned by the National Trust, open to the public and strongly recommended.

4

Chedworth Roman Villa
GLOUCESTERSHIRE

Colchester is about Roman politics and military organization; Hadrian's Wall is about loneliness and distant outposts on a bleak frontier; but if you want to know about Roman daily life – at least for those who could afford it – you must go to Chedworth. It is a magical place today, tucked away deep in the Cotswolds; but in Roman times it probably felt a good deal more accessible, standing as it does close to the Fosse Way, that magnificent Roman road that begins at Exeter and runs, in an almost direct line, north-eastward through Bath, Cirencester and Leicester to Lincoln – a total of some 270 miles. (You can, incidentally, follow it on foot for most of its length; in some short stretches the original paving-stones, complete with cart tracks, are still visible.) In the early days of the Roman occupation, before the legions advanced to the north and west, the Fosse Way constituted the frontier of the empire; later, however, when it was no longer so exposed, the part that runs through the Cotswolds seems to have become a favourite area for war veterans and others to settle in after their retirement; the remains of no fewer than twenty-two other villas have been excavated within ten miles of Chedworth, and there are doubtless many more that have yet to be discovered.

Villa is, quite simply, the Latin word for 'farm'; and it's easy to forget that Roman Britain was very largely an agricultural society – only some 10 per cent of the population lived in towns. But when we talk of Roman villas nowadays we mean something more like a well-to-do country estate, although it would also have been a working farm. Its fortunate owner would certainly have cultivated his land – or paid other people to do so – and much of his produce would have consisted of items recently introduced by the Romans: cabbages, carrots, cucumbers, radishes, celery, broad beans and walnuts. He may have tried also to grow vines, although the wine that he and his family drank at table would more probably have been imported from Gaul, together with figs and olive oil. The landed gentry were most likely to be Romanized Britons, for by the second century, when Chedworth was first built, the *Pax Romana* reigned and the land was (on the whole) at peace. Moreover there was by now relatively little continued immigration. Whoever he may have been, the first builder of this particular villa was a rich man, for he laid it out on a remarkably generous scale, its three sections framing a central courtyard in the Roman style. The result is one of the largest and most impressive villas in England.

Despite its size, Chedworth seems in those early days to have been fairly unpretentious; there is no sign of anything particularly showy. Early in the fourth century, however, the villa was transformed; it now became an elite gentleman's residence. A fourth wing was added, completely enclosing the courtyard and turning it into a proper Roman atrium, with an elegant colonnaded peristyle. Another addition was a series of astonishing bath-houses. The villa was already equipped to face the perishing Cotswold winters with the Roman system of hypocausts – basically underfloor heating; it now received a Turkish bath, a sauna and a cold plunge, all with superb mosaic floors.

It is these that are the pride and glory of Chedworth. All too often, such mosaics – and sometimes the entire monument that surrounds them – are protected by vast sheds of wood or corrugated iron, which not only make it impossible to enjoy them properly but also utterly destroy the surrounding landscape. Here, thanks to the National Trust, they are properly exposed to view, so that we can see them as they should be seen. Alas, those depicting Bacchic orgies have almost gone, leaving only just enough for us to see what fun they must have been; gone, too, is the personification of Autumn. But her sisters Spring, Summer and Winter have survived, and very splendid they are; not highly sophisticated perhaps, but high-spirited and full of life. Their creators obviously loved their job and, one suspects, had a first-rate sense of humour into the bargain.

We see floor mosaics all over the Roman world, in the furthest reaches of the empire. There is a vast palace in Sicily containing literally acres of them; while in Tunisia one gets the feeling that they must have adorned every floor of every room in every house. In England too, there are plenty, most of all, perhaps, at Fishbourne, near Chichester, where there is another so-called palace, larger and grander than Chedworth, which has been hailed by its owners, the Sussex Archaeological Society, as one of the greatest Roman buildings in the empire – a mighty claim indeed when one remembers the Colosseum. It boasts some truly magnificent mosaics – there is a justly famous one of a cupid on a dolphin – but it is sadly unatmospheric and institutionalized. I had thought at one moment of including it on this list, but no: Roman villas should be seen, not in those vast sheds, but in their proper surroundings of green hills, fields and woodland. Give me Chedworth, every time.

5

Fort of Housesteads
HADRIAN'S WALL, NORTHUMBERLAND

*H*adrian's Wall is, for most of us, pretty remote and comparatively inaccessible; but it repays the journey a thousandfold. Set in the wildest and most rugged part of England, originally fifteen to twenty feet high by seven to ten feet thick, it marches majestically for seventy-three miles right across the country from coast to coast, from the Solway Firth to the River Tyne.

It was Julius Caesar who first invaded Britain in 55 and 54 BC, but nothing much came of it: he seems to have been simply flexing his muscles with little more than a reconnaissance. Trade began, and developed as the years passed; but the land was effectively left in peace until AD 43, when the Emperor Claudius sent an army with orders both to conquer and to colonize. Ultimately, they did so; but they did not have it all their own way. Caratacus, leader of the Catuvellauni tribe in central England, and Boudicca, Queen of the Iceni in East Anglia, both put up a stiff resistance, and the Roman Governors, usually known as Legates, seldom escaped having to contend with one uprising or another. Gradually, however, they established themselves, making their new province as much like Rome as possible, building immense public baths as in Bath (q.v.), or fine, luxurious villas as at Fishbourne or Chedworth (q.v.).

Then, in the year AD 121, the Emperor Hadrian arrived in Britain to survey his most northerly outpost. Who, first of all, was he? Briefly, he was the greatest Roman emperor between Augustus and the fourth-century Constantine the Great. He was by origin a Spaniard, born almost certainly near what is now Seville, who became emperor after the death of his predecessor Trajan in AD 117. The empire covered a vast area, yet somehow, during his twenty-one-year reign, Hadrian visited every corner of it: always on the move, eating and sleeping rough with his men. Deeply cultured and an ardent Philhellene, he knew his Greek philosophers well, was no mean poet and did his best to make Athens the cultural capital of the empire. Finally he was the first emperor since Nero to wear a beard, setting a fashion for his successors that was to continue until Constantine.

Having heard rumours of a recent rebellion in the north of Britain, he marched up to the north and ordered the construction of the magnificent wall that bears his name. Most of it still exists today, looking quite magnificent as it strides across the Northumbrian hills. Only Hadrian could have done it. He designed it as an extended military base, with troops stationed in fortresses set at regular 500-yard intervals along its length, as a means of keeping out marauders from the north and marking the limits of a feasible Roman province. Of the fortresses, the most complete is the one the Romans called Vercovicium, which we generally know as Housesteads. The perfect monument to Roman military power, it is now the property of the National Trust, and administered by English Heritage. Built in stone probably around AD 124, it does not straddle the wall – as do all its fellows – with half of the building on barbarian territory; instead, it stands entirely on the south side, the wall itself constituting its northern defence. It possesses a small museum, but there is a larger one in the nearby fort of Chesters (Cilurnum).

The other most interesting site is actually a little to the south of the wall, but near enough to be mentioned in the same context. It is the camp of Vindolanda, and it was here that in 1973 archaeologists unearthed what are known as the Vindolanda Tablets – small, square pieces of wood, each bearing ten or twelve lines of handwriting, written in ink and in the Roman cursive script. Not surprisingly, most of them are concerned with military matters; a fair number, however, are a good deal more personal. Of these perhaps the best known is written by Claudia Severa, wife of the commander of another fort, to Sulpicia Lepidina, wife of the commander of Vindolanda, inviting her to her birthday party. It is one of the earliest examples we know of writing by a woman. Other examples take the form of what we might call laundry lists, and finally establish the answer to a question that has long tormented historians: yes, Roman soldiers did wear underpants.

And yet for me the essence of Hadrian's Wall is not the information that it reveals so much as the atmosphere that it creates. Standing at Housesteads – or anywhere else along its length – and gazing at it as it disappears over the horizon, suddenly it brings the long Roman occupation to life; we can imagine the poor legionaries, many of whom had marched from the Mediterranean or even the Balkans, standing guard on the watchtowers, fighting the cruel winds and the bitter cold as they gazed over the bleak northern hills where dwelt the barbarians – and, quite possibly, lurked the dragons – wondering why they had ever enlisted.

Others, however, may have felt more like Kipling's Roman centurion, having received his marching orders to return to Rome, and pleading to be allowed to stay:

. . . You'll take the broad Aurelian road, through shore-descending
    pines,
Where, blue as any peacock's neck, the Tyrrhene Ocean shines.
You'll go where laurel crowns are won, but – will you e'er forget
The smell of hawthorn in the sun, or bracken in the wet?

Let me work here, for Britain's sake – at any task you will –
A marsh to drain, a road to make or native troops to drill.
Some Western camp (I know the Pict) or granite Border keep,
Mid seas of heather derelict, where our old messmates sleep.

Legate, I come to you in tears – My cohort ordered home!
I've served in Britain forty years. What should I do in Rome?
Here is my heart, my soul, my mind – the only life I know.
I cannot leave it all behind. Command me not to go!

Anglo-Saxon England

Introduction

O ne of the chief difficulties confronting any would-be writer on Anglo-Saxon England is that we still know pathetically little about it. Documentary evidence is slight indeed: the most valuable, perhaps, is the *Anglo-Saxon Chronicle*, a collection of annals originally dating from the ninth century. Manuscript copies were circulated to all the leading monasteries, where they were independently updated. Then we have the *Ecclesiastical History* of the Venerable Bede, which begins with Julius Caesar's invasion of 55 BC and ends in 731, four years before Bede's own death. But there is relatively little else. *Beowulf*, a long epic poem probably written in the ninth or tenth century, provides any amount of local colour, but nothing solid to offer historians. For the rest we have to fall back on archaeology, which in the past century or so has made several spectacular discoveries, of which Sutton Hoo has been by far the most exciting.

The years following the departure of the Romans in AD 410 remain frustratingly obscure and deeply unhappy. England was left unprotected and rudderless. During the third and fourth centuries there had been increasing numbers of plundering raids by Anglo-Saxons from across the North Sea; henceforth 'the English', as they came to be called, could be expected every spring for a season of looting, burning, raping and sacking; then, probably around 450, they began to make permanent settlements. Over the next century these new settlers – Bede divides them into Angles, Saxons and Jutes, which is convenient but a serious oversimplification – spread the length and breadth of the country. It is at about this time that we hear of a great Romano-British leader, Ambrosius Aurelianus, who won at least one great battle against the English newcomers before passing – as King Arthur – into legend.

Thus, almost miraculously it seemed, out of all the chaos and devastation, a remarkable new civilization began to emerge. It began in 597, when Pope Gregory the Great despatched St Augustine on a mission to convert the Anglo-Saxons to Christianity. Augustine landed in Kent, where he made his headquarters in Canterbury and became its first archbishop, giving the city the religious primacy it still enjoys today. All through the following century the work of conversion continued. Occasionally there were clashes with the old British Church – which itself had not lifted a finger to convert the invaders – but the Synod of Whitby in 664 settled their differences and harmony was restored.

By this point great churches and monasteries were making their appearance for the first time, and were rapidly developing into centres of art and learning unrivalled anywhere in western Europe. Thus it was that by the eighth century Britain had succeeded in developing a new, surprisingly sophisticated and deeply Christian Anglo-Saxon society. But then came disaster: a new enemy, sweeping down from the north-east to destroy this society just as cruelly as the Anglo-Saxons had devastated the Romano-British before them: the Vikings. Their very first victim, in 793, was the monastery of Lindisfarne; and for the next seventy years they wrought destruction not only along the east coast but the south – where they reached as far as Cornwall – and even north to the Severn estuary. Then they too chose to settle. Those from Norway and Sweden went for the most part elsewhere: those who established themselves in England were the Danes.

Northumbria and Mercia were soon wiped out; only Wessex was left, and it was the Wessex King, Alfred, who alone succeeded in halting the Danish advance. Indeed, he did more. In the peace that he finally concluded with the Danish King Guthrum, English and Danes were accepted as equals and there is a reference to 'all the English race'. Alfred himself began to be described as 'King of the Anglo-Saxons'. Dying in 899, he established a dynasty, founded not on primogeniture but with each succeeding monarch elected by the great council of nobles and higher clergy – the Witanagemot – from all the members of the royal family. All through the first three-quarters of the tenth century the power of the royal house grew, as did the extent of its dominions. It was at this time, too, that England assumed its rough administrative shape, with the shires and counties that we know today. By the death of King Edgar in 975 the kings of England counted themselves among the leading rulers of western Europe.

Just four years later, however, there succeeded one of the most catastrophic kings ever to sit on the English throne. The thirty-eight-year reign of Ethelred the Unready, who succeeded only after the murder – in which he was deeply implicated – of his elder brother, saw a new wave of Viking attacks, which he did virtually nothing to stop. Instead, he embarked on a disastrous policy of appeasement, paying the aggressors no less than 22,000 pounds of gold – the infamous Danegeld. Worse still, in 1002 he gave orders for the massacre of the Danish communities that had been long established in the country and deplored the recent attacks as much as anyone.

As always, appeasement failed. The year 1009 saw a full-scale invasion by the Danish King Sweyn, and England found itself part of a vast Scandinavian empire, embracing not only Denmark but also Sweden and part of Norway. Ethelred fled, to everyone's relief, and died soon afterwards, and the Witanagemot elected Sweyn's son, Canute. And then a miracle happened. The former Norse raider transformed himself into an admirable Anglo-Saxon king. He married Ethelred's widow Emma of Normandy, adopted Anglo-Saxon traditions and customs, and single-handedly restored the kingdom of England to its former place among the European nations. He even attended the imperial coronation of the Emperor Conrad II in Rome, where he was received with the highest honours.

What is left today of Anglo-Saxon England? Architecturally, a surprising amount: at least fifty of our parish churches are of Anglo-Saxon origin. For the rest, apart from the Sutton Hoo hoard and some remarkable metalwork – the Alfred Ring in the British Museum is worth going a long way to see – all the greatest art of the period has survived in illuminated manuscripts, best exemplified by the Lindisfarne Gospels. The style is quite unlike that found anywhere else: more Celtic in origin with its repeated knot designs, but also clearly influenced by Byzantium, and by Carolingian art in Germany.

One last masterpiece stands alone, utterly individual and surely one of the most wholly enjoyable and entertaining works of art ever created: the Bayeux Tapestry. Commissioned by Bishop Odo of Bayeux, William of Normandy's half-brother, it is widely regarded as the work of Anglo-Saxon needleworkers. Whoever was responsible for it, it sings.

6

Sutton Hoo
SUFFOLK

A few miles from the Suffolk coast near Woodbridge, overlooking the River Deben and on a high ridge about 100 feet above it, a cluster of curious-looking mounds stands out against the sky. Until the summer of 1939 nobody bothered much about it, and the place remained virtually unknown. But then a team of archaeologists began to dig, and suddenly the name of Sutton Hoo – 'hoo' is an Old English word meaning the spur of a hill – was on everyone's lips. What they had unearthed was perhaps the most exciting discovery in the history of English archaeology, a discovery that threw a completely new light on England in what we used to call the Dark Ages: the Anglo-Saxon world of Beowulf, hero of this country's first great epic poem. *Beowulf* is actually set in southern Sweden; but in those days Scandinavia must have seemed even closer than it does today. In the absence of roads, land travel was practically non-existent, whereas the coast of Denmark was just a day or two away, a lot more easily accessible than London.

Ships were consequently of immense importance; and the central discovery at Sutton Hoo is a ship burial dating back to the early seventh century. Although the practice was also known in Ancient Egypt, this was essentially a Scandinavian idea, whereby a ship was used as a ceremonial container for the deceased, and for all the treasure that was buried with him. Sometimes indeed it formed a part of the treasure itself. At Sutton Hoo the wooden hull of the ship had rotted completely away, but its outline had been preserved in what was described by one of the archaeologists as 'a kind of crusted, blackened sand'. It was twenty-seven metres long, accommodated some forty oarsmen, could easily have sailed across the North Sea and very probably had.

But the ship was only the start; the contents were still more astonishing. The first surprise, though a negative one, was that there was no body; it had completely dissolved away. A few bones, however, would have told us comparatively little. What did survive was an astonishing wealth of precious objects that were buried with their owner. We have, first of all, his magnificent helmet of bronze, with a frontal mask. When found, it had been shattered to fragments by the collapse of the tomb roof, but it has now been painstakingly reconstructed. Brow, nose and mouth are all gilded, as is a short but heavy moustache; all combine to create a face – one that brings him instantly and vividly to life. Then there are his sword, with a gold *cloisonné* pommel decorated with garnets that must have come from India or Sri Lanka; his shield and spears; his lyre; and a wealth of superbly wrought jewellery – a great golden buckle, shoulder-clasps similarly of gold and garnets – a purse (of which the leather pouch has gone) that carried thirty-seven Frankish gold shillings, each from a different mint, drinking horns made from the horns of an aurochs (a wild ox now extinct) and a quantity of imperial silverware, bowls and spoons, that can have originated only in Byzantium.

Nothing on this scale had ever been discovered in England before. Now the great question remains to be answered: to whom did this glorious hoard belong? Who was the man buried amid such splendour? He must surely have been a king, or at least a great heroic warrior chieftain. We shall never know; the name of the early seventh-century Raedwald, King of the East Angles, has often been proposed and may well be right, but there is no proof – or, probably, ever will be. Perhaps, however, this is not so very important. What gives Sutton Hoo its power and fascination is the light it sheds on a sophisticated civilization of which we previously knew remarkably little, with what we did know often founded on myth and legend rather than serious historical documentation: a northern civilization centred on the North Sea, comprising East Anglia, Scandinavia, Normandy, Brittany and very probably Iceland, with commercial links that extended as far as Byzantium and perhaps even India. The Dark Ages, it seems, were not so dark after all.

As established treasure-trove, all the finds at Sutton Hoo were awarded to the landowner, Mrs Edith May Pretty; and Mrs Pretty then presented them to the nation. All the principal items from Mound 1 – site of the ship burial – went, quite correctly to ensure their proper conservation and security, to the British Museum; at the time they constituted the largest gift ever made to the museum by a living donor. They are now on permanent display in Room 41. The original finds dating from the excavation of Mounds 2, 3 and 4 in 1938 will be found at the nearby Ipswich Museum, in a specially designed Anglo-Saxon Gallery opened in 1996. Sutton Hoo itself, however, offers much that is of interest. There are regular tours of the site with knowledgeable guides, and the National Trust – which now owns and administers the property – has arranged an excellent Visitor Centre, where you can find the full (and extraordinary) story of the excavations and examine a life-size restoration of the ship itself.

There have been later archaeological campaigns, especially in the late 1960s and again in the late 1980s, and there will doubtless be further digs in future. Who knows how much more this thrilling site will yield?

7

Lindisfarne
NORTHUMBERLAND

*T*he Holy Island of Lindisfarne is not, it must be admitted, easy to reach. Tucked away in the extreme north-east corner of England, it is attainable only by means of a long causeway, negotiable for only a few hours a day at low tide. As Sir Walter Scott deplorably described it:

> *Dry-shod o'er sands, twice every day,*
> *The pilgrims to the shrine find way.*
> *Twice every day the waves efface*
> *Of staves and sandalled feet the trace.*

On the other hand it is, in its own rather bleak fashion, wildly beautiful; and it sums up, better than anywhere else I know, that extraordinary flowering of monastic culture in the area which directly preceded – and was largely destroyed by – the Viking raids.

The story of Christianity in the north-east began when Ethelburga, the daughter of King Ethelbert and Queen Bertha of Kent (see **Canterbury**) married Edwin, King of Northumbria, and easily converted him. (It was at a subsequent meeting of wise men in order to have this conversion ratified, that one of the Saxon nobles first uttered the famous simile in which life was compared to the swift flight of a sparrow through a lighted hall.) Only a few years later the Irishman

St Aidan, who had travelled with a party of monks from another holy island, Iona, off the west coast of Scotland, founded the monastery of Lindisfarne. The area, then, was from the first torn between two opposing early Christian traditions: the Roman, introduced by St Augustine, and the Irish/Scottish/Celtic as represented by St Columba and Aidan himself. The two traditions met at the famous Synod of Whitby, held in 664 principally to decide on the dating of Easter. The Romans won, and the complexion of the Church in the north-east was determined once and for all.

The monks who arrived with Aidan were the first inhabitants of the new monastery, which was devoted to two main purposes: first, the evangelization of the north of England; second, the copying of the sacred texts and histories of the early Church. This latter task was vitally important until the invention of printing eight centuries later, for how else could Christian – and classical – literature survive? At Lindisfarne as at Bede's nearby monastery of Jarrow, copying was a veritable industry. It was not, however, a cheap one: the skin of 100 calves was required to produce a single Bible. But Lindisfarne was lucky; one of its copyists was a monk named Eadfrith, and Eadfrith was the genius – the first great English artist whose name we know – who created the Lindisfarne Gospels, to this day one of the British Library's most treasured possessions. The volume is made still more interesting by the fact that an Old English translation of the Latin was added between the lines in the tenth century – the oldest extant translation of the Gospels into English. The initial letters in particular, with their strange, twisting, serpentine arabesques, are things to be wondered at; each is an individual, fully fledged work of art. Someone with plenty of time on their hands once counted the tiny red dots surrounding a single initial: the total came to 10,600.

The Lindisfarne Gospels were probably written for the shrine of St Cuthbert, Lindisfarne's most distinguished alumnus, who serves nowadays as the patron saint of Northumbria. Prior of the monastery before he was thirty, he soon found the austere monastic regime too soft for him and moved out to the uninhabited Farne Islands a little further off the coast, where he could more freely indulge in his habit of saying his prayers half-immersed in the freezing sea water and communing with the puffins. It was there that he died in 687. A party from Lindisfarne rowed out to collect the body, which was buried in the monastic chapel of St Peter.

A century later, however, a new and deeply unpleasant people appeared off the English coasts. In early June 797, according to the *Anglo-Saxon Chronicle*, 'dire portents appeared over Northumbria . . . immense whirlwinds and flashes of lightning, and fiery dragons were seen flying through the air'; and on the 8th Lindisfarne was utterly destroyed by Viking raiders. But the monks had taken no chances. Four years before, they had removed St Cuthbert's apparently uncorrupted remains and begun to seek a safer repository for them. Seven long years the search continued; but eventually the body was lodged in the then still embryonic Durham Cathedral where it remains today.

The Vikings continued to ravage the English coastal towns for the best part of three centuries. In my schooldays they were presented as unspeakable ruffians and villains, raiding, robbing and raping in all directions, swinging their blood-axes and lopping off heads, arms and legs wholesale. Nowadays we are told that the poor chaps have been greatly misunderstood, that they dropped in entirely because of over-population in their Scandinavian homelands and that they only wanted to trade. They even have a theme park (Jorvik) in York telling us how delightful they were. Well, yes, and it has to be admitted that in later years they produced some dazzling artefacts: the complete Viking ship in the Oslo Ship Museum must be the most beautiful sailing vessel ever designed. But there was plenty of head- and limb-lopping for all that: all too many English towns have their own horror stories to tell, and they can't all be made up. Besides, look what happened to Lindisfarne. All that remains of the glorious old monastery is a few sad ruins; and the rock is now crowned by, of all things, an English country house, built in the early twentieth century by Sir Edwin Lutyens.

8

St Peter on the Wall
BRADWELL-JUXTA-MARE, ESSEX

I thought long and hard before choosing Bradwell. There are far more important – and far more accessible – Saxon churches at, for example, Bradford-on-Avon in Wiltshire or Brixworth in Northamptonshire. Bradwell is hard to reach, and the church of St Peter on the Wall is some twenty minutes' walk from the end of the motor road; but it's worth it a hundred times over. Architecturally, it must be admitted, there is nothing very remarkable about this little church, built on the edge of what was the Roman fort of Othona – of which only a few stones remain – gazing out over the grey North Sea. But the importance of St Peter's lies not in how it looks but in what it is: in all probability, the oldest church in England of which so much of the original fabric has been preserved, having been built by St Cedd on the very spot where he landed from Lindisfarne in 653 on his mission to evangelize the East Saxon invaders. Some time in the seventeenth century the church was turned into a barn by a local farmer, who cut doorways for his carts; the roof and the floor too are modern, but none of that seems to matter. This grand old building, standing solitary and desolate where the long low flats slope down to the sea, retains a numinous quality like few other places in England.

The East Saxons were only one of three main tribes that

began crossing from what are now Germany and Denmark to eastern Britain in the early fifth century. The others were the Angles – who gave their name to England and seem to have come from a district called Angeln in Schleswig-Holstein, a little south of the Danish border – and the Jutes, who came from the Jutland peninsula in Denmark. They were probably joined by a handful of Frisians and Franks. Together, they are known as the Anglo-Saxons. Gradually they spread across the country, driving their neighbours, the indigenous Celts, further and further to the west, into the Scottish Highlands, the Welsh mountains and the wilds (as they then were) of Cornwall. The old Celtic language has died out in Cornwall, but still survives in Welsh and Gaelic, as well as in Manx, the language of the Isle of Man. Meanwhile the invaders developed their own language – Anglo-Saxon – which in turn became Old English, and finally the English that we speak today.

Gradually, too, they began to organize themselves, until the land was principally under the domination of seven small kingdoms: Northumbria, Mercia (central England), East Anglia, Essex, Kent, Sussex and Wessex. This last was ruled in the second half of the ninth century by the near-legendary Alfred the Great. By his day the Viking raiders had became a serious menace to the whole country. In 850 a Viking fleet, amounting – according to the *Anglo-Saxon Chronicle* – to no fewer than 350 ships, captured Canterbury and London. York fell in 867. In 869 the East Anglian King Edmund dared to resist: he was beheaded and impaled. The situation was saved by Alfred. After some months as a fugitive – this was when he burned the cakes – in 878 he managed to gather an army that completely crushed the Vikings at Edington. This gave him a long respite, during which he constructed a sort of early Maginot line of fortresses, which proved highly successful;

and when in 886 he entered London he began to be called 'King of the Anglo-Saxons'. I find it hard not to bang on about Alfred: he was also a legist and educationist, a shipbuilder and statesman; indeed, it was difficult to find any area of life in which he did not have his impact. Anglo-Saxon culture as we know it today was in very large measure due to him.

What was that culture? Considering that the Anglo-Saxons were dominant in England between the end of the Roman occupation in 411 and the Norman Conquest of 1066, we know surprisingly little about it – although, thanks to recent discoveries at Sutton Hoo (q.v.) and elsewhere, we are learning more all the time. Much of our knowledge comes from the principal work of Anglo-Saxon literature, the epic poem we know as *Beowulf*. It is a bloodthirsty story, the story of almost constant bloodshed and battle. Its eponymous hero fights three enemies: the villainous and terrifying Grendel, Grendel's mother and an unnamed Dragon. Grendel appears invincible, since his skin is impenetrable by any weapon; Beowulf deals with this problem by tearing his arm off at the shoulder. Grendel's mother too possesses an immense advantage: she lives at the bottom of a lake. This time Beowulf manages to seize a giant's sword – one that no one else can wield – from her armoury and beheads her (a feat still more remarkable when performed under water). With the Dragon, alas, he is less successful: he kills it, but dies from his wounds and is given a perfectly splendid funeral.

That – perhaps only slightly exaggerated – was the life of the Anglo-Saxons: violent and probably short, but enlivened by drink and carousal. G.K. Chesterton summed it up best:

How white their steel, how bright their eyes! I love each laughing
   knave;
Cry high and bid him welcome to the banquet of the brave.

Yea, I will bless them as they bend and love them where they lie,
Where on their skulls the sword I swing falls shattering from the sky;
The hour when death is like a light and blood is like a rose –
You never loved your friends, my friend, as I shall love my foes.

9

Offa's Dyke

HEREFORDSHIRE

*L*et's get the main facts sorted straight away. Who was
Offa? He was a powerful King of Mercia, and he reigned
from AD 757 to 796. What was his dyke? It was a massive
earthwork, up to 25 feet high and 65 feet across, stretching
some 177 miles – with a few interruptions, at points where it
wasn't necessary – all the way from Chepstow in the south to
Prestatyn in the north. Quite a lot of it still exists, in the form
of a high bank, with a deep ditch running alongside – enough
for there to be a recognized Offa's Dyke Path for long-
distance walkers. Expert opinion is divided – as expert opinion
nearly always is – over what precisely it was for; but to me it
has always seemed fairly clear that it must have been a line of
defence against the Welsh. It still follows – though only very
roughly – the present boundary between England and Wales;
and when it comes to a hill, or a range of hills, it invariably
passes to the west of them so that potential troublemakers are
always in sight.

Once again, we find ourselves wishing that we knew more
about the history of these Dark Ages. Apart from the *Anglo-
Saxon Chronicle* and the Venerable Bede our sources are sadly
thin on the ground. We must therefore be all the more grateful to a Welsh monk by the name of Asser, author of a life of
his close friend Alfred the Great, in which he writes: 'There

was in Mercia in fairly recent time a certain vigorous king called Offa, who terrified all the neighbouring kings and provinces around him, and who had a great dyke built between Wales and Mercia from sea to sea.' He probably had good reason to do so. After the last Roman soldier set sail from Britain in 410, there was no longer anything to bind the Celtic Welsh to the Anglo-Saxon English; and as time passed the Welsh began to see themselves more and more as a separate people. The Anglo-Saxons probably felt much the same – the more so since the Welsh had their own Celtic culture and spoke their own incomprehensible tongue – and there was no love lost between the two. Though he should obviously not be taken too literally, the nineteenth-century writer George Borrow informs us that 'it was customary for the English to cut off the ears of every Welshman who was found to the east of the dyke, and for the Welsh to hang every Englishman whom they found to the west of it.'

Thus, by the time of the Norman Conquest, England and Wales were effectively two different countries. The Normans, as might have been expected, adopted a rather more aggressive attitude than their predecessors, with any number of footloose younger sons trying to set up little baronies for themselves along the borders; this was the age of the first great border castles, such as Ludlow, Caerphilly and Chepstow, to name but three. But it was a full two centuries later – with the accession of Edward I in 1272 – that matters came to a head. For some time the activities of a certain Llewellyn ap Gruffyd had been causing concern; he had now won control over nearly all north and central Wales, his power was steadily increasing and in 1274 he refused to do homage to the new King.

That, Edward felt, was enough: three years later he mobilized the biggest army the Welsh had ever seen – some 800 knights and 15,000 infantry (more than half of them Welsh opponents of Llewellyn) and invaded. It was all over quite quickly: with the onset of winter Llewellyn gave in. This was not of course the end of the border fighting, which was to continue on and off for centuries to come; but it was enough for the King to order the building of a whole chain of castles, to serve as forward bases for English garrisons. Flint, Rhuddlan, Beaumaris, Conway, Caernarfon, Harlech, Aberystwyth all sprang up within twenty years of each other – and even these were just the beginning. To build them, Edward brought in architects and craftsmen from all over England, all of them subjected to the strictest military discipline. The buildings themselves represented, it need hardly be said, the *dernier cri* of castle design – Edward had learned a lot about it while in Palestine and Syria on the Ninth Crusade – but they also showed more than a streak of megalomania. Let me quote historian Simon Schama:

> In *The Mabinogion*, the cycle of early Welsh tales, there is mention of a king who had dreamed of a castle with high, coloured towers. That dream had been translated into reality at Constantinople, and at Caernarfon Edward created a Byzantium by the sea, with banded octagonal towers copied slavishly from the Theodosian walls of Constantinople. On top of the battlements he set the eagles of imperial Rome.

And the castles were not only in Wales; there are also no fewer than fourteen on the English side of the border. As Professor Schama goes on to say: 'this scale of castle-building [was] the most ambitious exercise in colonial domination ever undertaken anywhere in medieval Europe'. King Offa, as he sent his men off with their spades to create his great dyke, was starting something far, far greater than he knew.

Norman England

Introduction

*I*t is difficult for us to realize today the sheer impact on England of the Norman Conquest. It was like being invaded by Nazi Germany. Overnight, the English became second-class citizens. Their new masters seemed to be everywhere, curiously dressed and speaking a strange, incomprehensible language. But there was a new energy – almost an electricity – in the air; the Normans liked to get things done. Many of the old English institutions remained undisturbed, but there was a huge new administrative drive, culminating in that almost incredible achievement completed only twenty years after William's arrival, the Domesday Book. And then there was the building: not only magnificent constructions like the White Tower of London and Durham Cathedral, but vast quantities of castles and exquisite small parish churches, a surprising number of which still survive essentially unchanged.

But even the Normans couldn't be everywhere at once. In twenty years they had taken over and largely transformed southern and western England, but the north proved a good deal harder to pacify and strong measures had to be taken; William's campaign of 1070 showed an unprecedented brutality. The final results, however, were much the same: the complete Normanization of the ruling class, and the wholesale transfer of lands from the old English aristocracy to the newcomers. In, too, came all the intricacies of the feudal system. This assimilation, however, worked both ways. Culturally and socially speaking, the several thousand Normans, most of them noblemen or squires, were up against well over a million English. In the country, they made little difference; rural and agricultural society continued largely as it always had. We must also remember that relatively few Norman women had crossed the Channel; thus from the very beginning there was large-scale intermarriage – a fact that was to have its effect on both languages, ultimately producing the magnificently mixed tongue that we speak today.

Finally, the Norman Conquest made England, in a very real sense, a part of Europe, more closely linked to the Continent, indeed, than at any other time in our history until we joined the European Union. Later, from the fifteenth century onward, we were to drift away again; but for some four centuries the kings of England ruled also over vast areas of France – even if they did spend a good deal of their time fighting to maintain their possessions – and much of the wine industry, particularly around Bordeaux, soon fell into English hands. What prevented a still greater degree of integration was, above all, the weather. Had the English Channel been as tranquil as the Mediterranean, traffic across it – and consequently trade – would have been vastly increased; as things were, for perhaps eight months of the year the ships' captains of the eleventh and twelfth centuries intending to cross it needed all the skill and courage that they could muster. Those twenty-two miles of water remained a barrier – not an insuperable one, but a barrier all the same – and would continue to do so until our own day.

When William died in 1089, his lands were divided; his eldest son Robert took over Normandy, while England fell to his second son William, generally known – on account of his red hair – as William Rufus. Rufus was efficient enough at putting down rebellions, but was deeply unpopular; according to the *Anglo-Saxon Chronicle*, he was 'hateful to almost all his people and odious to God', this last presumably a reference to his bitter quarrels with the Church. In 1100 he died in a hunting accident – there were suggestions of assassination – in the New Forest and, being homosexual, unmarried and childless, was succeeded by his younger brother Henry I.

Henry's principal achievement was to wrest Normandy from his brother Robert, whom he kept imprisoned. The real tragedy of his life, however, was the death in 1120 of his only legitimate son in a shipwreck; in consequence, when he himself died fifteen years later the succession was angrily disputed. The crown was seized by his nephew Stephen, Count of Boulogne; but Stephen's claim was challenged by his cousin, Henry's daughter Matilda and her husband Geoffrey, Count of Anjou. The result was what was in essence a civil war, which largely destroyed the firm administration that Henry had so carefully built up. At last in 1153 it was agreed that Stephen should reign for the rest of his life, but that he should be succeeded by Matilda's son Henry. A year later Stephen died and Henry became king. Since he was the grandson of Henry I, it seems rather arbitrary that he should be seen as beginning a new dynasty, that of the Plantagenets. But so he is; and thus, after only four rulers, the Norman line came to an end.

Battle Abbey

EAST SUSSEX

*B*attle of Hastings, 1066: the best known date in all English history, and by far the most important engagement ever fought on English soil. Rather more obscure is the year 1070, when Pope Alexander II ordered William the Conqueror to do penance for all the bloodshed he had caused four years before. William accordingly vowed to build an abbey on the battlefield, and Battle Abbey was the result. Its high altar marks the spot where King Harold was killed – as the Bayeux Tapestry makes abundantly clear – by an arrow in the eye.

This was the last time that England suffered an invasion by a hostile foreign power (though we narrowly missed another in 1940) and, apart from the bloodshed, it did us nothing but good. Anglo-Saxon England was, I suspect, not really much fun. We needed a shot in the arm, and the Normans gave it to us. They were an astonishing people. It was only a century and a half since Rollo, the fair-haired Viking, had led his long-boats up the Seine, to be enfeoffed by the French King with most of the eastern half of modern Normandy. In 912 he and his chief followers were baptized, Thor and Odin giving way with scarcely a struggle to the feathery onslaught of the Holy Ghost. By the end of the century the old Norse language had been forgotten, the local law adopted. The Vikings had become Frenchmen.

For the English, the changes wrought by the Conquest were less dramatic: for one thing, there was no need to change their religion. But their government administration and their legal system were overturned and replaced, and their whole aristocratic ruling class was eliminated, to be replaced by Norman nobles. In the early years, this led to serious difficulties of communication: they spoke what we now call Middle English, their rulers spoke Norman French; there was no instant abandonment of the old language in favour of the new, as there had been in Normandy. Gradually, as was inevitable, the two languages merged into the half-Latin, half-Teutonic hybrid that we speak today; but the kings and their courts continued to conduct most of their business in French until the end of the fourteenth century.

William had landed his army at Pevensey on 28 September; he had therefore been in England for over a fortnight before meeting Harold's army on Senlac Hill, about six miles north of Hastings, on 14 October. His men were fresh; Harold's were exhausted, having just completed a forced march of some 200 miles in five days immediately after fighting a savage battle against the Norwegian King Harold Hardrada at Stamford Bridge, near York. William relied on his armoured and highly trained cavalry, together with several companies of archers, some with short bows, some with crossbows (here making their first appearance in military history); the English fought on foot, wielding heavy, two-handed Danish battle-axes, though they probably carried swords as well. True, the English occupied the higher ground; none the less, the odds were massively weighted on the Norman side, and it is a wonder that Harold had the success he did: at one moment he had the Normans on the run down the hill, and William's horse was killed from under him.

But then the Normans counter-attacked, and the tide

turned. Hitherto the English had defended themselves with an uninterrupted wall of shields. William ordered his archers to fire high, over this wall; and it was then, with the arrows coming down like rain, that Harold sustained his fatal wound. Finding themselves now without a leader – the King's two brothers had already fallen – the English fled the field. It was all over. The few remaining pockets of resistance were quickly dealt with, and William was crowned in Westminster Abbey on Christmas Day.

Of Battle Abbey itself, sadly little of the original Norman building survives, although several of the later monastic buildings are still there, including a splendid dormitory, with a fine vaulted chamber for the novices. The west range, which included the Abbot's Great Hall, was converted after the Dissolution of the Monasteries into a country mansion, which in the early eighteenth century was bought by a baronet appropriately named Sir Thomas Battle. One guidebook informs me that 'it was an all-girls' boarding school when Canadian troops were stationed there during the Second World War' – the girls must have had quite an education – and it is still a school today, though now for both sexes.

The ruins and the battlefield itself are now in the care of English Heritage. No other English battlefield has been so well preserved. You can tour it in about forty-five minutes on foot, and there are many signs – to say nothing of an excellent audioguide – to help you on your way. If you have no time for the full tour, then head for the west end of the lower terrace – where Harold drew up the right wing of his line – and look out across the now tranquil playing fields where, in a few nightmare hours, all English history was changed.

Only one trick is missed: the souvenir shop does not sell Stanley Holloway's superb recording, in a rich Yorkshire accent, of one of my favourite poems. It ends:

The Normans turned round in a fury,
And gave back both parry and thrust,
Till the fight were all over bar shoutin'
And you couldn't see Saxons for dust.

And after the battle were over,
They found 'Arold, so stately and grand,
Sittin' there with an eye full of arrer,
On 'is 'orse, with 'is 'awk in 'is 'and.

II

Hemingford Grey

CAMBRIDGESHIRE

*H*emingford Grey in Cambridgeshire is an astonishing house – not for its beauty, since it's not at all beautiful in the strictest sense of the word, but for its age and its quite extraordinary atmosphere. It must be one of the oldest continuously inhabited houses in England, or even in Europe, because it is built around – and inside – an early twelfth-century Norman hall. Of this several windows, of one and two lights, still survive; so too does the original doorway, which must have been approached, then as now, by an outer wooden stair. In the hall itself is an even rarer survival: a complete Norman fireplace, flanked by two columns with scalloped capitals.

This country boasts one or two fine cathedrals that are basically of the Norman period – though there are always later additions and accretions – of which Durham is the outstanding example; there are also quite a few unspoilt Norman churches. But that period covers only little more than a century – it came to an end around 1180 – so surviving Norman domestic architecture is rare indeed. The owner of Hemingford Grey would probably have been what we should now call a country squire. He would certainly not have been a great lord – his house is no castle; rather he would have been a lord's vassal, who had been granted possession of the land, known as a fief, in return for an undertaking to provide military service as and when required. He was relatively high in the feudal pecking order none the less; immediately below him were the freemen, who were essentially more humble farmers who paid rent for their land but were without military obligations; and below the freemen came the villeins.

Being a villein wasn't much fun. He would generally rent a small cottage, in return for which he was expected to work in his landlord's fields – or just possibly to provide domestic help in the manor house – for a given number of days a week; on the other days he could concentrate on his own fields, crops and livestock. One drawback to this system was that the weather treated landlord and villein in the same way: when the master's fields were ready to be harvested, so were the servant's – and the master's, it need hardly be said, always took precedence. Another was that, although technically free under the law, the villein was always tied to the same piece of land and was forbidden to move away without his landlord's consent. There were however compensations: on the days when he worked for the landlord, he could probably expect a good, nourishing meal. He also had the right to gather firewood in his master's forests, and – possibly on payment of a very small fee – to use his master's mills and ovens.

Finally he could console himself with the reflection that there was another class still worse off than he: the serf. The serf was little more than a slave. He owned no land, worked exclusively on his landlord's and lived on the landlord's handouts. Theoretically he owned nothing – not even his own clothes; in fact, however, he could sometimes earn a pittance by selling any surplus farm produce at the local market. Fortunately, too, most landlords seem to have felt a certain sense of responsibility to their serfs. They would do their best to protect them against the depredations of outlaws – not unusual in those troubled times – and would normally provide a helping hand in the event of sickness or famine.

If I seem to be harping on agriculture, this is because agriculture was by far the most important factor in medieval life. Most of people's time was spent in working the land, trying to produce enough food to carry them through for another year. Church feast days provided them with the only opportunity of resting from their labours; nobody ever took a holiday. For those who could afford the time, however, there were regular markets and fairs, the latter often providing entertainment in the form of musicians, acrobats and jugglers. And naturally, every town had its taverns – though these were regrettably rare among the smaller villages.

The other universal preoccupation was religion. Even if a small village had no tavern, it would almost certainly possess a church, and the principal services were attended by everyone, save those who were prevented by age or sickness. This universal attendance was, one suspects, prompted less by the love of God than by the fear of hellfire, which was assiduously preached from every pulpit. We have only to look at the vast 'doom paintings' that survive over many an ancient chancel arch to understand the terror they must have inspired – a terror that hung over every aspect of medieval life.

The only certain way of avoiding hell was to be totally absolved from all one's sins; and, at least for the better off, what more effective means was there of gaining such absolution than by going on a pilgrimage or, better still, a Crusade? The first Crusaders had left England in 1096 – three years later, they and their Frankish companions had captured Jerusalem – and had returned with many strange tales about distant lands; and all over Europe the pilgrim routes were thronged. Another attractive aspect of pilgrimages was that they cost nothing but a pair of stout walking boots;

accommodation was free at all the monasteries along the way. And as time passed, they became steadily more popular: at the end of the fourteenth century, Chaucer's Wife of Bath was boasting that she had been three times to Jerusalem.

None the less, life in Norman times was hard; it was also short. Even if you survived infancy, you would probably be dead before your children were grown up. A poor man – unless he worked in a great house – was nearly always hungry. Even a rich man was very seldom clean; the owner of Hemingford Grey and his friends probably all smelled like polecats. Privacy, too, was out, with master, mistress and servants all sleeping together in the Great Hall. Before you close this book, thank your lucky stars that you weren't born in the Middle Ages. I do, all the time.

12

Appleby Castle
CUMBRIA

*I*t is hardly surprising, in view of the almost constant fighting between England and Scotland in the Middle Ages,
that castles sprang up like mushrooms all along the border.
There are twenty-two of them still wholly or partly surviving,
seven in Cumbria and fifteen in Northumberland. Of these
Appleby is by no means the greatest or the grandest. It is not,
like Alnwick, the second largest inhabited castle in England
after Windsor; nor, like Lindisfarne (q.v.) is it spectacularly
beautiful. Rather is it typical of the chain of relatively minor
castles that sweeps across northern England between
Newcastle and Carlisle. The original early twelfth-century
building occupied, like most of its fellows, a fairly isolated and
lonely elevation looking down on to the River Eden; but it is
now virtually surrounded by the quite attractive little town of
Appleby. The principal survivor is the great square stone keep
of about 1170, one of the best preserved of its type remaining
in the country and known – for some mysterious reason – as
Caesar's Tower.

From this tower a long medieval curtain wall runs up to
another medieval tower – a round one this time – to the
Mansion, a rather grand seventeenth-century house built by
one of the great figures in the history of the north, the redoubt-
able Lady Anne Clifford (1590–1676). She owned at least two

neighbouring castles, Brougham and Brough, and in the days when the north-west was the best part of a week's journey from London she wielded huge power in the region. She was also an enthusiastic patron of the arts – and there weren't very many of those. (The delightfully named and quietly perceptive Bishop Rainbow of Carlisle noticed that 'her dress, not disliked by any, was yet imitated by none'.)

Were all these castles strictly necessary? On the whole, they were. For the English, the Scots have always been something of a problem. Assiduous readers of this book will know that already in the early second century AD the Roman Emperor Hadrian built a wall to keep them out, and for many centuries after that the various tribes along the still ill-defined border raided each other's towns and villages, abducted each other's women and rustled each other's cattle. Until the Norman Conquest, nobody did much about it; but in 1072 William the Conqueror ordered a strategically brilliant pincer movement against the Scottish King Malcolm III from the Clyde in the west to the Tay in the east, cutting Scotland effectively in two and forcing Malcolm to accept him as rightful King of England. (Though not, of course, of Scotland.) William's son and successor William II continued his father's work. In 1091 he repulsed an attempted invasion by Malcolm, obliging him to pay homage, and in the following year he built the castle at Carlisle, taking control of both Cumberland and Westmorland (together forming the modern Cumbria) which Malcolm had previously claimed for himself. It was during yet another border skirmish, at Alnwick, Northumberland, in 1093, that Malcolm finally received his comeuppance at the hands of a Norman army commanded by one of William's leading knights, Robert de Mowbray.

But the fighting went on. By 1135, with Stephen struggling with his cousin Matilda, England was involved in something

very like a civil war. The Scots seized their chance and recap-
tured Carlisle. By this time, however, it wasn't just a straight
contest between the English and the Scots; the barons of the
north had now exploited the situation to assert their independence from both kingdoms. It was Matilda's son, the
English King Henry II, who finally took matters in hand:
when the young Scottish King William I (the Lion) was captured at Alnwick in 1174 – having made the mistake of allying
himself with Henry's rebellious sons – Henry decided to make
an example of him. He first paraded him as a captive, feet tied
beneath his horse, then shipped him off to imprisonment at
Falaise and released him only when he had done formal
homage, both for his Scottish kingdom and for 'any lands
elsewhere'. Although this oath was in fact abrogated by
Henry's son and successor, Richard I (Coeur de Lion), it was
the basis for the perennial claim by the Plantagenet kings that
they were the feudal suzerains of the Scots – a claim that
in future years was to make mountains of trouble for both
parties.

In later centuries the basic hostility continued unabated, though there were plenty of periods when an uneasy truce prevailed. The situation was further complicated by what came to be known as the Auld Alliance, the traditional friendship between Scotland and France, the two of them drawn together by their cordial dislike of their common neighbour; and it became well-nigh intolerable with the appearance on the world scene of Mary Queen of Scots (see **Wingfield Manor**). It was not until 1603 that their two countries were united under a single king – James I of England was also James VI of Scotland – and not until 1 May 1707 that they were still more closely united under the name of Great Britain, with a single Parliament (in London, but with Scottish representatives) and a single flag, the Union Jack.

Even since that time, the relationship has continued a little prickly. In 1999, in what was generally accounted a significant step forward, Scotland obtained a Parliament of its own – though this did not stop it continuing to send members to Westminster – and at the time of writing, the Scottish National Party has become the ruling party in that Parliament, standing as it does for a totally independent Scotland. Whether it will ever obtain that objective seems to me unlikely, though I shall shed no tears if it does. At least we shan't have to build any more castles – or (dreadful thought) shall we?

Medieval England

Introduction

No one should ever think for a minute that the Middle Ages were an agreeable time to live. Even for the aristocracy, life was cold, uncomfortable and usually short, with hygiene almost non-existent, the food filthy, the drink not much better. But, in England at least, things were happening. The country was changing fast. The Normans had given it a shot in the arm, and now the people were beginning to reap the benefit. The feudal system that the Normans had introduced remained fully in force, and quite rightly: the delegation of authority to their vassals enabled the nobles to maintain control over their often widely distributed dominions while, at the other end of the scale, the peasantry wanted security from marauders and, on occasion, from invading armies. They paid for this security with much of their individual liberty, but in those lawless days most of them probably thought that it was well worth the sacrifice.

For the vast majority who continued to work the land, there was in the twelfth and thirteenth centuries a distinct improvement in the climate, while advances in agricultural methods – in particular in the design of the plough – made their labours perhaps one degree less arduous than in earlier times. By the fourteenth century it is estimated that up to half the peasantry possessed holdings of between fifteen and thirty acres, which would have yielded saleable surpluses of grain and animal products such as dairy produce and, above all, wool.

It is difficult to overestimate the importance of wool to the economy of medieval England. It was by far our most important export, and it formed the basis for our largest industry, textiles. Yorkshire, East Anglia and the Cotswolds in particular produced the finest wool in Europe. Until the fourteenth century, it was exported in vast quantities through the ports of the east coast to the Low Countries, where it was woven into cloth. Then the trade was seriously interrupted by the Hundred Years War, and England began a weaving industry of its own. The various processes necessary to produce the finished article generated several other profitable trades besides that of the weavers: fullers washed the cloth and broke down its fibres; carders combed it; and dyers gave it its colour. No wonder the country prospered.

Meanwhile for those in the professions or trades there was no shortage of employment. This was the golden age of building in England; much of our greatest architecture – the majestic castles, the breathtaking cathedrals like those of Salisbury, Ely or Wells, the innumerable exquisite parish churches – dates from this time. And two more trades, not particularly demanding in Norman days, were now taken to new heights of technical skill: that of the quarryman and the master stonemason.

There were catastrophes of course, by far the worst of which was the Black Death, that epidemic of the bubonic plague that struck England in 1348–50, killing perhaps two in five of the population. It was a good half-century before the country came anywhere near recovery. And there were wars: notably the Hundred Years War, which for the English had the great advantage of being fought exclusively in France, in a largely vain attempt to regain England's former possessions there;

and, through much of the fifteenth century, the first of our civil wars, delicately known as the Wars of the Roses: a misnomer if ever there was one. These later hostilities, by contrast, were confined to England; but, deeply unpleasant as they were for those engaged in them and for those with the misfortune to live on or near a battlefield, the vast majority of Englishmen and women were probably unaware of their very existence.

For the better educated – by which I mean the literate – intellectual life was beginning in the still embryonic universities of Oxford and Cambridge, and took a further huge step forward in 1476, when William Caxton set up England's first printing press in Westminster. Appropriately enough, the first book that he produced was Geoffrey Chaucer's *Canterbury Tales*, written in the reign of Richard II almost a century before. Though the language of the time was what is known as Middle English, there are plenty of modern versions available; but Chaucer's original is easily comprehensible with a little practice, and is well worth reading as the first undoubted masterpiece of English literature.

Perhaps the principal drawback the English had to contend with during the Middle Ages was the dynasty of the Plantagenets. After the near-genius of Henry II – who laid the foundations of our legal system – and with the not very shining exceptions of Edwards I and III, our rulers till the end of the fourteenth century were little better that dolts; the new century started rather more promisingly with Henrys IV and V, but then with Henry VI we were saddled with the worst of the lot – in youth a fool, in later life an imbecile. The series was completed by a playboy and a villain. (All right, I know that not everyone agrees about Richard III, but I stick to my guns.) And, because we were still a long way from constitutional monarchy, the people suffered. What a relief it must have been, after Bosworth, when the Tudors got a grip at last.

Stonehenge. The greatest and grandest of the stone circles of England, dating probably to 3,000–2,500 BC. Mysteries still abound. The inner stones seem to have been brought 160 miles from South Wales; how? Others are missing altogether; what happened to them? And what is the whole thing for, anyway?

Hadrian's Wall, Northumberland. There's no more evocative sight in England than that of this astonishing fortification, marching from coast to coast. Typical Hadrian too: no other Roman Emperor would have dreamt of building it.

Chedworth Roman Villa, Gloucestershire. The Romans loved the Cotswolds – the hills were a favourite place for their villas, which were essentially working farms. The early ones were probably simple enough, but as their owners grew more prosperous, floor mosaics proliferated. We're still some distance from Botticelli, but we're on our way.

Sutton Hoo, Suffolk.
In the whole history of English archaeology, can there ever have been more exciting moments than those of the discovery of the Sutton Hoo ship, and of that magical iron helmet which seems to be a living man?

Lindisfarne, Northumberland. Although there are few traces now left of the monastery or the Tudor castle that followed it – both having been rather surprisingly replaced by a country house designed by Sir Edwin Lutyens – the Gospels penned by the monk Eadfrith in *c.*700 AD are more spectacular then either. This, in case you failed to recognize it, is the opening page of St Mark.

St Peter on the Wall, Bradwell-juxta-Mare, Essex. This unpresumptuous-looking building is not haunted; but it possesses a quality of the spirit stronger than any other I know. It is also probably the oldest church in England, built in 653.

Offa's Dyke, Herefordshire. King Offa of Mercia seems to have been a formidable enough character, but he was no Hadrian – and, as he would probably have been the first to admit, his Dyke is no Wall. On the other hand he seems to have felt very much the same about the Welsh as Hadrian did about the Scots.

Battle Abbey, East Sussex. How incredibly lucky we are to have the greatest-ever strip cartoon to illustrate the greatest-ever battle fought on English soil. The Bayeux Tapestry is not only a superb narrative full of the captivating detail of eleventh-century life, it is also hilariously funny. Don't let anyone ever tell you that the arrow-in-the-eye story is a myth. It's all there.

Hemingford Grey, Cambridgeshire. Walk into Hemingford Grey and remind yourself: there were people living in this old Norman hall in the early twelfth century: doorway, windows, even the great open hearth are still there. Life has continued on this spot in fact, for just about nine hundred years.

Canterbury Cathedral.
I always think that Canterbury looks exactly the way our mother-cathedral ought to look. Can the same be said of our father-martyr Thomas Becket? What no representation of him makes clear is his enormous size – well over six feet, a giant in the twelfth century. They still keep one of his robes at Sens Cathedral; once a year – until it became too fragile – it was worn by the tallest canon, but he always had to pin it up.

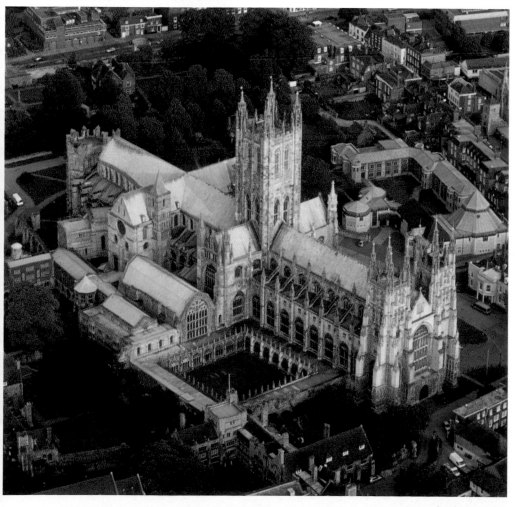

Runnymede, Surrey. The interesting thing about Runnymede is how unremarkable it looks – just an ordinary water-meadow like a thousand others, probably a meeting place for the old Anglo-Saxon Witanagemots. With apologies to my American friends, I feel that it has been rather spoilt by its modern memorials. It would have been better left to its one great memory, and to the birds, and to the wind over the grass.

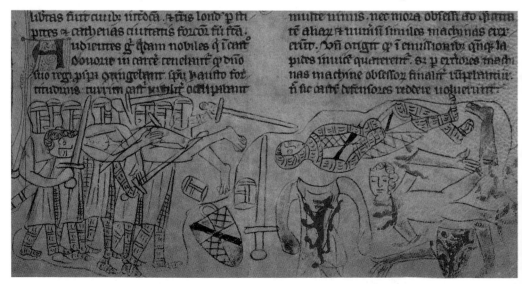

Church of St Lawrence, Evesham, Worcestershire. In Evesham, everybody can tell you about the Battle of Evesham in 1265; outside Evesham, alas, relatively few. The great battlefield remains its monument; the church where Simon de Montfort and his men prayed on the morning of the battle has long since gone. We are left with this contemporary illustration and a modern stained-glass window in St Lawrence's.

13

Canterbury Cathedral
KENT

*T*he heart, the mind and perhaps even the soul of English Christianity are encapsulated in the Cathedral Church of Christ, Canterbury. Its history goes back over fourteen centuries, to the year 597, when St Augustine arrived and converted King Ethelbert of Kent. (His wife Bertha, being French, was a Christian already and had presumably softened him up in advance.) After the King's baptism, followed by that of all his subjects, Christianity in England never looked back. Eventually Augustine settled in Canterbury and became its first archbishop.

There had been Christians in England in the third century – St Alban was martyred in 304 – but after the departure of the Romans the religion was at a low ebb; the old British Church, moreover, had shown no interest in converting the recent invaders, so this new wave of fervent missionaries, sent directly by Pope Gregory the Great, was vitally necessary if England were ever to become a Christian country. They and their successors were dramatically successful, and within a century or so the rapidly developing Anglo-Saxon culture was deeply imbued with the new faith.

Canterbury remained the ecclesiastical capital, as it still is today; but its popularity was hugely increased when in 1170 the most popular of all English medieval martyrs, St Thomas

Becket, was murdered within its walls. Only a very few years later St Thomas's magnificent shrine was, after Rome and Jerusalem, more visited than any other in Christendom. The story of the murder is well known: how four knights, hearing King Henry II's furious shout, 'Oh, who will rid me of this turbulent priest?' and taking it somewhat too literally, rode straight to Canterbury and ran the archbishop through with their swords. Henry, horrified, subsequently did penance – which included a ritual scourging – in the cathedral; he was haunted by the atrocity for the rest of his life. In further expiation he ordered the building of the shrine, which brought many thousands of pilgrims – and a great deal of money – to the city every year. Would that it were still there today; alas, it was destroyed on the orders of Henry VIII, who for good measure had the murdered archbishop also condemned as a traitor and a rebel. All that remains to mark the spot where he fell – in the north-west transept, just by the entrance to the passage that leads into the cloister – is the early thirteenth-century mosaic floor and an inscription on the wall above: THOMAS BECKET/ARCHBISHOP *SAINT* MARTYR/ DIED HERE/TUESDAY 29TH DECEMBER/1170.

Only a few feet away, on the south side of the Trinity Chapel, is the sumptuous tomb of Edward the Black Prince, eldest son of Edward III, who died in 1376. There he lies in gilded copper, armed cap-à-pie, on a high tomb chest with painted shields and beneath a painted wooden canopy. High above hang replicas of his funerary achievements: shield, helm, gauntlets and tabard. (The originals, or what is left of them, can be seen in the south choir aisle.) Opposite, on the north side of the chapel, stands the tomb of King Henry IV – who died in 1413 – and his queen, Joan of Navarre. Whereas the Black Prince was represented hieratically, these two effigies are obviously portraits. Solicitous angels adjust their pillows and crowns.

When you have finished seeing the body of the cathedral, don't miss the crypt. It is much older, going back to the early twelfth century and Norman times. Unlike the crypts of most other cathedrals, it is well above ground, has quite large windows and is full of light. It possesses two outstanding glories: the carved capitals of the supporting columns and the wall paintings in St Gabriel's Chapel on the south side. Walled up for nearly 700 years, they have kept all the freshness of their execution and the brilliance of their colouring; but the really remarkable thing about them is their unEnglishness. There is a spiritual, hieratic quality about them that speaks compellingly of Byzantium. Now early twelfth-century England had only one cultural link with Constantinople: Sicily, where the Norman King Roger II (1130–54) commissioned from Byzantine painters and mosaicists works as fine as any to be found in the imperial capital. Thus these paintings are, in their way, the counterpart of the mosaic portrait of St Thomas of Canterbury in the apse of the Cathedral of Monreale, placed there as a gesture of contrition by Henry II's own daughter, Queen Joanna of Sicily.

Next, the Cloister. This too is basically Norman work, though it was remodelled in the fourteenth century with the vaulting and the painted heraldic shields for bosses. If you walk clockwise round it, you will almost complete the circuit before you come, halfway along the east side, to the Chapter House. It comprises one vast single room, nearly 100 feet long, of immense height and profoundly impressive. The effect is largely due to the wooden roof of memorable splendour – the largest in England apart from that of Westminster Hall, which it comfortably predates.

So much – though there remains any amount more to examine and enjoy – for the cathedral and its monastic appurtenances, but these are by no means all that Canterbury has to offer. Although the city suffered seriously during the Second World War – a stick of bombs scored a direct hit on a building in which one of the cathedral canons was having his bath, with the result that the front wall collapsed and the canon, still in his bath, slid down the rubble into the High Street – there are a number of other ancient monuments that should not be ignored. You should not, for example, fail to visit St Martin's Church, probably the earliest place of Christian worship surviving in England. It is impossible to date with any accuracy; all we can say is that it is not later than the sixth century, and could be earlier. It was certainly here before St Augustine; it may have been founded by Bertha, soon after her arrival.

Finally you should nip down to Greyfriars, off Stour Street. The Greyfriars were Franciscans – they adopted their brown robes later – the first of whom arrived in Canterbury in 1224, while St Francis was still alive. This building, which probably served as the warden's lodging, dates from about half a century later. With its two arches spanning the river – here little more than a stream – and narrow lancet above, it is characteristically unassuming; but on a sunny morning it looks quite ravishingly pretty.

14

Runnymede

*W*ith the exception of London and Windsor, Runnymede is the most historic place on the River Thames, and every schoolchild knows – or should know – the reason why: it was here, on 15 June 1215, that King John was forced by his barons to sign Magna Carta, the Great Charter that is universally recognized as one of the cornerstones of English constitutional history.

Of all the monarchs who have ruled in England since the Norman Conquest, John was probably the worst – so bad indeed that no later king has ever taken his name. His elder brother Richard I (Coeur de Lion) runs him a close second; but this is largely because during his ten-year reign he spent less than six months in England. John too was often an absentee, but he was a disastrous ruler as well. In Richard's absence he raised a private army and took over the country; and when Richard, returning from the Third Crusade, was taken prisoner by Duke Leopold of Austria, John instantly proclaimed him dead and himself king – a piece of treachery for which Richard, rather surprisingly, forgave him. He was a violent man, who thought nothing of slaughtering thirty-two noble hostages during his Welsh wars; the story of his treatment of his nephew, Prince Arthur of Brittany, is movingly told in Shakespeare's play, *King John*.

But treachery and violence were by no means all. Excommunicated by Pope Innocent III in 1209, three years later John had no hesitation in handing the whole kingdom over to Rome, in order to get the sentence lifted and to gain an ally for his war against King Philip Augustus of France. Always short of money, he taxed his people until the pips squeaked: heirs were forced to pay a tax before they could inherit, widows before they could remarry. As for the barons, they were excused military service in return for the payment of what they called *scutage*, or shield-money. And what was there to show for all these extortions? Precious little. In 1214 John's army of some 15,000 men was smashed by King Philip's far superior force at Bouvines, between Lille and Tournai. This marked the end of all his continental ambitions. He was now so weak that he was obliged to sign Magna Carta the following year.

Which brings us to Runnymede. Why, one wonders, did the barons choose this beautiful but unremarkable little water-meadow by the Thames as the setting for the most important constitutional step since the Conquest? It seems that it had been a political meeting place ever since Anglo-Saxon times, that the very name means 'regular meeting place', and that it had been used for gatherings of the Witanagemot – the Anglo-Saxon gathering of elders – since the reign of Alfred the Great. The fact remains that it had not served in such a capacity for the best part of 200 years, so we are still uncertain.

As for the Great Charter itself, there is no greater mistake than to see it as a precursor of the Declaration of Independence, still less of the US Constitution. It was not, as has been wisely pointed out, a charter of liberty so much as a charter of *liberties*, a list of prohibitions that the King was required to observe. Thus it was not a birth certificate of freedom so much as a death certificate of despotism. Henceforth the law was not

simply the whim of the King; it was an independent institution that the King, like everyone else in his kingdom, was
bound to respect. Perhaps one of its most important provisions was the right of *habeas corpus*, by which nobody could be
held in confinement for more than a very limited time without proper trial.

Such is the reputation of this most celebrated of all historic
documents that it comes as something of a surprise to learn
that the more intransigent barons almost immediately rendered it unworkable. Far from ensuring a healthier relationship
between themselves and the monarchy, it led to a civil war
that soon became an international one when Prince Louis of
France (later Louis VIII) invaded England at the barons' invitation. Pope Innocent – who saw it not as an assertion of the
law against tyranny, but as a 'shameful and demeaning'
attempt at feudal insurrection against royal authority – was
predictably furious, and at John's request declared it null and
void on the grounds that it had been imposed upon the King
against his will. Later monarchs, however, reissued it in various bowdlerized forms, omitting the bits that they particularly
disliked or that they saw as a specific challenge to their own
authority.

As far as we know, there was no single, master copy of the
charter, and on any of the four surviving copies going back to
1215 you will look in vain for King John's signature; his royal
seal was deemed enough. Of the four, the one belonging to
the British Library is in the worst condition, having been
damaged by fire to the point where it is virtually illegible. The
best is that owned by Salisbury Cathedral. Of the other two,
one is kept in the House of Lords; the fourth, the property of
Lincoln Cathedral, is normally displayed in Lincoln Castle.
In 1939 it was sent to New York, to be put on exhibition at the
World's Fair; it was still there on the outbreak of war, when it

was sent to Fort Knox for the duration. Not until 1948 did it return to Lincoln; but it has revisited the US on several occasions since.

It would have been nice to have a copy at Runnymede; what you will find there are three memorials. The first is a monument to the men and women of the Allied Air Forces; the second is a circular classical temple to commemorate the charter itself by the American Bar Association in 1957; the latest was erected in 1965 to the memory of President Kennedy. It bears the inscription – taken from his Inaugural Address – reading:

> Let every nation know, whether it wishes us well or ill, that we shall pay any price, bear any burden, meet any hardship, support any friend or oppose any foe, in order to ensure the survival and success of liberty.

15

Merton College
OXFORD

*I*deally, I should like to have called this piece 'Oxbridge'. It would, first of all, have been a more accurate title; it would also have saved me from accusations of favouritism. But there: Oxbridge, useful as it is, refers to two different places, and for the purposes of this book I can choose only one. I plump for Oxford – not as an old alumnus but simply because it is the older of the two; and I plump for Merton College not because I went there (I didn't) but because it is the oldest of the forty-four.

The universities of Europe were the most important and valuable product of the Middle Ages. They began in the eleventh century as loose assemblages of teachers and students, and only very gradually coalesced into the institutions we know today. There seems to have been teaching of some kind going on at Oxford in the 1090s, and the numbers swelled dramatically after 1167, when Henry II banned his subjects from attending the University of Paris. Then in 1209, after what must have been quite a serious dispute with the people of the town, a discontented group departed in disgust and settled in the fen country of East Anglia, where they founded the University of Cambridge. Still, however, there were no colleges as we know them today; for the first of these we have to wait another fifty-three years.

Despite occasional claims by University College and Balliol, to Merton must go the distinction of being the oldest of all the Oxford colleges. Let no one tell you that 'Univ', as it is familiarly known, was founded by Alfred the Great; in fact it owes its existence to one William of Durham, who in 1249 left the university 310 marks to maintain a dozen advanced students of theology. Unfortunately, however, the earliest statutes were not issued until 1280, sixteen years later than those of Merton. As for Balliol, it was almost certainly founded in 1263, when John Balliol set aside eightpence a day for the maintenance of sixteen poor scholars, as a penance for having in 1255 kidnapped the Bishop of Durham; but once again the statutes came later, in the 1280s.

It was in 1262 that Walter de Merton, Chancellor of England and later Bishop of Rochester, obtained a licence to allot the revenues of two manors in Surrey for the support of 'clerks' studying at a university, and two years later he received royal sanction in a deed which still exists in the Merton Library. A further royal statute of 1274 specifically establishes the college at Oxford. It's interesting to note that all these foundations were originally set up in the form of scholarships, or bursaries. Poverty seemed endemic in the universities, and would continue to be so for a long time to come. When Sir Thomas More was disgraced in 1534, he told his children that at a pinch the family could always go to Oxford: 'Then may we yet like poor scholars of Oxford go a begging with our bags and wallets and sing Salve Regina at rich mens dores.'

Quadrangles – at Cambridge they are called 'courts' – soon came to form the focus of college life. Around them are grouped all the principal buildings of the college: the chapel, the hall, the library, the lodgings of the head of the college (Warden, President, Master or whatever the title may be) and rooms for dons and undergraduates. These rooms ushered in a significant change: previously, students had been obliged to live in religious houses or halls of residence – no other kinds of accommodation were available, since they were forbidden to lodge with the local townspeople. Now they could live in the colleges, in a new atmosphere of learning and study. In the Middle Ages, as well as theology and philosophy, they would learn the seven liberal arts of grammar, rhetoric, logic, arithmetic, geometry, astronomy and music; now, as medieval scholasticism gave way to the new humanism, they began studying the pagan texts in Latin and – after around 1400 if they were lucky enough to find a teacher – Greek. No longer did the lecturers concentrate on explaining the meaning of the early texts; now, with the Renaissance, there came a new spirit of enquiry.

From the beginning, the individual colleges possessed libraries of their own. Some, however, were obviously better stocked than others, and it became desirable to establish a library for the university as a whole. At Oxford the younger brother of King Henry V, Duke Humphrey, founded the first of these; most of it was broken up during the Reformation, the books being sold or destroyed, and in 1598 Sir Thomas Bodley decided to restore and extend it. He died in 1613 while the work was still in progress, but the Bodleian Library as we know it today was completed in 1624. The Cambridge University Library grew up at much the same time. Apart from the British Library, they are the largest in the country. Both are Legal Deposit Libraries, which means that they are entitled to claim a free copy of any book published in Great Britain and Ireland within a year of publication.

All this makes a university sound a somewhat grim affair; and so, in their early days, the great universities probably were.

But young students, particularly when gathered together, tend to be high-spirited, and the sudden relaxation of the discipline they knew in their schooldays is bound to have had an exhilarating and liberating effect. For 500 years at least there is evidence of unseemly behaviour – and not only among the undergraduates. In 1507 the Fellows of Magdalen were obliged to submit to an enquiry into their conduct. Its findings were not favourable:

> *Stokes was unchaste with the wife of a tailor.*
> *Stokysley baptized a cat and practised witchcraft.*
> *Gregory climbed the great gate by the tower, and brought a*
>   *Stranger into College.*
> *Kendall wears a gown not sewn together in front.*

And quite right too. It has often been pointed out that the purpose of a good university is to put back all the nonsense that was knocked out of one at school. As Max Beerbohm put it: 'I was an honest, good-humoured boy. It is Oxford that has made me insufferable.' But perhaps the pithiest comment of all was made by one Andrew Boorde in 1549:

> *A Mayster of Arte*
> *Is not worthe a Farte.*

16

Stained-Glass Window, Church of
St Lawrence

EVESHAM, WORCESTERSHIRE

S t Lawrence's Church in Evesham is a fine example of
what is known as the Perpendicular style of Gothic
architecture, which means that it is almost certainly of the
fifteenth century. The Battle of Evesham took place in
the thirteenth century – in 1265 to be precise – long before the
church was built. But tragically – apart from the battlefield
itself, which remains much as it was on that fateful 4 August
– there is no contemporary monument to one of the most
important military encounters in English history. Of the great
abbey, thanks to Henry VIII and the Dissolution, barely one
stone remains on another (though the separate Bell Tower
remains); so St Lawrence it will have to be. The window in the
church is Victorian; but it depicts the last hours in the abbey
of the wild, idealistic, impetuous and utterly impossible Simon
de Montfort before he rode out to his extremely unpleasant
death. (De Montfort was in fact King Henry III's brother-in-
law, though only after seducing his sister and making her
pregnant – a circumstance that hardly improved relations
between them.)

People tend to forget – and the schools are unlikely to teach
them any more – that England has in fact seen not two but
three civil wars in its history, the first every bit as significant
as the second and third. This war was effectively a struggle for

power between the King and the barons, of which the first major manifestation had been the signing of the Great Charter by King John in 1215; in the ensuing decades it had grumbled on, and it once again came to a head in April 1258 when John's son Henry III found himself faced at Westminster with de Montfort and six other leading barons, demanding that the King should immediately dismiss his foreign counsellors and hangers-on: 'Let the wretched and intolerable Poitevins and all aliens flee from your face and ours as from the face of a lion, and there will be glory to God in the heavens and peace to men of goodwill.' Henry, we are told by the chronicler Matthew Paris, swore a solemn oath at the shrine of St Edward (the Confessor) that he would fully and properly amend his old errors and show favour and kindness to his native-born subjects. He also agreed to the establishment of a committee of twenty-four to draft reforms.

The crucial meeting was held on 11 June at Oxford. What it achieved was, in essence, the abolition of the absolute monarchy. The sovereign powers of the crown were transferred to a permanent standing committee appointed by the barons and the Church. All foreign noblemen were to be expelled. (De Montfort himself had rather awkwardly been born in France, but an exception was made in his case.) The future government would be English through and through. Henry gave his reluctant assent, but his son Edward was by no means prepared to surrender the royal powers so easily. Simon made the mistake of leaving the country for France, and without his fierce charisma the prince managed over the next two or three years to sow considerable dissension among the barons, one or two of whom came to sudden and unexpected ends. When Simon de Montfort returned in 1263 he found to his fury that the King had recovered many of his strategic castles and had even gained papal absolution, releasing him from his oath.

War was now inevitable. On 14 May de Montfort defeated the King's army – which included the famous Robert the Bruce of Scotland – at the Battle of Lewes. He failed to capture Henry himself, who had taken refuge in a local priory; but his victory was complete enough to allow him to dictate peace terms, which included Prince Edward's becoming hostage for his father's good behaviour. De Montfort then took a step that probably brought England nearer to the status of republic than at any time before the execution of Charles I, still four centuries in the future. He demanded that each shire and many of the most important boroughs should send two *elected* members to a parliament to be held the following year in 1265, simultaneously calling on them to provide enough armed men to form a people's army. To be sure, the parliament didn't last long and its deliberations bore little similarity with those of the House of Commons as we know it today; but they represented the beginnings of a representative government far more broadly based than any other in still feudal and absolutist Europe.

Prince Edward, however, had escaped from his custody and was more active than ever. As for de Montfort, success had by now gone dangerously to his head: he was arrogant, domineering, power-hungry and, it was rumoured, increasingly corrupt. His former popularity had virtually evaporated. Meanwhile Edward's whirlwind activities in the Welsh border country were undermining the baronial forces, suborning some, dividing others, until at last, in the high summer at Green Hill, just north of Evesham, he was ready to bring de Montfort to battle. At eight in the morning, the two armies rode out on to the field in a melodramatically raging thunderstorm which quickly turned the ground to mud. The barons fought valiantly, but their 5,000 were hopelessly outnumbered by two to one and had no chance. Simon himself was unhorsed, then fought on foot until he was killed. His last words, we are told, were 'Thank God'. What followed was a massacre. Few if any prisoners were taken; the wounded were stabbed to death where they lay. De Montfort's hands, feet and genitals were cut off, these last hung around his neck. His great castle of Kenilworth, however, refused to surrender. It held out for a five-month siege, falling only when the last of its defenders were dying of cold and hunger.

Thanks largely to the energy, courage and brilliant diplomacy of his son, King Henry III's crown had been saved. He gave thanks by completing the new shrine in Westminster Abbey of his hero, the royal saint Edward the Confessor, whose remains were transferred four years later to their new resting place. When Henry himself died in 1272 – once again an absolute monarch – his coffin was laid there while his own magnificent tomb was being prepared. Despite the length of his reign – fifty-six years – he is largely forgotten today, perhaps because there is something curiously colourless about him; he was a monarch to whom things happened, rather than one who made things happen. Dante includes him in the *Divine Comedy* as 'the King of simple life', sitting dolefully outside the gates of Purgatory. It seems a harsh judgement; but perhaps one sees what he means.

17

Middle Temple
LONDON

*I*n England there are four Inns of Court – professional legal associations, to one of which all members of the English Bar must belong. They are Lincoln's Inn, Gray's Inn, and the Inner and Middle Temple. They originated in the thirteenth century as hostels, or schools for student lawyers; the layout of each is not unlike that of an Oxford or Cambridge college, with church or chapel, hall, library and offices – known as 'chambers' – for literally hundreds of barristers. In this short survey, the Middle Temple must stand for them all.

It occupies the western half of what was called the Temple, the headquarters of the old Knights Templar until they were dissolved in 1312. The church – which also serves the Inner Temple – was consecrated in 1185 by the Patriarch of Jerusalem. It is circular, like all the Templar churches, built on the model of the Rotunda in the Church of the Holy Sepulchre in Jerusalem. Many of the knights are still there; their effigies lie not, as one might expect, on pedestals but on flat stone slabs set directly into the pavement, like wounded men just brought in after a battle.

In Anglo-Saxon and early Norman days, justice – if it could so be described – was decided by trial by ordeal, or occasionally by combat. English law really began with Henry II, one of our greatest kings. Henry inherited a troubled kingdom.

England was recovering from a civil war between two of the Conqueror's grandchildren, Stephen and Matilda, both of whom had had resort to mercenaries; and the trouble with mercenaries is that when the fighting – and the regular payment – is over they take to villainy and crime. This too was the century of the Crusades, which meant that many wealthy landowners were away from home for three or four years at a time, their castles falling prey to vandals and squatters. The King was consequently obliged to take firm action. Trial by ordeal was too deeply entrenched to be completely eliminated – it was to continue spasmodically for another two or three centuries – but it was Henry who, with the Assize of Clarendon in 1166, laid down that future trials should be based not on magic or mumbo-jumbo but on *evidence*. Twelve years later, in 1178, he appointed five members of his household 'to hear all the complaints of the realm'. They must, one feels, have been distinctly overworked; but now at last a proper legal system was beginning to evolve, and by the thirteenth century there had developed a whole team of professional judges and magistrates, who were no longer selected only from senior members of the clergy but who now included representatives of the knightly class. By now, too, the judges were travelling the country 'on circuit', which means that each was assigned to his own region and worked exclusively – or at least largely – within it. This was known as the Assize System; it continued until 1971.

Henry's other great problem – indeed, the one for which he is chiefly remembered – was the Church. It was enormously rich; after the crown, it was by far the largest landowner in England. Its members were not even obliged to obey the laws of England if they conflicted with Church governance. Thus it was effectively operating as a kingdom within a kingdom, with its own system of Church courts which were responsible not to the King but to the Pope. Already in 1164 his so-called Constitutions of Clarendon (not to be confused with the Assize, mentioned above) had attempted to reduce ecclesiastical interference from Rome; but Thomas Becket, his newly appointed Archbishop of Canterbury, had refused to accept them and had fled to France. In 1170 the Pope was on the verge of putting the entire country under an Interdict – a sort of national excommunication under which all church services were forbidden. Henry prevented this by allowing Becket to return; but, as everyone knows, by the end of the year Thomas Becket was dead (see **Canterbury Cathedral**).

The next English king to institute a major step forward in the administration of justice was Edward I (1272–1307). It was during his reign, in 1285, that 'good and lawful men' were commissioned to keep the King's peace. These men were the first Justices of the Peace, more usually known as magistrates. Basically untrained as lawyers, they nevertheless handled, with efficiency and despatch, about 95 per cent of the judicial work carried out in England. By now the foundations of English law were firmly in place. Obviously, there was a long way to go – but so there is today. The law is constantly evolving, constantly developing, constantly changing; and it always will.

A word now about Middle Temple Hall, a perfectly magnificent structure completed in 1573 with a wonderful double hammerbeam roof of oak and an oaken screen to match. Almost miraculously, both survived the German bombers in the Second World War. The long table, called the Bench Table on the low dais at the end, is twenty-nine feet long and made from a single oak tree. It is said to have been a present from Queen Elizabeth I. The small table in front of it, known for some obscure reason as the Cupboard, is made of wood from the hatch of Sir Francis Drake's ship the *Golden Hind.*

The hall was also used for plays, masques and other entertainments: on 2 February 1601 it saw an early performance of Shakespeare's *Twelfth Night*. It is still in active use today, for legal dinners, lectures and the like.

18

Great Coxwell Tithe Barn
OXFORDSHIRE

The manor of Great Coxwell in Oxfordshire was given to the Cistercian Order in 1203 by King John, for the founding of an abbey. The monks immediately set about farming there, which they must have done with remarkable success, since almost exactly a century later, at the very beginning of the fourteenth century, they found it necessary to build a perfectly enormous barn, one of the largest of its kind surviving in England. Measuring some fifty yards in length and fifteen across – giving it a total floor area of over 5,500 square feet – it is the size of a modest parish church; like a parish church it has a central nave and two side aisles, to support the weight of its steeply sloping slate roof. The walls, thick and sturdy, are of lovely mellow Cotswold stone. Obviously, it was built to last.

Tithe barns were intended to hold a tithe – that is to say a tenth – of the produce of any given manor, which represented the amount that legally had to be paid to the Church. Great Coxwell is generally known as a tithe barn, and may indeed have been one for some of its history; but it was already Church property – being part of a monastic grange – which had by now come under the control of the Abbey of Beaulieu in Hampshire, and its very size suggests that it would have originally been intended to store all the produce of the grange rather than a relatively small proportion of it. But unfortu-nately no contemporary written records have survived, so we shall never know for sure.

At the time the barn was built, agriculture would have been based on the open field system, in which each village was sur-rounded by three huge fields, one of which would lie fallow every year according to the practice of crop rotation. Each of these fields would be divided into small strips of roughly half an acre each, and each villein would be allocated a certain number of strips in each field – perhaps thirty or so – which he would farm. The strips themselves would be widely scattered, so that no one found himself with all the good land, or all the bad. The peasant farmer's work was never done, and his life was hard. In 1395 the French chronicler Jean Froissart wrote:

It is the custom in England, as with other countries, for the nobility to have great power over the common people, who are serfs. This means that they are bound by law and custom to plough the field of their masters, harvest the corn, gather it into barns, and thresh and winnow the grain; they must also mow and carry home the hay, cut and collect wood, and perform all manner of tasks of this kind.

'The Labours of the Months' was a favourite late medieval theme, to be found on innumerable illustrated manuscripts or stained-glass windows, or carved around church doors. The first three months of the year were given over to the making and repairing of farmyard implements, mending fences, spreading manure and ploughing. April and May was the time for sowing the seed, harrowing and digging ditches; June and July for haymaking, sheep-shearing and the weeding of crops. In August came the harvest, after which there was threshing, more ploughing and tending the fruit trees. Finally, in the last months of the year, there was the back-breaking task of gathering acorns for the pigs, followed by the killing of such livestock as was necessary, salting or otherwise preserving it to survive the coming winter. Throughout the year, regardless of the season, the weather dominated everything. Frosts were the worst. Just one severe late frost in the growing season could kill off an entire crop, leaving a whole village without sustenance for a year; and while rain at the right time was welcome and indeed essential, heavy downpours at harvest-time could flatten the corn and make harvesting it almost impossible. Farmers knew that they were hostages to fortune, and lived in constant suspense. And then, to top it all, there were the taxes. Not only the tithe, though that was quite bad enough; there was also the rent to be paid to the landlord. True, it was nearly always payable in kind – peasants had little loose cash – but it remained a crippling imposition on a poor family in a hard year.

Meanwhile the women, it need hardly be said, worked every bit as hard as their menfolk. Quite apart from the duties of motherhood, if the family had a few sheep, the wife would tend them, shear them, spin the wool and sew the clothing. A really bright (and probably attractive) girl might go into service with the local lord. Her life would not be greatly improved if she found herself working in his kitchen or laundry; but there was always a chance that she might be taken on as a seamstress or even an embroiderer. In any case she could reasonably expect to be a good deal better fed and housed than if she had stayed at home.

Not that the life of a rural lord was all that comfortable either. He and his family may have had enough to eat, but at least in the summer the meat was probably off, the milk sour and the butter melted. There was little variety and the cooking was doubtless atrocious. *Merrie England* it may have been; but I can't think how.

19

Ightham Mote
KENT

*T*he approach alone is unforgettable: a steep descent, twisting down one of those narrow, leafy Wealden lanes, gives no suggestion of what lies ahead. Then, suddenly, there it is – almost too good to be true, so perfectly preserved, so complete and self-contained in its seclusion as to make you wonder if you have not yourself slipped back into the Middle Ages: the fourteenth-century manor house of everyone's dreams, part timber-framed, part good vernacular Kentish ragstone, its walls dropping sheer, on all four sides, into the calm, almost miraculously clear waters of the moat. Few houses in the country have existed for so long, and remained so pure and unspoilt, as this.

Late medieval England was still a fairly dangerous place to live, but it was gradually getting safer. A gentleman of some means no longer required a castle in which to bring up his family, and as security became less necessary he was able to give more and more consideration to comfort. But a degree of protection was none the less advisable, and this was the perfect solution to the problem: a moated manor house. In the fifteenth and sixteenth centuries there must have been a good many surviving; today I know of only two – Ightham and Baddesley Clinton in Warwickshire. Both, I am delighted to say, are owned by the National Trust.

As political conditions improved, the owners of Ightham replaced the old drawbridge with a modest bridge of stone; but the house still looks much as it did when it was built by Sir Thomas Cawne in the reign of Edward III. At its centre there remains Sir Thomas's Great Hall; but already the function of these halls was changing. They continued to be the focus of the domestic life of the house, and – at least on feast days – the squire and his wife would make a point of eating at the great table, invariably set on a low dais at the far end; but by this time personal privacy – a luxury almost unknown in former days – was becoming ever more desirable. Leaving the hall to their servants – who would eat and sleep in it as well – the gentry would normally withdraw to take their meals in a smaller room called the solar, which was usually to be found up a short flight of stairs behind the dais. (This practice had the additional advantage of allowing them to enjoy better food than that which they provided for the staff.)

The owners of Ightham were well-to-do members of the knightly class, certainly accustomed to considerably better provender than that described in the previous article. There would have been plenty of meat, above all mutton, pork, chicken and in certain areas venison. Beef too, though this was perhaps a little less common, requiring as it did greater investment in land. Of fish there was a wide variety: cod and herring above all for those who lived within reach of the sea; trout, perch and occasionally salmon for those who depended on lakes and rivers. Eggs and milk, cream and cheese were of course always available in the local markets, as were fruit and vegetables; on the other hand rice was unknown, as were potatoes, the first of which were introduced only in 1536; it was to be another 100 years or more before they became generally popular.

Efficient preservation was, as ever, a problem. Some foods,

such as fruit, could be dried; others could be salted, smoked or pickled; but all too often it was necessary to disguise the taste of something that had well passed its sell-by date; hence the enormous importance of spices – above all pepper, saffron and ginger. Honey also helped, as did almonds, which were widely used for thickening. So, at the richer tables, did cooking wine, which produced dishes not unlike our own *boeuf bourguignon*. But then wine was a luxury. There had been rich vineyards all over southern England in Roman times; by the Middle Ages, however, whether through climate change or merely because our Dark Age invaders preferred ale and mead, Englishmen had largely given up the cultivation of the grape; virtually all our wine was imported from Europe. Most of it came from Bordeaux, which in those days was still under the English crown, though Burgundy, the Rhône and the Rhine all produced their share.

Over all, it must never be forgotten, loomed the huge shadow of the Church, which considered eating and drinking far too pleasurable not to be strictly controlled. To most Christians, meat was forbidden for a full third of the year, and all animal products except fish – but including eggs and dairy products – were prohibited during Lent. During particularly severe fast days, the number of meals allowed was reduced to one; normally there were two – dinner at midday and a lighter supper in the early evening. Breakfast was avoided by the gentry, though tolerated for men doing hard physical labour.

Alfred, Lord Tennyson's 'lonely moated grange' is a deserted, gloomy, Gothic sort of place – not surprisingly, since it provides the backdrop to one of the most depressing poems in the English language. Ightham, though unquestionably lonely and moated, seems to me to radiate contentment. Almost continuously inhabited for well over 600 years, it is a happy old house, comfortable in its skin, giving itself no airs and graces yet possessing a deep serenity that casts its spell over all who visit it. It contains no great treasures, nor is it classically beautiful; but no one can doubt, as they gaze upon it safe behind its moat, that there is magic in the air.

20

Merchant Adventurers' Hall
YORK

*T*hough it may not look it from the outside, the Merchant Adventurers' Hall is one of the most important buildings in York. The Great Hall itself was completed by 1368, and is the largest timber-framed building anywhere in the United Kingdom that is still used for its original purpose – for the Company of Merchant Adventurers exists to this day. Nowadays not all of them, it has to be said, are merchants, and I suspect that few if any could be described as adventurers; but they are still – as they always have been – occupied with charitable works in the city, they still worship in the same chapel and they still meet together under the same roof.

Nor were the Merchant Adventurers of York the only representatives of their kind. They had affiliated companies in London, Norwich, Exeter and several other cities, all principally engaged in the wool trade with Flanders, the Low Countries and the Hanseatic ports. They and they only were allowed to export cloth from England – a privilege that made many of them extremely rich; at bottom, however, their company was only a glorified guild, one of perhaps 200 that existed in England in the late Middle Ages.

These guilds began with the understandable tendency of craftsmen and tradesmen to associate themselves with others pursuing the same line of business. In doing so, they had several objectives. First, they could keep out the cowboys – doubtless as prevalent in medieval times as they are today. Second, they could fix prices and wages, welfare and working conditions. Third, they could exercise strict quality control, imposing severe punishments for poor workmanship. Finally they could provide help, financial or practical, to those of their number who were sick, old or otherwise in trouble. Membership, however, was not to be had for the asking. It was available only to master craftsmen, and to achieve such distinction a boy had to serve an apprenticeship for anything up to ten years, working in return only for his keep and clothing. After this was completed he would become a journeyman, now paid for his labours but still working under the supervision of a master. At last, when he had acquired enough experience and skill, he would submit a sample of his work to the guild for its approval. If this were granted, then – but only then – could he become a master in his own right and set up an independent business.

In the provinces, many towns were effectively run by their guilds; in one of them, Southampton, the medieval ordinances have survived; although a number of them go back to the thirteenth century and even earlier, they still have the power to surprise:

> . . . And when the gild shall sit, the alderman is to have, each night so long as the gild sits, two gallons of wine and two candles, and the steward the same . . . And the lepers of La Madeleine shall have the alms of the gild, two sesters [roughly eight gallons] of ale, and the sick of God's House and of St Julian shall have two sesters of ale . . .

> . . . And when the gild sits, and any gildsman is outside of the city so that he does not know when it will happen, he

shall have a gallon of wine, if his servants come to get it. And if a gildsman is ill and is in the city, wine shall be sent to him, two loaves of bread and a gallon of wine and a dish from the kitchen; and two approved men of the gild shall go to visit him and look after his condition . . .

. . . No one shall go out to meet a ship bringing wine or other merchandise coming to the town, in order to buy anything, before the ship has arrived and come to anchor for unlading; and if anyone does so and is convicted, the merchandise which he shall have bought shall be forfeited to the king.

As time went on, it was inevitable that members of a given guild would gather together in one particular district or street. In the *souk* of many oriental cities and towns this practice continues to be followed today: I still flinch at memories of deafening coppersmiths and stinking tanners. But the tendency is visible in this country as well: we have only to think of the tailors in Savile Row, the booksellers in the Charing Cross Road, the trilby-hatted diamond merchants in Hatton Garden – or, heaven knows, the bankers and financiers of the City of London.

But the City is a rather special case. Of course the old guilds, there and everywhere, are long since gone; but they have direct descendants in the form of the City Livery Companies, so called because their members wore a distinctive uniform, or livery. You have only to look at London's Guildhall – the largest hall in England after Westminster – in which the Lord Mayor of London, the sheriffs and other senior officials are all elected, to understand the part that these companies still play in the life and administration of the City. Their members are no longer even remotely reminiscent of their horny-handed forebears, their resplendent halls a long way from the benches and workshops of past centuries; but they proudly maintain their trade names – the Goldsmiths, the Apothecaries, the Fishmongers and indeed the Merchant Adventurers – to remind themselves, and us, of the noble old traditions from which they have sprung.

21

Fobbing

ESSEX

Not many people know about Fobbing, a small and nowadays fairly inconsequential village in Essex, on the north side of the Thames estuary. Nor, I suspect, have thousands flocked to admire the metal sculpture that was erected there in 1981. But 1981 was a 600th anniversary; and what Fobbing witnessed on 30 May 1381 was the beginning of the most serious crisis faced by an English king since the Norman Conquest. It is known as the Peasants' Revolt.

To find the reasons we have to go back some thirty-five years to the Black Death, which had wiped out some 40 per cent of Englishmen and had consequently resulted in an acute shortage of labour. Suddenly the average villein or serf had found himself no longer tied to his lord, but a marketable commodity able to sell his labour to the highest bidder. The only trouble was that Richard II's government, in a desperate attempt to hold down spiralling prices, fought back; and in 1381 it trebled the existing poll tax, demanding it indiscriminately from rich and poor alike.

This was a disastrous mistake. The townsfolk of Fobbing and the neighbouring village of Brentwood flatly refused to pay; and when Chief Justice Sir Robert Belknap arrived to investigate, he was set upon and was lucky to escape with his life. Meanwhile the revolt spread quickly across the river into

Kent, where the castle at Maidstone was attacked and its prisoners set free. Among them was a fire-breathing priest called
John Ball, who had been imprisoned and excommunicated by
the Archbishop of Canterbury and who preached to the insurgents – by now gathered at Blackheath – a highly inflammatory
sermon which included the well-known couplet:

When Adam delved and Eve span,
Who was then the gentleman?

At Maidstone too there had appeared an undeniably cha-
rismatic ruffian named Wat Tyler, who now assumed the
leadership of the entire revolt. On his orders, the rebels
descended on London, where London Bridge was opened to
them. They sacked the Temple and the huge palace at the
Savoy belonging to John of Gaunt – the King's uncle – then
turned and joined forces with a separate band of insurgents
under a man calling himself Jack Straw, finally coming to a
halt in Highbury Fields and Mile End, where King Richard
II rode out to confront them.

For any ruler, it would have been a courageous act. Richard
was just fourteen. He had been on the throne since he was
ten, but heretofore his reign had been uneventful. Now he
was to be tested. He rode, we are told, confidently forward to
the rebels' camp. He found them reasonable, but determined.
They knelt, and assured him of their loyalty, but demanded
that the 'traitors' in his government should be surrendered to
them at once. Richard replied that no man was a traitor until
he was tried; but if any were found guilty, they would be willingly handed over. All the other demands – they included the
dismissal of several of his most unpopular ministers and the
effective abolition of serfdom – he immediately granted, then
bade the negotiators a cordial farewell. He had capitulated on
almost every point; but he had at least established friendly

relations. There seemed no reason why the insurgents should not now disperse.

Richard had, however, a nasty shock coming. On his return to the Tower he found that, despite a 1,200-man garrison, the mob had somehow forced its way in. A group of them had burst into the chapel and seized those they found at their devotions, including the Treasurer Sir Robert Hales and the Archbishop of Canterbury Simon Sudbury; these unfortunates were dragged out to Tower Hill and executed on the spot, after which their heads were paraded through the city and set up on pikes at London Bridge. They had even laid hands on the King's mother, though she had come to no harm.

Richard, with what seems quite remarkable courage, decided on a further confrontation – this time at Smithfield, then as now the principal cattle market of the capital. On this occasion he saw at once that Tyler was dangerous: success and all that bloodletting had gone to his head. As their discussion went on, his manner grew ever more arrogant and overbearing; and at last Sir William Walworth, the Mayor of London, could bear it no longer. He barked out an order; at once a group of his men set upon Tyler, pulled him off his horse and cut him down with a broadsword.

Here was a moment of supreme danger. The rebels surged forward; the royal party, outnumbered many times over, could easily have been massacred. It was Richard once again who saved the situation. He held up his hand for silence and, speaking very quietly, asked them what more they wanted. He was their king, and had granted all their requests. Why did they not now hold their peace? Gradually the tumult died down. Richard, meanwhile, was determined to avoid punitive measures. Tyler's head was substituted for Sudbury's on London Bridge, but all his followers were pardoned.

It was the King's finest hour. Alas, after this magnificent beginning he seemed to go steadily downhill, becoming ever more unreasonable, ever more tyrannical, until his final deposition as the fourteenth century drew to its close. He did not, it need hardly be said, keep the promises he made to Wat Tyler; on the other hand, the villeins and serfs would never again be so despised and downtrodden as they had been before. They had shown their teeth; and those who had taken advantage of them and profited by their poverty now treated them with a new respect. Their rulers had narrowly escaped a massacre. They would never risk such a thing happening again.

22

Eton College Chapel

BERKSHIRE

*I*t is distinctly ironical that two of England's most distinguished centres of learning should have been the creations
of the dottiest of its monarchs. Henry VI had come to the
throne at the age of nine months, and by the time he entered
his teens it was clear that he was quite unfitted to rule. He was
not then actually simple-minded – that came later – but he
was ridiculously easily led and alarmingly lacking in political
judgement. Nevertheless he wanted to cut a dash, and by the
time he was twenty he was obsessed with two immense building projects: the first at Eton, just across the river from his
castle at Windsor; the second at Cambridge. Though technically they were to be only chapels, he was determined that
they should be bigger than any church or even cathedral in
England.

It was somehow typical of him that he knew nothing about
the twin colleges – Winchester and New College, Oxford –
that Bishop William of Wykeham had founded some sixty
years before; when the penny eventually dropped in 1443, all
the old plans were scrapped, and seven years of work at Eton
had to be demolished. Henry's original idea had been for
twenty-five scholars in each of his foundations; this figure
was now increased to seventy, for no other reason than to
put William in the shade. Because the King wasn't really

interested in scholarship: he was interested in religion, and above all – as his secretary's letters to Rome make clear – in the sale of indulgences, by which credulous people might be persuaded to pay good money for the remission of their past sins. (They could get it for future sins as well, but that came in rather more expensive.)

In 1461, when he was forty, Henry was very understandably deposed; and although he had a very brief return to power before his murder in the Tower of London ten years later, his successor Edward IV ordered all work at Eton stopped when only the chapel's eight eastern bays, out of a projected eighteen, had been completed; the rest were scrapped. Unlike its sister chapel at King's, Cambridge, whose fan-vaulting – not completed until the reign of Henry VIII more than half a century later – is one of the wonders of England, the chapel at Eton was hastily finished off with the cheap wooden roof that it retained till the 1950s. Only then, after the deathwatch beetles had done their worst, did it receive the bogus but effective fan-vaulting that we see today.

But the greatest treasure of the chapel is something that even King's cannot match. It is those astonishing wall paintings that adorn the north and south walls, the finest in northern Europe. They are the work, it is believed, of four master painters, possibly Flemish, in the college between 1479 and 1487. Over sixty-five feet long, those along the north side illustrate the miracles of the Virgin – to whom the chapel is dedicated – while those on the south tell a story, popular at the time, about a mythical empress. In the wave of Puritanism that hit England in the mid-sixteenth century, the college barber was paid to 'wipe them out'; fortunately he simply covered them over with a layer of whitewash. Gradually they were forgotten, and it was only in 1847 that they were rediscovered. Even then they had to wait till 1923 to be restored and properly revealed by the removal of the stall canopies that obscured them.

Eton was not the first of our public schools – which is, of course, precisely what they were not. Winchester, founded in 1382, was almost sixty years older; but for several centuries to come none of these schools – which taught little except Latin and Greek – seems to have made much impact. We hardly hear of them till the nineteenth century; then, suddenly, they multiplied dramatically and become a force to be reckoned with. The towering figure, who left his mark on almost all the public schools of the nineteenth and twentieth centuries – though he died at forty-seven – was Dr Thomas Arnold, who became headmaster of Rugby in 1828. For him, religion and the classics were almost the only subjects worth teaching; but he was also the high priest of what became known as 'muscular Christianity', emphasizing the importance of games to instil a sense of manliness and fair play, and introducing the system of fagging to promote both the imposition and the acceptance of discipline. His advocacy of the stiff upper lip did not, however, altogether succeed in concealing his own emotions. As a friend of his remarked: 'A man who could burst into tears at his own dinner-table on hearing a comparison made between St Paul and St John to the detriment of the latter, and beg that the subject should never be mentioned again in his presence, could never have been an *easy* companion.'

But whatever the doctor's social graces, we can now see that his legacy to the public school system – and through it to the whole philosophy of English education – was dangerously flawed. In my own Eton days, we still did two or three hours of the classics a day, as compared with an hour of mathematics, French or history and perhaps two hours of science a week. Underlying it there must have been some almost instinctive feeling that technology was not altogether for gentlemen. In England and Wales in 1913, for example, in all branches of science, technology and mathematics, only 350 students graduated with first- or second-class honours; in Germany, 3,000 graduated in engineering alone. In the modern curriculum the balance has been partially righted; yet even now, I suspect, the baneful melody – and indeed the malady – lingers on. To this day, our educational system gives no cause for pride.

23

Bodiam Castle

EAST SUSSEX

O ne's first sight of Bodiam seems almost too good to be true: everybody's idea of the perfect medieval castle, totally symmetrical, set in a moat broad enough to rank as a small lake and in a quite remarkable state of preservation. Its strategic purpose is less immediately apparent, but this too becomes clear when one remembers that in the 1380s, when it was built by Sir Edward Dalyngrygge, the Hundred Years War was going full blast and French raiding parties from across the Channel were a constant menace. The River Rother, more navigable then than now, enabled them to penetrate deep into the hinterland: Rye and Winchelsea had both been burned to the ground in the previous decade. Fortunately, by the time the castle was finished, England had regained control of the Straits of Dover. Bodiam in fact saw no fighting until 1655, when it was besieged by the Parliamentarians; but that is another story.

The Hundred Years War: its very name is an understatement. Though occasionally punctuated by short periods of uneasy peace, it actually lasted for 116 years, from 1337 to 1453. Essentially it was a struggle for the throne of France between two rival royal houses, the Valois and the Plantagenets. Unfortunately the latter happened to be kings of England as well, so what might otherwise have been a domestic tiff turned into bitter international strife. Our King Edward III – who already ruled over Gascony – had a good legal claim, his mother Isabella having been the sister of the last French King, Charles IV; but he was still a boy of just sixteen. His rival, Philip of Valois, was only Charles's cousin; but he was a grown man, already regent, and – unlike Edward, who was away in England – he was on the spot. He quickly had himself crowned, and that was that.

Or should have been. It is fascinating to speculate how European history would have been changed had Edward's claim prevailed, with England and France united under a single crown. But the lawyers continued to argue; Edward further irritated the French by invading their old ally, Scotland; and in 1337 Philip confiscated Gascony, 'on account of the many excesses, rebellions and acts of disobedience committed against us and our royal majesty by the King of England, Duke of Aquitaine'. This was the last straw. On 7 October Edward formally claimed not only Gascony but France as well, declaring himself 'King of France and England'. The Hundred Years War had begun.

The fact that – apart from those few raids across the straits – the war was fought entirely on foreign soil was, obviously, a blessing to the English; but it in no way diminishes its importance in our history. In the mind of every English schoolboy of my generation, only Trafalgar and Waterloo eclipsed the glorious victories of Crécy in 1346, Poitiers in 1356 and Agincourt in 1415. Militarily speaking, too, the war signalled a new age. In feudal days, a peasant was bound to give a fixed amount of military service to his lord in return for the right to farm his land; but now the old feudal system was rapidly disintegrating, giving way to the introduction of mercenary standing armies, shot through by their very nature with a new discipline and efficiency.

The last three battles mentioned above were won not by French cavalry but by English archers. There was nothing new about longbows: the Welsh in particular had been using them to disastrous effect since the twelfth century. But by the fourteenth century the English had made vast improvements in both design and technique. With a good bow in the hands of a practised professional, an arrow could be shot for some 400 yards, and at 100 was easily capable of penetrating a suit of armour. In battle, however, a corps of archers would seldom bother with precise marksmanship. Putting its trust in quantity rather than quality, it would launch hundreds, perhaps thousands, of arrows high in the air, so that they would come down on the enemy like a deathly hail from the sky. The chronicler Froissart claimed that at Crécy in 1346 they even blacked out the sun. For the French, who had put their trust in Genoese crossbowmen, it was a massacre.

Strangely enough, the superiority of pedestrian, plebeian archers over noblemen on their caparisoned chargers was a lesson that the French were never able to learn. There were sixty-nine years between Crécy and Agincourt, but in 1415 it was still the same story: a mounted charge into a hail of arrows, one falling horse tripping up a dozen others, wounded men bowed down with the weight of their armour struggling through mud and blood until the inevitable surrender. But, although the French may have lost the principal battles, they won the war. By the 1450s they had gradually recovered all the early Plantagenet gains, and expelled the English from all French territory except for a few square miles around the port of Calais. But they had done so at immense cost: what with the fighting, the famines, the epidemics – including the Black Death in 1348–9 – and the marauding mercenary armies who, when their business was done, always turned to banditry, the French had lost, probably, two-thirds of their population.

And virtually all the destruction had taken place on their side of the Channel.

The Plantagenets, on the other hand, had managed to transfer, for well over a century, prodigious quantities of plunder to *their* side; with the result that England probably finished the war a good deal richer than when it began it. None the less, it had been taught a lesson. Had King Edward reined in his ambitions, not only would countless lives have been saved on both sides, but he might also have kept Gascony for his family. England might hang on to Calais till the days of Bloody Mary; but never again would it cast covetous eyes on its nearest – if not always its dearest – neighbour.

24

Wool Hall

LAVENHAM, SUFFOLK

Of all the villages of Suffolk, Lavenham – pronounced with a short 'a', as in *have* – is the most enchanting. It is a monument to the huge boom in the wool industry that occurred between about 1380 and 1550, and seems to have changed amazingly little since. Here you will find not just individual timber-framed houses but whole streets of them, their overhanging jetties leaning and lurching like drunken platoons. The Guildhall in the Market Place was built in the 1520s by one of the three guilds founded to regulate the wool trade. Another, now known simply as the Wool Hall, dates from 1464; it stands on the corner of Lady Street and now forms part of the Swan Hotel.

The fact that the Lord Speaker of the House of Lords – formerly the Lord Chancellor – sits on the Woolsack, which is exactly what it claims to be, is a constant reminder of the importance attached to the wool trade. It flourished above all in two regions of England: East Anglia and the Cotswolds. In both you will find what are still known as 'wool churches' – immense and magnificent buildings, often out of all proportion to the small town or village from which they rise. Lavenham has a terrific one, second only to its neighbour, Long Melford. (In the Cotswolds, Cirencester and Chipping Campden are among the best.) These churches demonstrate, better than anything else could, the fabulous wealth of their benefactors, the late medieval wool merchants, some of whom, by the end of the fourteenth century, had become rich enough to replace the Florentine financiers who underwrote the royal debts.

What caused this extraordinary boom that made all their fortunes? First, the growth of the weaving industry in the Low Countries – and particularly in Flanders, where the weavers of Bruges, Ypres and Ghent joined those of Lombardy to provide a permanent and highly profitable market for high-class wool; and second, the sudden desperate shortage of labour that followed the Black Death in the mid-fourteenth century. Arable farming is hugely labour-intensive; but it takes relatively few people to look after a flock of sheep. Admittedly, you need more than shepherds: the sheep must be shorn and the wool carded before being bagged, trans-ported and sold. This carding is – or was – a long and laborious process, in which the wool is untangled with the use of special boards set with short spikes and the fibres roughly aligned, much in the same way as we comb our hair. (At this point perhaps we should spare a thought for St Blaise, the only Christian martyr to have been *combed* to death, who is in con-sequence the patron saint of wool carders. He is also extremely efficacious for those with fish bones stuck in their throat.)

By the year 1400 the wool merchants were exporting some 35,000 sacks a year. So profitable was the trade that it was not surprising that it should attract the attention of successive kings, who taxed it mercilessly. Edward I was the first to do so; without his tax on wool 'the Hammer of the Scots' could never have afforded his campaigns in Scotland – or in Wales either, for that matter. His grandson Edward III went fur-ther, using the by now steadily increasing revenue to finance his struggle with France that was to develop into the Hundred Years War. Edward III's chief objective, as we know, was the

French crown; but he was also responding to an appeal from the burghers of the Flemish cloth towns for support against their French masters.

Yet alas, however fertile the goose may be, it can lay only a certain number of golden eggs; and Edward's demands began to do serious damage to the trade. The result was that, rather than pay crippling duties on its wool exports, the merchants began building up a weaving industry of their own, and many of the Flemish weavers, only too happy to escape the miseries of war and of French domination, came over to England and set up their looms in Norfolk and Suffolk, the West Country and the Cotswolds, and even as far north as Cumbria.

So it was that by the middle of the fifteenth century England was not only producing enough cloth for its own purposes; it was exporting it to Europe. In those days before factories had been heard of, this was of course a home and family industry, with whole villages loud with the clattering of looms, one in every cottage, all engaged in that almost magical process by which raw wool is transformed into fine cloth – cloth that would eventually find its way to the thriving markets of Norwich in the east, Bristol and Gloucester in the west and Kendal in the north.

But danger loomed. As the industry flourished there was need for more wool, which meant more sheep, which in turn meant more land to graze them on. Gradually, as the population began to increase again after the Black Death, the peasants found that with all the fields now full of sheep there was less and less demand for agricultural labour. Simultaneously the sheep farmers began to enclose the common land with fences and hedges, squeezing the peasants and increasing their rents until they were forced to leave. 'Then,' wrote Sir Thomas More, 'what else can they do but steal or go about begging?' In fact there was one other alternative: they could rebel – which, quite often, they did. One particular revolt, in Norfolk in 1549, needed 13,000 government troops to suppress it. When it was over, about 3,000 rebels had been killed or injured, their leaders hanged for treason.

This tragedy, however, cannot be ascribed to the wool trade; it was the result, quite simply, of human greed. The trade itself, over some two centuries, brought prosperity – or relative prosperity – to many thousands; it benefited the shepherds, the fullers, the carders, the dyers and, we hope, the purchasers. It produced, at Lavenham and elsewhere, much dazzling architecture. For, as the old advertisements used to say:

> *It proved again the old, old rule,*
> *There is no substitute for wool.*

25

Courthouse
LONG CRENDON, BUCKINGHAMSHIRE

*L*ong Crendon is one of those ridiculously pretty Chiltern villages that regularly appear on Tourist Board postcards and calendars; but it is a good deal more than that. The manor was the property of one Walter Giffard, who was created Earl of Buckingham by William the Conqueror, and it was granted a Royal Charter to hold a weekly market as early as 1218. Its greatest interest for us today, however, lies in its medieval courthouse, a fifteenth-century timber-framed building in which justice was dispensed from the days of perhaps Henry V (and not later than Henry VIII) until those of Queen Victoria. Since the building now belongs to the National Trust, the courtroom on the upper floor is open to the public; the lower, which did duty as the village poorhouse, is privately occupied.

Long Crendon was lucky: not all villages in the Middle Ages had a courthouse of their own. Those that did not would use the parish church, or the hall of the local manor house; at a pinch the court could even be held outdoors, under or beside the oldest tree in the village. These courts would have been of a relatively simple kind – the equivalent, perhaps, of a magistrate's court today. In the absence of anything resembling a police force, it was up to the villagers themselves to arrest offenders. Their duty was to raise the alarm – calling all their neighbours to their aid – then to pursue the miscreant and hold him until help arrived. Similarly, it was incumbent on the neighbours to drop whatever they were doing and join the chase, shouting to others – who might not have heard the original alarm – to join it too. The result was the traditional 'hue and cry', an excitement hugely enjoyed by all and a welcome break in the normal monotony of village life.

Even at this relatively humble level, trial was by jury, the members of whom could be of any rank, including villeins and serfs. All, together with any witnesses, were on oath, and verdicts had to be unanimous; but the practice differed from our present system in that the jury, being composed of members of the local community, was not expected to be impartial. On the contrary, jurymen were encouraged to base their decision not only on the evidence but also on their personal knowledge of the accused. The punishments were most often a fine, the money going into the village coffers; but when the offence had been against the whole village rather than a single individual this would be supplemented by given amounts of time in the stocks, or – less frequently – the pillory.

What sort of offences were committed in a medieval village? Serious crimes, of course, were normally referred to the local Assizes; but where lesser transgressions were concerned, we have a reasonably clear idea. A fair number of the manor records have survived; here are a few extracts from those of Yalding in Kent, dated 1334–5:

Joanna Cheeseman: fined 2s. for failing to protect her daughter; 1s. for allowing her pigs to roam without rings.
Stephen Webb: fined 6d. for moving boundary stones in the field.
Matilda Bigge: fined 2d. for not grinding her corn in Hugh de Audley's water-mill.
Thomas Brooker: fined 1d. for arriving late for haymaking.

Adam Fleete: fined 3d. for harbouring a stranger overnight.
Gilbert Baker: found not guilty of failing to stop her [*sic*] son
   Thomas from taking a tench from the lord's fish pond.
Richard Wood: found guilty of stabbing Thomas Godfrey with
   a knife while the two men were mowing together; *fled*.

More surprisingly, there are records of permissions granted by the court for such requests as to leave the village, to have a son taught to read and write, to remain unmarried or to arrange the marriage of a daughter.

So much for the courthouse; what about the poorhouse below it? In the Middle Ages, the poor were looked after by the monasteries; after the dissolution of these by Henry VIII and throughout the sixteenth century, however, their life was hard indeed. It was not until 1601, during the reign of the Elizabeth I, that provision was first made for 'the impotent poor' – those who were too old or infirm to work. Parents and children were expected to look after each other; for the rest, responsibility was thrust on the parishes, which were allowed to levy special rates for the purpose. Wealthy men or women with charitable inclinations, or just occasionally an unusually rich parish, might endow a row – or sometimes a complete foundation – of almshouses. Many of these still survive today, and very beautiful a number of them are. Those who managed to find a place in one of these were lucky indeed. For the rest, the poorhouse – later known as the workhouse – beckoned.

Vagrants were a special case. According to a law of 1547, they were to be punished with two years' servitude and branding with a 'V' for a first offence and death for the second. Nor were they eligible for parish poor relief; for this, every applicant had to prove a permanent domicile, known as a 'settlement'; if he could not do so, he was forcibly transported to the parish nearest to his place of birth, or at least to one with which he could prove a long connection. Some paupers were moved over hundreds of miles, with each parish through which they passed liable to provide food and lodging for a single night.

As you climb the steep, steep stairs of Long Crendon Courthouse, thoughts of village life in the Middle Ages swim into your mind. They do not paint a very pleasant picture: even for the young, healthy and well-to-do, that life was tough; it was also rigorously circumscribed. Civilization as we know it today came to us only after a thousand years of struggle, of suffering, of unspeakably hard work on the part of our ancestors. We, its beneficiaries, have good cause to be grateful.

26

Towton Cross
YORKSHIRE

You could easily miss it – a slightly battered stone obelisk, some seven feet high, surmounted by a rather undersized Maltese cross within a wheel. It stands by the side of the B1217 a mile or so south of the little village of Towton in Yorkshire, immediately opposite the Cocksford Golf Club. And it marks the bloodiest battle ever fought on English soil.

The Battle of Towton took place on Palm Sunday, 29 March 1461, in a blinding snowstorm. It was the ninth battle of the Wars of the Roses, and the sixth victory for the House of York; but before we talk about it, we should perhaps talk a little about the Wars themselves. They were in essence the fault of three kings – one excellent, one mediocre and one hopeless. The first was King Edward III. He was in many ways magnificent, but he made one bad mistake: he had far too many children, including seven sons, and in those days when the rules of the royal succession were not set in concrete as they are today, this was courting disaster.

His eldest son, the Black Prince, predeceased him, so on Edward's death the throne passed to the prince's son, Richard II. The second, mediocre, king was Henry IV, also Edward's grandson but only through his *third* son, John of Gaunt, Duke of Lancaster; in 1399 Henry had deposed Richard, thereby showing that a member of a junior branch of the family could overthrow a legitimate ruler. The third, hopeless, king was Henry VI, grandson of his usurper namesake, who proved incapable of holding his kingdom together. One of his countless mistakes was to exclude from his government the man who, being descended from Edward's second son (as well as his fourth) had perhaps a better claim to the throne than he did. This was the hugely ambitious Richard, Duke of York, who, when Henry suffered a complete mental breakdown in 1453, seized the opportunity to make himself Protector of England.

Then, in January 1455, the King recovered his reason. As a recent historian has pointed out: 'if Henry's breakdown was a tragedy, his recovery was a national disaster.' He tried to undo all that Richard had done; Richard fought back; and for the next thirty years the Wars of the Roses – with Lancaster represented by the Red Rose, York by the White – cast their shadow over England. During this period the crown was to change sides no fewer than six times, control of the feckless and unhappy King being seized first by one side, then by the other. At the end of 1460 Richard of York was killed at the Battle of Wakefield, and the overall command of the Yorkist forces passed to his son Edward, Earl of March (later King Edward IV). The scene was set for Towton.

To a very considerable extent, the Battle of Towton was decided by the weather. The Lancastrian army was believed to number about 42,000 men, including almost half the peerage; Yorkist numbers were probably slightly smaller, some 36,000. In addition the Lancastrians occupied the stronger position, on higher ground and with good fields of fire for their archers; theoretically, therefore, the victory should have gone to them. But they had reckoned without the weather. The Yorkist archers had the wind behind them; they could loose showers of arrows into the enemy ranks, then quickly retreat out of range when the Lancastrians attempted to retaliate. And even the retaliation was easier said than done, for the Lancastrians were half blinded by the snow, which was now driving straight into their faces. Their only chance was to advance on Edward's men; combat at close quarters was never pleasant, but anything was better than those arrows.

And so the battle turned from long-range archery to hand-to-hand fighting, and it was savage indeed: no quarter was given on either side. Often it had to break off for a few minutes, while the dead bodies were pulled out of the way. It continued until the early afternoon when, for the Yorkists, a miracle occurred. Suddenly there arrived a sizable contingent from East Anglia, under the command of the Duke of Norfolk. The Lancastrian left, finding itself outnumbered and outflanked, fled the field – and the rout began. Already the bloodshed had been hideous; but it is generally believed that more men died after the battle was over than while it was in progress. One reason is that both sides were resolved that no prisoners were to be taken; if any man had the misfortune to fall into enemy hands, the best he could hope for was to be swiftly and effectively despatched. But there were also the little River Cock and several other streams, all swollen by the early spring rains. Their fragile wooden bridges collapsed under the weight of the panic-stricken fugitives; hundreds were drowned, hundreds more cut down as they stood helplessly on the banks. One of the fields where they died still bears the name of Bloody Meadow today.

The Lancastrians never really recovered from Towton; but neither did they give up the war. Ten years later they suffered another crushing defeat at Tewkesbury, where Edward, Prince of Wales, the King's only son, met his death; in the abbey nearby, the inner face of the sacristy door is covered with metal plates made from the armour of those who died with him. This really was the beginning of the end; less than three weeks later, King Henry himself died in the Tower, almost certainly murdered.

Some years after Towton, Richard III founded a memorial chapel on the site, 'in token of prayer and for the souls of the men slain at Palme Sunday field'. Of this chapel – which was never finished – Towton Cross probably formed a part; centuries later it was found in a hedgerow and erected in its present location. It is known locally as 'Lord Dacre's Cross', but it is nothing of the kind. Lord Dacre – who fought at Towton – is buried (with his horse) in Saxton churchyard, a little way down the road.

27

Tower of London

S eldom, if ever, do Londoners visit the Tower – any more than Parisians go up the Tour Eiffel or New Yorkers struggle off to the Statue of Liberty – but our loss is far greater than theirs; for the Tour and the Statue are both artefacts of the nineteenth century, whereas Her Majesty's Royal Palace and Fortress – to give it its proper name – is almost as old as London itself.

Well, not quite. It was not there in Roman or Anglo-Saxon days; but the central, almost cubical White Tower, the castle keep that gave the whole vast complex its name, was built by William the Conqueror in 1078. There are those alive today who will live to celebrate its thousandth anniversary, though there were few indeed who rejoiced at its construction. In the words of the King's biographer William of Poitiers: 'he saw that it was of first importance to overawe the huge and brutal populace'. At first the Tower was considered – as William had intended it to be – a symbol of oppression, inflicted by the foreign invader upon his newly conquered people; and was deeply resented in consequence. This resentment increased still further after 1100, when it came to be used as a prison.

From the beginning, however, it was also a royal residence. This double purpose was in no way surprising: the Norman kings and their Plantagenet successors habitually lived in castles, and no castle was complete without a good set of dungeons. The Conqueror could never have slept in his White Tower – he was dead ten years before it was ready for occupation – but his sons William II (William Rufus) and Henry I may well have done so, and his grandson Stephen made it his official residence. During the reign of Richard Coeur de Lion at the end of the twelfth century expansion began in earnest, and by that of Edward I (1272–1307) – whose bedchamber has now been reconstructed – the Tower looked much as it does today. We know that Richard II was living there at the time of the Peasants' Revolt in 1381 (see **Fobbing**), and it was continuing to perform its double duty on the accession of Richard III in 1483 and the arrival of his two nephews, 'the Princes in the Tower'.

One of these princes was in fact the rightful King, the thirteen-year-old Edward V; the other was his brother, Richard, Duke of York, who was ten. In order to claim the throne, the King had – without a shred of evidence – declared both illegitimate and imprisoned them in the Tower. For the first few weeks, in the summer of 1483, they were seen practising archery in the dry moat; then, suddenly, they disappeared and were never heard of again. During renovations to the White Tower in 1674, the skeletons of two children were found under the chapel staircase. Since they seemed in all likelihood to be the remains of the princes, Charles II ordered that they should be buried in Westminster Abbey, where they still rest. In 1933 they were exhumed, in an attempt to establish their identity once and for all; but such tests as were then available proved inconclusive. Nowadays, thanks to DNA, a definite identification might well be possible; but there are, so far as I know, no plans to examine the bones again – so the mystery, such as it is, remains.

I say 'such as it is' because, despite the efforts of the novelist Josephine Tey – whose book, *The Daughter of Time*, is well worth reading – several other historians and the vigorous Richard III Society, there has always seemed to me little doubt of Richard's guilt. While the princes lived, they were always a possible focus for rebellion. If it had been known for a fact that he had had them murdered, the popular outcry might have had much the same effect. A simple disappearance, with nothing ever admitted or confessed, was from his point of view by far the wisest solution.

The Tower posseses a palace of its own, though it is more famous for having been in the sixteenth century the favourite place of imprisonment and execution for the rich and prominent – and indeed the royal. On 1 June 1533 Anne Boleyn set out on a damask-covered litter from the palace for her coronation at Westminster, and the whole Tower was decorated in her honour. A little less than three years later, on 19 May 1536, she was beheaded on Tower Green – at her own request, with a sword rather than an axe. (A special swordsman had to be brought over from France.) She was buried in the Chapel Royal of St Peter ad Vincula on the Green. Poor Anne was followed in 1542 by King Henry's fifth wife, her cousin Catherine Howard. She too had been accused of infidelity, and with considerably greater reason. On her way to the Tower she had to pass under London Bridge, where she saw the heads of her two lovers, Thomas Culpeper and her secretary Francis Dereham, impaled on spikes. She was executed – it was an axe this time – on 13 February 1542, and was buried like her predecessor in St Peter ad Vincula. Her ghost is said still to haunt the White Tower, where she is often spotted carrying her head under her arm.

Among the prisoners in the Tower were the future Queen

Elizabeth I (imprisoned by her sister Bloody Mary), Guy Fawkes, Sir Walter Raleigh, the Archbishop of Canterbury William Laud, Rudolf Hess and – briefly – the Kray twins, the last offenders ever to be held there. So far.

Tudor England

Introduction

*B*eginning with the accession of Henry VII in 1485 and ending with the death of Queen Elizabeth I in 1603, the Tudor period coincided almost exactly with the sixteenth century. Henry had married Elizabeth of York, uniting the Houses of York and Lancaster; thus, after the chaos and confusion of the Wars of the Roses, he was able to restore the power and stability of the English monarchy and so to inaugurate a long and welcome period of domestic tranquillity. This was still further guaranteed in 1502, when he concluded his 'Treaty of Perpetual Peace' with Scotland, confirming it by the marriage of his daughter Margaret to the Scottish King James IV. This did not, as he had hoped, destroy the Auld Alliance between Scotland and France; but it did result in the union of the English and Scottish crowns under Margaret's great-grandson James I and VI, who was to succeed Queen Elizabeth in 1603.

With Henry's son Henry VIII came the break with the Roman Catholic Church, as a result of the refusal of Pope Clement VII to grant an annulment of his marriage to Catherine of Aragon so that he could marry Anne Boleyn. This fortunately coincided with the rise of Martin Luther and the ensuing Reformation, which Henry enthusiastically espoused. It also made possible his Dissolution of the

Monasteries (see **Fountains Abbey**) which – despite the incalculable cultural loss – brought in some £1.3 million, a prodigious sum of money in those days, effectively transforming the country's economic condition.

The religious persecutions by Henry and Catherine's only child, 'Bloody' Mary, who followed the short reign of her half-brother, the sickly Edward VI, caused an indelible stain on the Tudor record; but Mary reigned for only five years before being succeeded by Elizabeth, under whom the period reached its apogee. For many people, indeed, Elizabeth's reign marks the golden age of English history. It certainly saw an extraordinary flowering of poetry, music and above all drama, with Shakespeare, Marlowe, Ben Jonson, John Webster and many others providing a constant supply of superb material for the theatres, which had suddenly become hugely popular to all classes. It also saw – especially after the defeat of the Spanish Armada in 1588 – a new patriotism and pride. Edward and Mary together had left the land deeply demoralized and very nearly bankrupt. By the time Elizabeth died after a forty-five-year reign she had transformed England from a weak, second-rate country riven by civil war to one not far short of being a major power, with a well-organized and efficient government and a magnificent new navy manned by superb seamen. This she was able to do since she was a child of both the Reformation and the Renaissance. The Reformation had ensured that the Church was no longer the way to advancement; high office was now in the hands of great noblemen, such as Lord Burghley and his son Robert Cecil. Religion had lost its pre-eminence, although not its power to disrupt. There were still many executions, much torture, particularly of Roman Catholic clergy, although in view of the number of Catholic plots and conspiracies against her we cannot judge Elizabeth too harshly. But rather than God,

Middle Temple Church, London. The story of the Knights Templar, and their contemptible persecution by King Philip the Fair (what a misnomer) and Pope Clement V has haunted me all my life. The circular – as always – Temple Church and the effigies seemingly strewn at random over the floor move me every time.

gaudebunt campi ꞇ omnia
eis sunt.

Great Coxwell Tithe Barn, Oxfordshire. Life was hard in the fourteenth century, as the peasants prepared the great sheaves, a tenth of which were bound for the tithe barn. One hopes that the life of the gentleman on the left (above) may have been infinitesimally cheered by his inspection of the bottoms of his female co-workers – but alas, in fifteen years or so the Black Death would probably have done for them all.

Ightham Mote, Kent. The house breathes a calm perfection unlike any other house I know in England. It has been described as looking like a stage set; but no house could be less dramatic or less showy. It is simply a moated manor house of the fourteenth century which time has forgotten.

Fobbing, Essex. One is always impressed, when confronted by fourteenth–fifteenth-century miniatures, by the tidiness of everything. How beautifully the two armies are drawn up; how completely under control the King looks in both his depictions. In fact, face to face with a murderous rebel at just fourteen, this must have been one of the tensest moments of his life.

Wall paintings, Eton College Chapel. You could ask many an Old Etonian about these wall paintings and be greeted by a look of blank astonishment. Even on guided tours, most guides either ignore them or dismiss them with a wave. But here are, quite simply, the finest frescoes in northern Europe, telling us everything about the clothing, the fashions and the ordinary day-to-day life of England in the late fifteenth century.

Bodiam Castle, East Sussex. Bodiam looks exactly like a fourteenth-century miniature of itself in somebody's Book of Hours. It does so, firstly, because it never saw a shot fired in anger for well over two and a half centuries until the Civil War; second, because it has a moat, which has prevented the local farmers raiding it for its stone.

Tower of London. Here, at the City's eastern limit, on the edge of the river and actually straddling the remains of the old Roman wall, is the greatest military bastion in all England. A fortress, prison and royal palace; from its very beginnings, the Tower was all three. It was also the very nucleus of London, around which the whole burgeoning metropolis was gradually to grow.

Long Crendon Courthouse, Buckinghamshire. No judicial architecture could ever conceal its purpose better than Long Crendon. A pretty little row of tradesmen's cottages, perhaps, or just possibly almshouses; certainly not a court of law, let alone a workhouse.

Hampton Court Palace, Middlesex. Cardinal Wolsey built it; Catherine Howard haunts it; William and Mary were to adopt it and nearly double it in size; but Henry VIII – and Henry VIII only – *is* Hampton Court. That monstrous personality seems to inhabit every nook and cranny of the building.

Fountains Abbey, Yorkshire. The sheer magical beauty of Fountains makes it the most perfect and most poignant illustration of Henry VIII's Dissolution of the Monasteries, of the vandalism, the depredations and the losses, and of the tragic unnecessity of it all.

Martyrs' Memorial, Bury St Edmund's, Suffolk. There are many episodes in English history of which we should be ashamed: the murder of Becket, the fates of Edward II and Richard II, the Wars of the Roses, the Princes in the Tower . . . But Mary's martyrs are the worst; we can only hang our heads.

Wingfield Manor, Derbyshire. Most of the queens in the sixteenth century lived at least part of their lives under threat of execution, while no less than four (Anne Boleyn, Catherine Howard, Lady Jane Grey, Mary Queen of Scots) actually suffered it. Poor Mary surely knew that it was only a question of time, which she passed making ravishing tapestries like this one.

East Budleigh, Devon.
This splendid picture shows the sheer quality of Sir Walter Raleigh: merchant-adventurer, explorer, poet, historian, romantic, swashbuckler, seducer – and, incidentally, our first smoker.

Buckland Abbey, Devon.
This, the greatest of the three 'Armada Portraits', hangs at Woburn Abbey in Bedfordshire. Behind the Queen are two different stages in the defeat of the Armada: on the left, the English fireships are threatening the Spanish fleet; on the right, the ships are being driven on to a rocky coast. The Queen's hand resting on the globe covers the Americas, probably suggesting her plans for expansion.

she was now free to glorify herself, and so she did, elevating monarchy to a level bordering on the divine. Her annual progress through the country was designed to show herself to as many of her people as she could, although a visit from the Queen, who travelled with her entire court, was so ruinously expensive an honour that only the grandest of houses could sustain it. Not since the days of Byzantium had rulers arrayed themselves in such splendour as we see in her portraits, splendour which was praised to the echo by some of the finest poets England had ever produced.

Of course it couldn't last. The last decades of the sixteenth century were marked by a series of disastrous harvests, followed by rocketing food prices. Unemployment rose; dissatisfaction grew. By the late 1590s, the legend that was Elizabeth was wearing thin. For almost fifty years she had put on a magnificent show; but now, as she aged, the illusion of the Virgin Queen became harder and harder to sustain. She died between two and three o'clock in the morning on 24 March 1603. There must have been some relief, but all over England there was the feeling that a great epoch had ended.

28

Hampton Court

SURREY

*H*enry VIII may have been matrimonially unfortunate, but he was lucky in his chief ministers. For most of the first half of his reign he had Cardinal Archbishop Thomas Wolsey, for most of the second Thomas Cromwell. Henry being Henry, he was idiotic enough to get rid of both of them, and paid dearly for his stupidity – but not before both had given him signal service.

The two men could hardly have been more different. Cromwell was content to be an *éminence grise*, but there was nothing grey about Wolsey. He wore magnificence the way he wore his cardinal's scarlet and purple robes; it was part and parcel of the man. And the foremost symbol of that magnificence was the palace he built for himself just outside London, at Hampton Court. In the words of the architectural historian Sir John Summerson, the palace shows 'the essence of Wolsey – the plain English churchman who nevertheless made his sovereign the arbiter of Europe and who built and furnished Hampton Court to show foreign embassies that Henry VIII's chief minister knew how to live as graciously as any cardinal in Rome'. But Wolsey didn't enjoy his palace for long. It was completed only in 1525, and just three years later, knowing that his downfall was approaching, he presented it to the King. If, however, he was hoping to placate Henry, he was disappointed: the following year saw him stripped of his government office and property, including his sumptuous London residence at York House which the King, not content with Hampton Court, also appropriated for himself. By the end of 1530 he was dead.

The cause of his disgrace was what was called 'the King's Great Matter': the annulment of Henry's marriage to Catherine of Aragon so that he could marry Anne Boleyn. He desperately needed a son to succeed him, and it was by now clear that Catherine was not going to give him one. He felt, however, that he had a strong case for an annulment, since she had previously been married to his deceased brother Arthur. His own marriage to her had thus been contrary to canon law, and had needed a special papal dispensation; but he now claimed – and in all probability had genuinely persuaded himself – that that dispensation should never have been given, and that their failure to produce a son was a sign of divine displeasure. Wolsey was using all his considerable diplomatic skills with Pope Clement VII, who might well have been only too pleased to meet the King's wishes – after all, the Reformation was well under way and an annulment was a small enough price to keep England in the Catholic fold – but for one consideration: Catherine was the aunt of the Emperor Charles V, with whom the Pope had at all costs to keep on good terms. So he dithered; and the King, as we know, took the law into his own hands. Wolsey had failed. Wolsey had let him down. And Wolsey paid the price.

At this time Henry possessed more than sixty palaces and houses; on the other hand his court numbered over 1,000, which few if any of them could accommodate. On acquiring Hampton Court, he therefore lost no time in enlarging it, quadrupling the size of the cardinal's already enormous kitchen and adding the Great Hall, under whose carved hammerbeam roof he would in later years regularly dine in state, with whomever happened to be queen at the time.

Doubtless because of his remarkable matrimonial history, Henry has always enjoyed the reputation of being a great lover of women; he seems if anything to have been the reverse. Anne Boleyn was probably the only one of his wives whom he genuinely loved – though even with her he was quite often stricken with impotence – but his love failed to save her from execution. Jane Seymour, at number three, granted him his dearest wish when she bore him a son in 1537. After this the problem of the succession became slightly less acute; but Jane died soon after giving birth, and the future Edward VI was a sickly child whose survival could by no means be guaranteed. (He was in fact to die at sixteen.) At least one more royal prince was needed for the future safety of the throne.

In Henry's eyes the two princesses were no substitute; England had never had a reigning queen, apart – arguably – from the twelfth-century Matilda, who had spent her entire reign battling with King Stephen for the crown. So another potential mother had to be found. His fourth wife Anne of Cleves was a non-starter – Henry was completely unable to perform – and so his eye fell on Anne Boleyn's cousin, Catherine Howard. This one too ended in tears. Poor Catherine could not bear sleeping with Henry, who by this time weighed 300 pounds and had a festering and foulsmelling ulcer on his leg which had to be drained daily. A sudden pregnancy gave the game away, and one day towards the end of 1541, while King and Queen were at Mass in the Hampton Court chapel, the news was broken to Henry of her adultery. She was dragged away screaming, to be beheaded shortly afterwards in the Tower (q.v.); her ghost is still regularly seen running along the gallery leading to the chapel.

Finally there came Catherine Parr. She must have possessed

considerable courage, but fortunately entertained no lovers; indeed she hardly needed to, since she had already had two husbands and was to have another after Henry's death, less than four years after their marriage. None of this prevented her, however, from writing a book called *Lamentacions of a Synner* – long out of print.

29

Fountains Abbey
YORKSHIRE

*T*he first view of Fountains Abbey takes your breath away. Here, surely, are the most sublimely beautiful monastic ruins to be found anywhere in Europe – which is to say anywhere in the world. They stand romantically in a secret, densely wooded valley, and their setting has been still further improved – it could so easily have been destroyed – by the attentions of an inspired eighteenth-century landscape gardener working for John Aislabie, owner of the Studley Royal estate nearby. The roofs of the great monastery and its outbuildings have all gone, as has of course the glass; but much of the original fabric is still there, including almost all the church itself. In consequence we have no difficulty in imagining how Fountains must have looked in its heyday, before King Henry VIII dealt it its deathblow.

We can argue for ever about the Dissolution of the Monasteries, that terrifying series of decrees by which, between 1536 and 1541, the King disbanded no fewer than 825 religious communities – and not only monasteries but also priories, friaries and convents – in England, Wales and Ireland, appropriating their incomes for himself and disposing of their assets. Ten years before, such a step – it represented the largest legally enforced transfer of property in our history since the Norman Conquest – would have been impossible, the English Church still being subordinate to the Pope; but having failed to get his annulment (see **Hampton Court**) Henry had now broken with Rome, and by the Act of Supremacy (1534) had become Supreme Head of the Church in England. Henceforth he could do as he liked.

And, it must be admitted, he had a case. By the beginning of the sixteenth century, the monasteries controlled more than half the Church's total income. They were too many, too powerful and too rich. By this time, too, there seems to have been a dramatic fall in their moral standards. The countless reports of impropriety and vice elicited by Thomas Cromwell's witch-hunters were almost certainly exaggerated; but there can be little doubt that in all too many foundations the old monastic vows were honoured more in the breach than the observance, and that in the richer monasteries the monks were doing themselves proud. None the less, they did not deserve their fate. In 1536 the work began: long processions of ox-carts would wind their way to one monastery after another, where they would load up the silver, the plate, the books, the reliquaries and everything else of value, and carry it off to the royal treasury. Then the demolition would begin, stripping the lead from the roofs, smashing the glass and such statuary as the carts had left behind. Nor was it only the monasteries that suffered: there were many holy shrines – the greatest of them all was St Thomas Becket's at Canterbury – at which pilgrims had left votive offerings of priceless gold and jewellery. These too were stripped bare.

In the south of England and in northern Europe, there was surprisingly little public protest. Henry's actions, drastic as they were, reflected a good deal of contemporary thinking. The Reformation was going from strength to strength. In 1521 Martin Luther had published his *De votis monasticis*, in which he maintained that monastic life had no justification in the

Scriptures and was incompatible with the true spirit of Christianity. He had gone on to argue that monastic vows had no meaning and that no one should feel bound by them. That same year the German province of his own Augustinian Order voted that every member should be allowed to renounce his vows, resign his office and get married. (In Luther's home town of Wittenberg, all but one did so.) By the 1530s the Church, and in particular the monasteries, were under fire throughout northern Europe. What, people began to ask, did all those monks do all day? In former times they performed an essential service by their copying of books; but since the invention of printing some three-quarters of a century earlier, this was no longer necessary.

In the north of England, however, feelings ran high; and in 1536 there was a serious insurrection in Yorkshire, centred on the city of York itself. Although basically a popular movement, it was supported by numbers of the local nobility and gentry, and it proposed to take the form of a march to London with a petition to the King. Its leader, a local lawyer named Robert Aske, emphasized its peaceable intentions by calling it the Pilgrimage of Grace; but its demands were far-reaching indeed. It called for an immediate halt to the Dissolution; for the restoration of the Pope as Head of the Church; for Parliament to be freed from the constant pressure exerted by the crown; and for the dismissal from power of Thomas Cromwell. It seems hard to believe that Aske and his friends could have deluded themselves into thinking that the King would have listened to them for a minute; in any case, they paid dearly for their naïveté. Over 200 of them, including Aske himself, were arrested and executed, the executions being carried out in cities and towns all over the north in order that it should be made perfectly clear that the King meant business.

Wandering through Fountains, we are reminded again and again of those nightmare years, of the centuries of monastic tradition so cruelly uprooted and of the extent of our artistic and architectural loss. Perhaps the monasteries had grown too big for their boots, perhaps they did need thinning and pruning; what they did not need was wholesale vandalism – vandalism that has rendered the whole country immeasurably the poorer, and has left on King Henry's far from immaculate reputation the most indelible stain of all.

30

Launceston Castle

CORNWALL

You can see it for miles: a typical Norman motte-and-bailey castle built on a high natural mound, dominating – as castles should – the surrounding landscape. It was begun by William the Conqueror's half-brother within a year or so of the Conquest; the central round tower was added in the thirteenth century. But Launceston Castle was also a focal point of one of the few rebellions in which the West Country was exclusively involved: a rebellion that we can now see, with all the wisdom of hindsight, as having been doomed before it started – the Prayer Book Rebellion.

When Henry VIII made himself Supreme Head of the Church in England he didn't stop at the Dissolution of the Monasteries. He knew that if he were fully to shake off the influence of Rome, the whole liturgy must be changed; and the first thing to go would have to be the Latin Mass. The question was, what should take its place? The King's most trusted ecclesiastical adviser was his Archbishop of Canterbury, Thomas Cranmer; and Cranmer, whenever he had time to spare from solving His Majesty's seemingly endless matrimonial difficulties, gave much thought to this problem. He was ideally placed to do so since, quite apart from his own impressive theological scholarship, he had served as Henry's Ambassador to the Emperor Charles V; and while in Germany he had had discussions with many of the leading Lutheran thinkers, including a certain Andreas Osiander, whose niece he had actually gone so far as to marry. Since the Catholic Church forbade clerical marriage, he could hardly have nailed his Protestant colours more firmly to the mast.

Henry died – to everyone's relief, including his own – in January 1547, leaving the throne to his son by Jane Seymour, the nine-year-old Edward VI. Two years later there appeared the first version of the Protestant Book of Common Prayer. How much of it is Cranmer's own work we shall never know. It was, as the King James Bible was to be sixty years later, the work of a committee; but Cranmer's, certainly, was the guiding hand. Here, for the first time, was set out the theology of the English Reformation. Although there were a number of old recusant families who refused to renounce their treasured Catholic faith – and were to suffer horribly for it in the years to come – most of the nobility and gentry accepted the new Prayer Book willingly enough. The major landowners had, after all, acquired countless acres of formerly monastic property after the Dissolution; they had every reason to welcome the new regime.

But many ordinary people up and down the country were appalled, above all in Devon – where the old religion had been particularly strong – and Cornwall, where the speakers of the old Cornish language pointed out that while they could understand a good deal of the Latin, they couldn't make head nor tail of the English, which many of them had never even heard spoken. They had already suffered the loss of the Cornish monasteries, which had done much to preserve their cultural heritage; to lose their beloved Mass as well was for them the last straw.

After the prohibition on all religious processions following the Pilgrimage of Grace, commissioners were despatched all over the country to root out every item of popish paraphernalia, and indeed every sign and symbol of Catholicism. This was the first hideous bout of iconoclasm in England – the second was to come with Oliver Cromwell's Commonwealth in the next century – and it was no wonder that it unleashed a storm. In April 1548, while one of the Cornish commissioners, William Body, was cheerfully hacking away at the statues and windows of Helston church, he was set upon and stabbed to death. As a result, twenty-eight Cornishmen were rounded up and taken at gunpoint to Launceston Castle, where they were publicly hanged, drawn and quartered. But that was only the beginning. In January 1549 Parliament passed the so-called Act of Uniformity, whereby the services laid down in the Book of Common Prayer were made compulsory in all churches. On Whit Sunday, the day on which the new law was to take effect, the congregation of the church of Sampford Courtenay in Devon flatly refused. The new liturgy, they complained, was 'but lyke a Christmas game'. They forced their priest to don his old vestments and to say Mass as usual. Justices hurried in to restore order, and that evening one of the protesters was run through with a pitchfork on the church steps. War had been declared.

But it was war not only against the government; it was also against the gentry, who were resented for their wholesale enclosure of common lands and bitterly blamed for the rampant inflation of recent years, during which wheat prices had quadrupled. The cry soon went up: 'Kill all the gentlemen, and we will have the ceremonies as they were in King Henry's time!' As the Duke of Somerset, Protector of the Realm during King Edward's minority, confessed: 'Indeed all hath conceived a wonderful hate against the gentlemen and taketh them all as enemies.' Many of the old families fled for their lives; some took refuge on St Michael's Mount, until the rebels, burning huge trusses of hay, forced them into surrender.

At the end of June the combined Devonians and Cornishmen marched to Exeter, in the hopes that the city would rally to their standard. It refused, and endured a five-week siege in consequence. By the end the population was almost starving; it was saved by the arrival, not a moment too soon, of an army of nearly 9,000 men under the command of Lord John Russell, first Earl of Bedford. It included 160 Italian arquebusiers and 1,000 German *Landsknechts*, and

when battle was at last joined on 5 August the bloodshed was terrible; Lord Grey, who was in command of the foreign mercenaries, reported that in all his long military experience he had never seen the like. The rebels had fought like tigers, but they had no chance against an army of trained, disciplined and heavily armed professionals. Relatively few survived.

The Book of Common Prayer, by contrast, lives on to this day.

31

Martyrs' Memorial
BURY ST EDMUNDS, SUFFOLK

D espite everything, it's hard not to feel sorry for Bloody Mary. All right, she executed 284 Protestant martyrs, most of them burned at the stake – some, though not all, are commemorated at Bury St Edmunds, where they met their deaths – but an unhappier woman has never existed. The only child of Henry VIII and Catherine of Aragon, she was intelligent and unusually musical, but her eyesight was poor and she suffered from agonizing migraines, which were probably made worse by the steadily deteriorating relations between her parents and her father's increasing frustration at his inability to obtain an annulment from the Pope. She was, meanwhile, kept ruthlessly separated from her mother. Then, after the break with Rome, Archbishop Cranmer ruled that Henry's marriage to Catherine was void and his marriage to Anne Boleyn valid. Mary was consequently declared illegitimate. No longer was she heir to the throne; that position now passed to Anne's newborn daughter Elizabeth, to whom she was sent to serve as lady-in-waiting. Not surprisingly, she firmly rejected the new dispensation. Henry continued to forbid her to visit her mother, who was by now on her deathbed; he even denied her permission to attend the funeral. Such was her anger that she refused to speak to him for three years.

After Anne's execution in 1536, Elizabeth was downgraded just as her sister had been; and only two weeks after the axe had fallen their father married Jane Seymour, who obediently produced a son, herself dying shortly afterwards. The two girls remained illegitimate, but were now restored to the line of succession; when her father was between marriages Mary even acted as his hostess. But on his death in 1547 everything changed again. With Edward VI still a child, the Regency Council was dominated by fervent Protestants; Mary, who clung doggedly to her Catholic faith, was forced to keep a very low profile and remained in constant danger of her life. Then in July 1553 the fifteen-year-old Edward died in his turn. She should legally have succeeded him; but he and his advisers, terrified that she would drag the country back into the Catholic fold, had arranged that the throne should pass to Henry VIII's sister's granddaughter, his safely Protestant great-niece Lady Jane Grey. On 10 July 1553 Lady Jane was proclaimed queen.

Mary, however, was having none of it. She gathered together a small military force, and support for her rival dwindled rapidly. On 3 August she made her triumphal entry into London; Lady Jane and her husband were sent to the Tower (they were beheaded later) and Mary, by now thirty-seven and desperate for a child, settled down to finding a husband. At this point her cousin the Emperor Charles V suggested that she should marry his only son Philip – obviously a superb match, Philip being as fervently Catholic as Mary was, quite apart from being the heir to vast territories in Europe and the New World. As to his physical qualities, Charles had only to send her Titian's full-length portrait, now in the Prado; on looking at it, the Queen instantly declared herself to be in love.

The feeling was not, alas, mutual. In July 1554 the marriage took place in Winchester Cathedral – two days after the couple's first meeting – but, as Philip frankly confessed to a friend, it 'was concluded for no fleshly consideration but in order to remedy the disorders in this kingdom and to preserve the Low Countries'. Nevertheless, two months later the Queen was showing all the signs of pregnancy, a state that her doctors unanimously confirmed. (The only one to express uncertainty was her husband.) The baby was due in June 1555, but by early July nothing had happened and suddenly the bulge disappeared. It had been a *grossesse nerveuse*, a false pregnancy which made poor Mary not only miserable but a laughing-stock. Philip – whom she seems genuinely to have loved – couldn't bear the embarrassment and fled to the wars. His wife was left alone, still childless and with precious little hope of ever being anything else.

Her religious policy, meanwhile, was as disastrous as the Protestants had feared, if not worse. She had the marriage of Henry and Catherine once again declared valid – confirming the illegitimacy of her half-sister Elizabeth – and the Church was once again subjected to Rome. Protestants were declared heretics, and heresy was punishable by death. In February 1555 the executions began; they continued until the Queen's death three years later. Most of the victims were burned at the stake. Among the first was the Bishop of Gloucester. The former archbishop Thomas Cranmer was forced to watch the burnings of two of his closest colleagues, Bishops Nicholas Ridley and Hugh Latimer. In an attempt to escape a similar fate he recanted his Protestant faith, but it was no use: Mary refused a reprieve, and as the flames licked around him he withdrew his recantation.

No wonder the Queen acquired her nickname; she richly deserved it. It should be remembered, however, that although she was much the worst of the persecutors, many of those who met their deaths were far from blameless themselves. Many Catholics had died for their faith under Edward VI, many more were to do so under Elizabeth. Bishop Latimer had personally presided in 1538 over the slow roasting of a Franciscan friar, John Forest. And the situation was no better in Europe; only four years after Mary's death several hundred Protestants were massacred in France, where the bitter Wars of Religion continued till the end of the century. In short, there were martyrs on both sides; both sides behaved – by our standards – abominably.

Much of the responsibility must lie with the violence of the age and the odious fanaticism that prevailed. But the shame remains.

32

Wingfield Manor
DERBYSHIRE

*T*here were two Queen Marys in the later sixteenth century, and it is hard to say which was the more miserable. The fervent Catholic Bloody Mary has already made her appearance in this book; she died in 1558 and was succeeded by her half-sister, the Protestant Elizabeth. The curtain rises on Mary Queen of Scots.

Now, concentrate for a moment. In 1543 Mary had been crowned Queen of Scotland at the age of nine months; two months before that, she had already been betrothed to Henry VIII's five-year-old son Edward; but Mary's mother, the French Mary of Guise, had managed to overturn the contract. Henry VIII, furious, sent an army into Scotland – it was known as the Rough Wooing – and early skirmishes soon turned into an all-out war, which continued into the reign of Edward VI. Edward had been on the throne only seven months when the English slaughtered 10,000 Scots at the Battle of Pinkie. The French now came over to help their old Scottish ally, and King Henri II offered to take Mary to France for safety; in return she would be betrothed to his son, the Dauphin François. In 1558 the couple married in Notre Dame, and the following year François succeeded to the French throne.

Mary was now Queen of France and Scotland; and, being

the great-granddaughter of Henry VII, was heir to the throne of England too, should its Queen die childless. This would mean England's return to the Catholic faith, which, after the horrors of the preceding reign, Elizabeth refused to contemplate. The situation improved a little from her point of view when young François died a year after his accession, leaving no issue. Mary was no longer the French Queen, and seeing her mother-in-law Catherine de' Medici – who had always hated her – moving in for the kill, hastily returned to Scotland.

Scotland, however, was in the throes of the Reformation, and Mary proved quite unable to handle it. There followed a series of disasters, which need not concern us here. It need only be said that in 1565 Mary married her cousin Lord Darnley, and in 1566 gave birth to the future James VI of Scotland, who was ultimately to succeed Elizabeth as James I of England. Darnley was murdered the following year, and Mary – who had somewhat ill-advisedly taken a third husband, the Earl of Bothwell, three months later – was accused of complicity. In 1568 she was forced to flee across the border to England and fling herself on Elizabeth's mercy.

What was Elizabeth to do? Mary was a Catholic; she was also her heir. Willingly or not, she was bound to be the focus of a whole series of Catholic conspiracies to return the country to the Roman fold. Within a year of her arrival in England there was a major rising in the north, with the object of marrying her to the Catholic Duke of Norfolk, getting rid of Elizabeth and putting the two of them together on the throne. After this was suppressed, 750 of the rebels were executed on the orders of the Queen. As Elizabeth had feared, the plot proved only the first of many, all aimed at replacing her with Mary. The only long-term answer to the problem was to keep her under close supervision; and so began the poor woman's long, sad progress from one castle to another – never quite imprisoned, for she was allowed to keep her various court ladies with her, but watched every moment of the day and night. First she was held at the Castle of Carlisle, then at Bolton, Tutbury, Chatsworth (not of course the present house), Sheffield: so the list goes on.

By now Elizabeth was coming under more and more pressure from her advisers to accept the only ultimate solution to the problem, execution; but she could not bring herself to do so. Mary might have abdicated her throne, but she was still an anointed queen; besides – although they had never met – they were second cousins. So poor Mary continued her enforced peregrinations, which took her three times to Wingfield Manor in Derbyshire, then under the care of the Earl of Shrewsbury. Shrewsbury, who was the fourth husband of Bess of Hardwick, was one of the kindest of her keepers; he used to take her out riding and hawking, and even allowed her to take the waters at nearby Buxton. (She also worked with Bess on a superb set of needlework hangings, now to be seen at Oxburgh Hall in Norfolk.) Wingfield is – or was – more a castle than a manor house. Today it is ruined, as are virtually all the castles at which Mary stayed, when they are there at all; but it remains hugely impressive, with a vast vaulted undercroft in which she is said to have played a sort of primitive tennis with her ladies.

At last Elizabeth's Secretary of State Sir Francis Walsingham took matters into his own hands. 'So long as that devilish woman lives,' he wrote, 'neither Her Majesty must make account to continue in quiet possession of her crown, nor her faithful servants assure themselves of safety of their lives.' He now engineered an elaborate plot of his own: to deceive Mary into thinking that letters could be smuggled to and from her agent in Paris and her devoted supporter Anthony Babington in London. Mary fell obligingly into the trap and entered enthusiastically into the plan that Babington outlined to her, for her own liberation and Elizabeth's murder. At the trial that followed, she inevitably tried to deny everything, but in vain. She was found guilty of treason and sentenced to death.

Still Elizabeth hesitated; but at last she was obliged reluctantly to sign the warrant for Mary's execution. It took place at Fotheringhay Castle in Northamptonshire on 7 February 1587. Her ladies removed a black outer gown and two petticoats, revealing a dress of brilliant scarlet – the liturgical colour of martyrdom in the Catholic Church. Then she knelt and was beheaded, the executioner using a bloody butcher's axe that had previously been used on animals. As the Jesuit Robert Southwell wrote, eight years before he was himself martyred:

> *A Prince by birth, a prisoner by mishap,*
> *From crown to cross, from throne to thrall I fell.*
> *My right my ruth, my titles wrought my trap,*
> *My weal my woe, my worldly heaven my hell.*
>
> *By death from prisoner to a prince enhanced;*
> *From cross to crown, from thrall to throne again,*
> *My ruth my right, my trap my style advanced*
> *From woe to weal, from hell to heavenly reign.*

33

Buckland Abbey

DEVON

*A*fter Buckland Abbey – originally a thirteenth-century Cistercian foundation – was dissolved by Henry VIII it was bought by a certain Sir Richard Grenville, whose grandson, Sir Richard, was famous in song and story as one of Queen Elizabeth's leading sea-captains; and he, in his turn, sold it to his still more celebrated rival, Sir Francis Drake: politician and pirate, slaver and privateer, and circumnavigator of the world.

Born in 1544, Drake started young. Master of his own ship at the age of twenty, he first crossed the Atlantic three years later with his cousin Sir John Hawkins, with whom he soon found himself trapped by the Spaniards in a Mexican port. He escaped, but from that moment he conceived a detestation of Spain, and became determined to do it all the harm he could. It was in December 1577 that he set off on a punitive expedition against the Spanish fleet in the Pacific. The September following he slipped through the Straits of Magellan, but violent storms destroyed all the ships except his own, the *Golden Hind*. Henceforth he was alone, sailing up the western coast of the New World, raiding Spanish ports and capturing Spanish ships as he went, then pressing further and further north in search of a western entrance to the fabled Northwest Passage; but the cold drove him back, and it was in a more temperate latitude – though we don't know precisely where – that he set off across the Pacific. The rest of his journey took him to the Moluccas – where his ship was caught on a reef and very nearly foundered – and thence by slow stages to the Cape of Good Hope and up the west coast of Africa. He sailed into Plymouth on 26 September 1580 with the fifty-nine surviving members of his crew and a huge cargo of oriental spices and Spanish treasure. That same year he bought Buckland, which was to remain in his family for several generations.

The stories of Drake's continuing depredations are legion, to the point where threats of *El Draque!* are still used to frighten Spanish babies; while all English schoolchildren were brought up on the story of his 'singeing the King of Spain's beard' at Cadiz. But we must now leap forward to 1588 and the ultimate triumph of Elizabethan sea power, the defeat of the Spanish Armada. King Philip had long been contemplating an armed invasion of England, over which he still claimed to reign; after Elizabeth's execution of Mary Queen of Scots he delayed no longer. This new expedition was to be a Crusade; it was blessed by the Pope; the 160 ships, carrying a total of 180 priests and monks on board, all wore red Crusader crosses on their sails. The fleet was to sail from Lisbon, across the Bay of Biscay and up the Channel to the French side of the Straits of Dover, where it would pick up the invasion army under the command of Philip's nephew the Duke of Parma and carry it across to England.

It all sounded so simple; but it wasn't. The commander, the Duke of Medina Sidonia, had no experience of the open sea; nor, it soon appeared, did a lot of his ships, built as they were for quiet Mediterranean waters rather than furious Atlantic storms. A violent tempest off Corunna wrecked several of the larger vessels and dispersed many of the others as far as the Isles of Scilly. The duke wrote there and then to Philip telling him that his great fleet was utterly incapable of fulfilling the role he had assigned to it; but the King, it need hardly be said, took no notice, and in mid-July 1588 the Armada rounded Cape Finisterre and entered the Channel, the English by now closely following its progress. The English had collected some 200 ships altogether, including twelve privateers owned by the joint commanders Lord Howard of Effingham, Hawkins and Drake.

On the 19th, the Spanish were sighted off the Lizard. Immediately the chains of beacons sped the news to London, and the long-drawn-out battle began. There were many encounters as the fleet beat its way slowly up the Channel, and gradually as it advanced the English learned more and more to their advantage. Perhaps the most important lesson was that the Spanish gun crews were trained to fire only a single broadside each as a prelude to boarding the enemy ship; but their heavy vessels found it impossible to bring the lighter, nimbler English ships within grappling range. The English meanwhile could come in to 100 yards or less and maintain a constant bombardment with little fear of retaliation.

By the time the Armada anchored off Calais on 27 July it was clear that the whole project was doomed. That night the English managed to spread more panic with their eight fire-ships, regular men-o'-war that had been filled with pitch, brimstone, gunpowder and tar before being set alight and released downwind among the closely packed Spanish fleet. By now the charred and shattered vessels were in no condition to transport an army, but this hardly mattered: there was no army to transport. Parma's troops, their numbers much diminished by epidemic, were in confusion and would not be ready to board for at least another week. The English defence force of 4,000 under the Earl of Leicester would clearly not be needed after all. None the less, they were still assembled at Tilbury when on 8 August the Queen came to address them:

> ... I know I have the body of a weak and feeble woman; but I have the heart and stomach of a king – and of a King of England too, and think foul scorn that Parma or Spain, or any prince of Europe, should dare invade the borders of my realm: to which, rather than any dishonour should grow by me, I myself will take up arms ...

So how was the Armada to return? There could be no retreat down the Channel; the only hope was to continue to the north, around Scotland and Ireland into the North Atlantic. Supplies of food and water were short, the horses were flung overboard, and some of the ships were literally tied together with cables. Many were wrecked off the Scottish coast, many more off the Irish. During that nightmare journey about 5,000 sailors were lost by drowning or starvation, more than had died in the fighting. Of the 160 ships that had set out, only 67 limped home, with some 10,000 exhausted men.

The English had lost fewer than a hundred – and not a single ship.

34

Globe Theatre

LONDON

*B*y far the most exciting aspect of the cultural renaissance that took place during the reign of Queen
Elizabeth was the rediscovery of the English language. One
or two earlier writers such as Chaucer, or perhaps John
Skelton, had glimpsed its possibilities, but its poetic potential
was largely untapped. This is hardly surprising; in the early
years of the century artistic patronage was still in the hands of
the Church, and Latin remained the language of learning and
culture. But then, with the Reformation, the whole picture
changed. Latin of course continued to be indispensable to any
man with pretences to education, but English suddenly began
to reassert itself as never before, emerging as an instrument of
rare beauty and unparalleled richness. Still fresh, fluid and
easily malleable, it now showed itself capable, in the right
hands, of producing poetry as sublime as has ever been written.

And whose were those hands? No longer was writing largely
the duty of grubby, ink-stained scholars and clerks; now fine
goose-quills scratched away in the exquisitely tended, sensitive
fingers of wealthy young gentlemen, often with positions at
court. The Queen herself wrote poetry; so did Sir Philip Sidney
and Sir Walter Raleigh, and many of their friends to whom the
gift was denied at least gave their support and patronage where
it was needed. And so, at last, a national literature began to

emerge, and with it came that uniquely English phenomenon, a popular national theatre, dominated by the four great
giants of the Elizabethan stage: Ben Jonson, John Webster,
Christopher Marlowe and William Shakespeare.

The first public theatres – one called the Curtain and one
known quite simply as the Theatre – were built in London
around 1576, but safely outside the northern walls. That way
they were out of reach of the always puritanical City Fathers,
who would have closed them down if they could. Indeed, they
tried on several occasions; fortunately the theatres, quite apart
from their huge popular appeal, enjoyed enthusiastic support
in high places, not excluding the Queen herself. Before long
they began to spread south of the river, to Southwark and
Bankside, and it was there, in 1599, that Shakespeare, with
Richard Burbage and four other friends, built the Globe.

The present reconstruction of the Globe, opened in 1997 on
almost – but not precisely – the same site, strives to be as close
to the original as possible, and is also fairly typical of the other
theatres of the time. Basically it is the 'wooden O' described
by the Chorus in *Henry V*, but it is also a great deal more than
that; one is always surprised by the complications of the
Elizabethan stage design, far more elaborate than that of our
modern theatres. Within the O, an apron projects out into
the middle of the pit; behind it, the rear part of the stage is
covered by a roof, supported on columns, and includes a gallery with balcony, for use by musicians and for special effects
such as the balcony scene in *Romeo and Juliet*. Most of the
audience would simply stand in the pit; the more distinguished would sit – pretty uncomfortably – in any one of three
tiers that ran round three sides of the stage.

Of the several acting companies who played these theatres,
the most prominent – and the one to which Shakespeare
belonged for most of his professional career – was the Lord

Chamberlain's Men, founded in 1594. Its star was Richard Burbage, who played Hamlet and Othello; later, in the reign of James I, he would go on to play King Lear and Macbeth.

There were at this time no actresses; the female roles were all played by young boys. It was only after the Restoration in 1660 that women regularly took to the stage. All the companies worked on a repertory system, seldom if ever presenting the same play for two days running or even repeating themselves in the same week. Costumes were elaborate, and extremely expensive, and companies jealously guarded their voluminous wardrobes. Few concessions were made to historical accuracy in the plays they furnished, however, the actors generally wearing contemporary clothing – including items they were not, in normal life, allowed to wear. Sumptuous costumes were all part of the spectacle; all Shakespeare plays were played in 'modern dress'.

What we find difficult to understand today is the astonishing fertility and sheer energy of the Elizabethan theatre, and the variety and richness of the literature it produced. We are looking at a period of some seventy years at the most, from 1575 to 1642; most of the plays written during this time have certainly been lost, yet the number that have survived amounts to well over 600. Who, one wonders, were all these playwrights? One or two – Marlowe for example – went to university; but the vast majority were self-made, self-educated men. Many of them probably held down other jobs as well; there was little enough money to be made – perhaps £6 or £7 per play and no copyright. If, as happened more often than not, a playwright worked in collaboration with others, the profits would be even less. Shakespeare did exceptionally well for himself, but only because he was also an actor and – more important still – a shareholder in the company.

How lucky we are that he lived when he did. Had he been born half a century later, he would have reached his prime around 1642, that terrible moment when all the theatres in the country were darkened, and our still burgeoning dramatic tradition went into eclipse. Great indeed would have been our loss. Even as things were, we had eighteen long years to reflect on the miseries of Puritan fanaticism – until the joyfully restored Charles II switched the lights back on.

35

Raleigh Monument

EAST BUDLEIGH, DEVON

S ir Walter Raleigh was the archetypal sixteenth-century
courtier, adventurer and poet. Alone, he seems to sum
up the whole Elizabethan age. Born in East Budleigh in 1544,
after seventeen years as a landowner in Ireland (to which he is
said to have introduced the potato), in early 1582 he appeared
at the royal court, where – through his good looks, his intelligence, his poetry and his immense charm – he soon made a
name for himself. But court life alone he found too tame; he
longed for a challenge, and in 1584 at the age of thirty he
organized an expedition to the New World, to set up what
he hoped would be 'the Colony and Dominion of Virginia',
named, of course, after his Virgin Queen.

To his considerable disappointment, she refused to let him
join the party. Had he been able to do so, the project might
not have ended in failure as soon as it did. The early colonists
had little idea of the hardships awaiting them, and consistently antagonized the local Indians, on whom they depended
for their food; but the real problem was that no one had any
idea of how much such a colony would cost, and the money
put up by Raleigh and his friends proved to be nowhere near
adequate. (It did however prepare the way for several subsequent colonies, which were funded by joint-stock companies
and consequently proved a good deal more successful.) Still, it

was a splendid attempt, and it won Raleigh his knighthood. He was certainly not discouraged, because in 1587 he had another try, establishing a settlement on Roanoke Island. Alas, the second attempt was no more successful than the first: in 1590 it was found that all the colonists had disappeared, the only clue to their fate being the mysterious word CROATOAN, carved into a tree trunk.

Queen Elizabeth was deeply fond of Raleigh. She gave him a splendid house in the Strand and the estate of Sherborne in Dorset. But somehow she never quite trusted him with one of the great offices of state. He would obviously have loved to play a swashbuckling part in the defeat of the Armada in 1588; instead he found himself in charge of the coastal defences of Devon – none of which was required when the moment came – and the local military levies, which proved equally useless. It was a pity that just three years later he seriously blotted his copybook by eloping with one of the court ladies-in-waiting, Elizabeth Throckmorton, without first seeking Her Majesty's permission; his position was hardly improved by the fact that she was eleven years younger than him, and heavily pregnant at the time. One wonders whether she was the lady whom my favourite seventeenth-century writer, John Aubrey, had in mind when he wrote:

> He loved a wench well; and one time getting one of the Mayds of Honour up against a tree in a Wood ('twas his first Lady) who seemed at first boarding to be something fearful of her Honour, and modest, she cryed, sweet Sir Walter, what do you me ask? Will you undoe me? Nay, Sweet Sir Walter! Sweet Sir Walter! Sir Walter! At last, as the danger and the pleasure at the same time grew higher, she cryed in the extasey, Swisser Swatter Swisser Swatter. She proved with child, and I doubt not but this Hero tooke care of them

both, as also that the product was more than an ordinary mortal.

Possibly it was. But there was nothing that the Queen hated more than people interfering with her court ladies, and she sent both Sir Walter and Miss Throckmorton to cool off in the Tower.

It was several years before Raleigh returned to favour. Meanwhile in 1594 he managed at last to assuage his thirst for foreign adventure. Somehow word came to him of Manoa, a great golden city in what is now Venezuela, at the headwaters of the Caroni River; and in the following year he set off to find it. Like its predecessors, the expedition proved a failure; but he himself was more than satisfied. At last he had seen the New World for himself, rather than sending other people there; he too had sought, even if he had not actually found, the legendary El Dorado; and the book that he wrote on his return, *The Discovery of Guiana*, certainly could not have been accused of understatement.

Finally, in March 1603, the Queen died. Just four months later, on 19 July, Raleigh was arrested on a charge of treason against the new King, James I. He was found guilty, but conducted his own defence with such skill that James commuted his punishment. He spent the next thirteen years in the Tower, writing the first volume of his *Historie of the World*, dealing principally with Ancient Greece and Rome. He seems to have been treated with all consideration – conjugal visits were certainly allowed, since his son Carew was born in 1604 – but he had probably long put aside all thoughts of release when, in 1616 at the age of sixty-two, he was ordered to conduct a second expedition in search of El Dorado. His elder son Walter was to accompany him. All might have been well if his men had not attacked a Spanish outpost on the Orinoco.

Walter was killed, and on Raleigh's return a furious Spanish Ambassador demanded that his death sentence should be reinstated. On 29 October 1618 he was beheaded at Whitehall. As he rested his neck on the block, his last words were to the headsman: 'Strike, man, strike!', and his epitaph was his own:

> *Even such is time, which takes in trust*
> *Our youth, our joys, and all we have,*
> *And pays us but with age and dust,*
> *Who in the dark and silent grave*
> *When we have wandered all our ways*
> *Shuts up the story of our days,*
> *And from which earth, and grave, and dust*
> *The Lord will raise me up, I trust.*

It is worth, I think, adding a small postscript. As everyone knows, it was Sir Walter Raleigh who introduced tobacco into England – and, through England, into just about everywhere else. Many people today wish he hadn't; but there are two enjoyable things to remember about the statue by Vivien Mallock, which in 2006 the local MP, Hugo Swire, arranged to have erected in East Budleigh, the village of Sir Walter's birth. The first is that the entire cost – it came to £30,000 – was met by British-American Tobacco. (It was, come to think of it, the least they could have done.) The second is that the statue was unveiled in the week when the new anti-smoking laws came into effect in England and Wales.

Stuart England

Introduction

The Stuarts fit just as neatly into the seventeenth century as the Tudors did into the sixteenth, with James I (James VI of Scotland) coming to the throne in 1603 – Elizabeth, the Virgin Queen, having died childless – and Queen Anne expiring in 1714. The two centuries, however – particularly after the accession of Charles I in 1625 – could hardly be more different.

The reign of King James was, to a very large extent, a continuation of that of Elizabeth; we actually have a word, 'Jacobethan', to cover them both. Even its most notorious event, the Gunpowder Plot of 1605, had several predecessors at the end of the previous century, just as the foundation of the first British colonies in the New World – at Jamestown, Virginia, in 1607, in Newfoundland in 1610 and at Plymouth, Massachusetts, in 1620 – were all the consequences of previous voyages of exploration. Shakespeare continued to write plays – *Macbeth*, *King Lear* and *The Tempest* were all written in James's day – as did Ben Jonson, John Webster and several others. Another genius to bridge the two reigns was one of the country's most glorious poets, John Donne. And let it never be forgotten that it was James who authorized the new translation of the Bible – the only world-class masterpiece ever created by a committee.

With the accession of Charles I, however, the whole complexion of England seems to change, as the spectre of religion immediately rears its head. Just a few weeks after his accession he caused grave parliamentary concern by marrying the Roman Catholic French princess Henrietta Maria. He did his best to allay the members' fears by undertaking to maintain all the existing restrictions imposed on recusants (the old English Catholic families), but then made a secret treaty with Louis XIII promising him help in his action against the Protestant Huguenots at La Rochelle. For the next fifteen years he seemed determined to antagonize Parliament in any way he could, in 1629 proroguing it and reigning for the next eleven years as an autocratic tyrant. Such stupidity and insensitivity almost beggars belief. The civil war that followed was very largely due to him, and even though he did not deserve execution – after all, few people do – he must take responsibility for much of the bloodshed of that nightmare time.

True, the eleven years under the Commonwealth were very little better, perhaps worse, since they affected not just the two warring factions but the entire country. During that grey, Puritan night everything that made life worthwhile seemed to be banned: the theatre, gambling, dancing, even Christmas. Few people indeed failed to welcome the Restoration; at last life was fun again. True, in the 1660s two disasters struck in swift succession, the Great Plague and the Great Fire; but the latter was followed by the rebuilding – to its huge advantage – of St Paul's, and the creation of some fifty superb churches – even though all too many of them were to be destroyed in the Blitz of 1940.

Of the dethronement, after only three years, of the Catholic James II, of the peaceful invasion of the Dutchman William of Orange and his Stuart wife Mary, and of the twelve-year reign of Queen Anne – England's most boring monarch –

little need here be said. Politically, indeed, the seventeenth century in England was deeply uninspiring. In the cultural field, however, in the arts and especially in the sciences, it blazed. This was the age of John Milton and Robert Herrick; of Samuel Pepys and Thomas Hobbes; of Anthony van Dyck and Sir Peter Lely; of William Harvey and Sir Isaac Newton; of Sir Christopher Wren, Sir John Vanbrugh and Nicholas Hawksmoor. And it saw the foundation of the Royal Society. Few countries indeed could boast a more distinguished record.

36

Coughton Court
WARWICKSHIRE

*T*he Throckmortons were recusants – members of the small group of English Roman Catholics who refused to abjure their faith after the Reformation. The family has lived at Coughton – pronounced 'Coaton' – for some 600 years, and the house reflects its turbulent history. The present house is essentially the creation of Sir George Throckmorton, who inherited the property at the beginning of the sixteenth century, and it was he who built the magnificent stone gatehouse – one of the finest of its kind in the country – that stands at its entrance.

Coughton was originally conceived as a regular quadrangle, enclosed by timber-framed ranges; but it is somehow typical of the house's history that the east wing – which contained the chapel – was destroyed by a Protestant mob at the time of the Glorious Revolution in 1688, when the Catholic James II was driven from the throne and the Protestant William of Orange arrived from the Netherlands to take over. Already before that time, however, it had borne witness to the stubborn faith of its owners. In 1584 Sir George's great-nephew Francis had been executed for having acted as a secret go-between for Mary Queen of Scots and the Spanish Ambassador, who were conspiring to overthrow Queen Elizabeth and restore Catholicism in England by putting Mary on the throne. This conspiracy was very similar to that known to history as the Gunpowder Plot, with which Coughton once again has a close association. Both had the same objective: the assassination of the Protestant monarch, who would then be replaced by a Catholic; and both had the same result: ignominious failure.

The Gunpowder Plot was in essence an attempt to blow up the House of Lords during the State Opening of Parliament on 5 November 1605. This, it was confidently hoped, would result in the death not only of the King himself but of his close family, together with the bishops, the senior judges, all the members of the Lords and a good many of the House of Commons. Meanwhile King James I's nine-year-old daughter, the Princess Elizabeth – who was third in the line of succession – would be kidnapped from where she was living at Coombe Abbey, near Coventry, and installed on the throne as queen. (She would presumably have had to be forcibly converted on the way.) The instigator of the plot was a good-looking young aristocrat by the name of Robert Catesby, whose mother was a Throckmorton. He quickly found an ally in his friend Thomas Wintour, who in turn recruited one John Wright. These were later joined by Thomas Percy and another fanatical Catholic, Guy Fawkes. During the weeks that followed, the number of conspirators gradually grew to thirteen, but it was these five who worked out the details of the plot, and who gave the orders.

During the summer of 1605, a total of thirty-six barrels of gunpowder were secretly transported to Westminster and concealed in the undercroft of the House of Lords – more still was to come in September – but already Catesby had approached the principal English Jesuit, Father Henry Garnet, and without revealing his plans had aroused Garnet's suspicions. Soon afterwards he made his confession to another

Jesuit, Father Tesimond, doubtless trusting that the seal of the confessional would prevent the information from going any further; but Tesimond felt that he must discuss what he had heard with Garnet who, having tried in vain to dissuade Catesby, wrote to a colleague in Rome warning him, though only in very general terms, that revolution was in the air.

By this time rumours of the plot were rapidly spreading; but the conspirators' fate was sealed when, on 26 October, a certain Lord Mounteagle received an anonymous letter warning him not to attend the Opening of Parliament 'as he tendered his life'. He of course at once showed it to all his colleagues, and by Friday, 1 November it was in the hands of the King. Accordingly, three days later, the House of Lords was thoroughly searched and there was found not only the gunpowder store but Guy Fawkes himself, carrying a lantern (which is now in the Ashmolean Museum at Oxford). He was immediately arrested, enduring two days of torture on the rack before he confessed.

Meanwhile several of England's leading Catholics, including one or two close relations of the conspirators and the two Jesuit fathers Garnet and Tesimond, were gathered at Coughton, where on 6 November Catesby's servant Thomas Bates arrived with the fateful news. The women were released after questioning; but most of the men were not so lucky. Several were arrested; Father Tesimond fled to the Continent, but Garnet was executed and Nicholas Owen – his servant, who had become famous for building 'priest's holes', places of refuge for Catholic priests – died under torture. As for the conspirators themselves, they suffered various fates. Catesby with a few others took refuge in Holbeche House in Staffordshire and was shot dead when the building was besieged by the Sheriff of Worcester on the following day; most of the rest, including Fawkes, were tried in Westminster

Hall and subsequently hanged, drawn and quartered in Old Palace Yard.

Of them all, only Fawkes is still remembered; how strange it is that the name of a relatively obscure member of an unsuccessful conspiracy four centuries ago should still be known to every child – and adult – in the country, and even have a day, 5 November, called after him. No other Englishman, alive or dead, can say as much.

37

Battlefield of Naseby
NORTHAMPTONSHIRE

'Saint and Martyr' or not, it is hard to believe that any king could have behaved quite so stupidly as King Charles I. First, there was his marriage to the Catholic Henrietta Maria; then there was the obvious contempt he showed for Parliament. He believed devoutly, as his father James I had believed before him, in what was known as the Divine Right of Kings: that God had put him on the throne and that he could do no wrong. This meant that he had no need of parliamentary approval for his actions, which must always be above reproach. When in 1629 Parliament incurred his displeasure over a relatively minor issue, he lost his temper and dissolved it the same day, imprisoning eight of its leading members, thus turning them, quite unnecessarily, into martyrs. For the next eleven years – the Eleven-year Tyranny – he ruled without a parliament at all.

How he got away with it for so long heaven knows; but with every one of those years he was laying up more trouble for the future. He insisted, for example, on his own particular brand of High Anglicanism as upheld by his Archbishop of Canterbury William Laud; this infuriated the Puritans, who suspected him of reintroducing Catholicism. When they complained, he had them arrested, in some cases chopping off their ears. Meanwhile they were heavily fined if they refused to attend Anglican services.

When Parliament at long last reassembled in November 1640 it was resolved to stand no more nonsense from the King. First – largely by implied physical threats – it forced him to sign a warrant for the execution, on grounds of high treason, of his right-hand man Thomas Wentworth, Earl of Strafford; then it passed what it called the Grand Remonstrance, a list of all its grievances since the beginning of the reign, many of which were asserted to be part of a vast Catholic conspiracy. Soon afterwards came the news of a rebellion in Ireland, but Parliament refused Charles's demands for the funds needed to deal with it, many of the members fearing that the forces he raised might be used later against themselves.

Meanwhile there had been an invasion by the Scots, who were at this time occupying Northumberland and Durham; and the King suspected – rightly, for once – that certain parliamentarians had been colluding with them. On 3 January 1642 he commanded Parliament to give up five members on grounds of high treason. It refused, whereupon he resolved to arrest them, personally, by force. Unfortunately for him, news of his intention reached Parliament before he did, and the five members managed, just in time, to make their escape. The King, seeing that 'his birds had flown', stamped out angrily. By now, the situation was serious. A week later, fearing for his own safety and that of his family, he travelled north and started to raise an army. Parliament too began to arm. Finally, on 22 August, Charles raised his royal standard in Nottingham, and on 26 October – with the ultimately inconclusive Battle of Edgehill – the Civil War began.

At the outset of the fighting, most of the country remained neutral; but as it spread, more and more of the population found itself swept up in the conflict. At first the Parliamentarians tried to maintain that the war was not being fought actually against the King, but rather to deliver him from his evil advisers. When the Parliamentarians appointed the Earl of Essex as commander of their army, his instructions were 'to rescue His Majesty's person . . . out of the hands of those desperate persons who were about them'. But as battle succeeded battle and feelings became ever more bitter, the fiction was gradually abandoned.

For two years the war raged, its fortunes swinging first in one direction, then in the other; the ultimate victory, it seemed, could go either way. The decisive battle – it was in fact the twenty-second encounter in the war – was fought at Naseby in Northamptonshire on 14 June 1645. Commanding the Royalist forces, which numbered some 12,000, was Prince Rupert of the Rhine, the King's German nephew and one of the outstanding cavalry generals of the day; confronting them was the Parliamentarians' New Model Army of perhaps 15,000, raised principally by Oliver Cromwell and commanded jointly by himself and Sir Thomas Fairfax. The battle began at about nine o'clock in the morning; on that fateful day, however, Prince Rupert's habitual genius deserted him, and by noon the Royalists' cause was lost. They fled the field, the Roundheads in hot pursuit, chasing them for a good twelve miles from the field and slaughtering all those they caught. Only about 4,000 escaped, and many of those were badly wounded. Charles's commissariat, with copious supplies of arms, powder and ammunition, was captured; so, still more disastrous, were many of his private papers, containing plans to bring Irish Catholics and foreign mercenaries to England. These were immediately published by Parliament.

After Naseby there was no longer any doubt of the outcome of the war; King Charles's army had been effectively destroyed. The scene of the battle looks peaceable enough today; but those placid open fields saw the most decisive battle fought on English soil since Hastings, nearly 600 years before. There would not be another of comparable importance till the Battle of Britain, nearly 300 years after.

38

Banqueting House
LONDON

*D*ecisive as the Battle of Naseby turned out to be, it didn't mean the end of the fighting. Charles and what remained of his army struggled on, suffering defeat after defeat until the Parliamentarians' siege of Oxford, from which the King escaped in April 1646 – only to put himself in the hands of the Scottish Presbyterian army at Newark. Thenceforth it was a sad story of imprisonments, escapes, re-arrests and flights, while Charles constantly tried to negotiate agreements with various factions that might restore him to the throne. During one of these – it was known as the Engagement and was concluded in the last days of 1647 – he persuaded the Scottish Covenanters to invade England on his behalf, agreeing in return to establish Presbyterianism in the country for three years. In the following year they did so, starting what was technically the Second Civil War; but in August 1648 they were destroyed at Preston, and Charles's last hope was gone.

It was the Engagement that proved his ultimate undoing. Until then, there was a good chance that he might be reinstated, this time as a constitutional monarch with drastically limited powers; now, while in captivity and defeat, he had provoked another war, and had done so by making a secret treaty with the Scots: 'a more prodigious treason,' said Cromwell, 'than any that had been perfected before'. In the minds of the Parliamentarians, only one course was now left open: His Majesty must be brought to trial.

Never before had the English tried a king. Edward II, Richard II and Henry VI had been deposed, Richard III had been killed in battle; but to place the monarch in the dock and to subject him to the full process of the law – that was altogether without precedent. Charles went further, claiming that it was illegal; when asked to plead, he consistently refused. 'I would know,' he repeated, 'by what power I am called hither, by what lawful authority?' The sixty-eight special commissioners, appointed by a special Act of Parliament to sit in judgement over him, had their reply ready. The King of England, they claimed, was not a person but an office; and the holder of that office was entrusted with a limited power to govern, 'by and according to the laws of the land and not otherwise'. The indictment did not spare its punches:

> The King . . . For the protecting of himself and his adherents in his and their wicked practices, to the same ends hath traitorously and maliciously levied war against the present Parliament, and the people therein represented . . . The wicked designs, wars, and evil practices of him, the said Charles Stuart, have been and are carried on for the advancement and upholding of a personal interest of will, power and pretended prerogative to himself and his family, against the public interest, common right, liberty, justice and peace of the people of this nation.

Many witnesses were heard, but the conclusion was foregone. Charles was condemned to be beheaded. Fifty-nine of the commissioners signed his death warrant.

Just as the occasion itself was unprecedented, so too was the place of execution. In King Charles's day Henry VIII's old Palace of Whitehall still covered an immense area in

Westminster. Despite its size, it had originally contained no Banqueting House. James I had built one, but it had barely been completed when in 1619 it was burned to the ground; James ordered an immediate replacement from the fashionable architect Inigo Jones, who had made his name designing masques for performances at court. Jones was a Renaissance man through and through; he had travelled in Italy, where he had closely studied the recent work of Andrea Palladio; and his refined, classically inspired building must have looked odd indeed in the middle of the rambling Tudor palace. At the same time, facing as it did a huge open courtyard, it made a perfect stage set for the drama that was to be enacted.

The date was fixed for Tuesday, 30 January 1649. It was a bitterly cold morning and the King, conscious that any sign of a shiver would surely be misinterpreted as fear, had put on two thick shirts before stepping out from the northernmost of the large first-floor windows on to the huge wooden platform specially erected. (Uncharacteristically, Jones had committed an architectural solecism by giving the façade an even number of bays, so that it has no central window; the platform extended over at least four of them.) Charles had given much thought to his speech from the scaffold, but it would have been inaudible to all except those standing there with him. His last words were 'I shall go from a corruptible to an incorruptible Crown, where no disturbance can be.' The story is taken up by Andrew Marvell:

> He nothing common did or mean
> Upon that memorable scene,
>   But with his keener eye
>   The axe's edge did try . . .
>   But bowed his comely head
>   Down, as upon a bed.

It was severed at a single stroke.

The normal practice after an execution for treason was to lift up the head by the hair and show it to the crowd. This was done; but the traditional words 'Behold the head of a traitor!' were not uttered. In another break with tradition, Oliver Cromwell allowed the head to be sewn back on to the body, so that it should be presentable when Charles's family came to pay their respects. Just over a week later, on the night of 7 February, the body was buried in St George's Chapel, Windsor Castle, and one of the darkest chapters of English history came at last to an end.

39

St Bartholomew's Hospital

LONDON

Not many hospitals still working today were founded in the twelfth century; St Bartholomew's, always known affectionately as Bart's, owes its existence to Rahere, a court favourite – some say jester – of King Henry I, who established it in 1123 in thanks for his recovery from a nasty bout of malaria contracted during a pilgrimage to Rome. At the same time he founded a priory at St Bartholomew-the-Great across the way (now the oldest church in London), himself becoming its first prior. The hospital also – most unusually – possesses its own museum, which recounts not only the history of Bart's itself but also that of medicine and medical care over the past 900 years. In the early years of its existence it was ruled by a master, whose servant was expected to live permanently in the infirmary, 'to wait upon the sick with diligence and care in all gentleness'; but the sick were not its only responsibility: it also extended its charity to orphans and outcasts, and always of course to the poor.

European medicine was slow to develop. Hard as it may be to believe, until the seventeenth century many of the theories and teachings of the second-century Greek physician Galen of Pergamum still held sway. Hospitals might be able to deal after a fashion with broken limbs, or the results of minor accidents; but there was no understanding of disease, and if the natural powers of resistance of the human body were insufficient there was little that they could do. Consequently death rates were high. The most fortunate patients were those who were able to entrust themselves to the great hospital run by the Knights of St John of Jerusalem in Rhodes or – after that island fell to the Turks in 1520 – Malta. (Both buildings still survive, and are fascinating to visit.) Particularly where infectious diseases were concerned, their success rate was far higher than anywhere else. It is only in relatively recent times that we have discovered the reason: the huge wealth of their order allowed the Knights to serve their patients with food and drink in vessels of silver plate – which of course were infinitely more hygienic than the rough wooden cups and porringers, all crawling with bacteria, used in other hospitals.

In 1381 Wat Tyler was brought to Bart's after having been stabbed by the Lord Mayor during the Peasants' Revolt (see **Fobbing**), but before the hospital could do anything for him he was dragged out again by the King's men and beheaded on the spot. Then in 1537 the neighbouring priory was dissolved by Henry VIII and all its revenues confiscated; Bart's too was financially stricken, but just about survived until, seven years later, the King was persuaded to refound it. In 1568 Dr Rodrigo Lopez became its First Physician. By origin a Portuguese Jew, he is thought by many to have been the model for Shakespeare's Shylock; alas, in 1594 he was accused of complicity in a Spanish plot against the Queen and found guilty of treason. He was hanged, drawn and quartered.

In English medicine, the first major breakthrough came thanks to William Harvey, who was born in Folkestone in 1578 and at twenty-four graduated with high distinction as a doctor of medicine from the University of Padua. That same year he gained his second doctorate at Cambridge and then settled in London, where he soon became a Fellow of the

College of Physicians and accepted an offer from Bart's. There he was to work until his retirement, not only as a hospital doctor but as an outstanding lecturer – his lectures being illustrated with dissections – and researcher. His private patients included many of the highest in the land, among them the Lord Chancellor Sir Francis Bacon, and his career reached its climax when in February 1618 he was appointed Physician Extraordinary to King James I and, after the King's death in 1625, to his successor Charles I. He accompanied Charles wherever he went, including on his many hunting expeditions. Harvey, it is said, had only to see a fallen stag to pounce upon it, slit it open and start dissecting on the spot.

The outbreak of the Civil War added a new duty to his other responsibilities: that of tending the wounded. When the King was obliged to retreat to Oxford, Harvey went with him, acquired his third doctorate ('Doctor of Physick') from the university in 1642 and – 'unmindful,' we are told, 'of the clatter of arms and of the constant marching and counter-marching around him' – settled at Merton College, becoming its warden in 1645. By this time he was sixty-seven, in those days an old man, and a childless widower; it was time for retirement. Resisting all attempts to lure him back to Bart's, he settled with his brothers in London. He died at Roehampton, probably of gout, on 3 June 1657. He was seventy-nine.

But the achievement for which Harvey is best known was his discovery of the circulation of the blood. It was all explained in his book *De Motu Cordis*, which was dedicated to Charles I and published in Frankfurt – to cash in on the already flourishing annual Book Fair – in 1628. The basic fact came as no surprise; physicians had long suspected it, even known about it in general terms. But Harvey was the first to describe the whole system, as he had meticulously worked it out by scientific experiment – not only on humans, but on pigeons, unborn chickens, even eels and shrimps. He had, he wrote, suffered many moments of near-despair, moments when he was 'tempted to think . . . that the movement of the heart was to be comprehended only by God'; and even when his book was safely in print, there were many who still remained faithful to their beloved Galen and violently condemned the new teaching. This, however, Harvey seems to have accepted with a shrug. He was by this time probably the most famous physician in the western world, honoured by everyone from the King down; he could afford to rest on his many laurels, and let the rest of the world – like his unfortunate predecessor Dr Lopez – go hang.

40

Oliver Cromwell's House
ELY, CAMBRIDGESHIRE

Nobody in English history ever wielded as much power as Oliver Cromwell, a fact the more remarkable in that until the age of forty he lived as an obscure yeoman farmer, showing no sign of future greatness. In all Europe, the only man who could boast a comparable rise is Napoleon Bonaparte, though fortunately Cromwell had no interest in foreign adventures. Unlike Napoleon, too, he died while still in command. And there is one more similarity between the two men: the division of opinion about them since their deaths. There are those who see Oliver Cromwell as a heroic defender of liberty against royal oppression; there are others for whom he was no more than a cruel and dictatorial regicide.

His pretty timber-framed house still stands in the city of Ely, where he settled in 1636 after early years spent in his birthplace of Huntingdon. It was almost certainly there that he underwent dramatic spiritual awakening which convinced him that the Reformation had gone nowhere near far enough, and that Catholic beliefs and practices must be exterminated. By this time, however, he was a Member of Parliament, and in 1640 he moved his family to London. On the outbreak of the Civil War he recruited a troop of cavalry, and rose rapidly to the rank of lieutenant-general of the horse, fighting in every major engagement. He showed himself completely fearless – but on certain occasions similarly devoid of mercy: following his capture of the strategically important Catholic fortress of Basing House in Hampshire, he ordered the execution of 100 of its garrison; and after the arrest and trial of the King, he was the third to sign the death warrant.

From 1649 to 1651 Cromwell was away on campaign, first in Ireland – where, thanks to his massacres and wholesale dispossession of Catholics, his name is detested to this day – and then in Scotland, where Charles II had been proclaimed king. His army smashed the Scots at Dunbar, capturing Edinburgh; but they somehow recovered, and in the summer of 1651 supported Charles in an invasion of England. The result was the Battle of Worcester, where Cromwell scored another decisive victory, Charles barely escaping with his life. After several hours concealed in an oak tree in the park of Boscobel House and two days in priest's holes there and at Moseley Old Hall nearby – tree, house and hall all survive to this day – Charles fled across the Channel.

Returning to London, Cromwell began showing his political strength. He also revealed a new degree of intolerance. In 1653, angry with Parliament, he entered the chamber with a body of musketeers and dissolved it by force; and on 16 December of that same year this action was retrospectively legalized when he was sworn in as Lord Protector, with power to call and dissolve parliaments at will. His first objective, he maintained, was 'healing and settling' the nation after the civil wars and the execution of the King, establishing political stability. This he managed in large measure to do; he was less successful, however, in his second objective, which was to institute a programme of spiritual and moral reform according to strict Puritan principles.

The Protectorate was effectively a monarchy under another name, with Cromwell – by now signing himself *Oliver P.* –

showing himself every bit as autocratic as Charles I had ever been. He divided the country into eleven separate districts, each under a 'Major General', who was responsible not only for law and order and the collection of taxes, but also for public morality. Virtually every occupation except church-going – which was of course compulsory – was considered sinful and consequently banned. The theatres were closed, as were the alehouses; horse racing, cockfights and even dancing were prohibited; severe penalties were imposed for blasphemy and drunkenness. Not surprisingly, the English – among whom true Puritans formed a small minority – were resentful and indignant, and as the decade advanced Oliver P. and his government grew ever more unpopular, not only with the people but with Parliament as well. Only military force kept them in power.

In 1658 the Protector was stricken with a grave infection of the kidneys; and on 3 September – the seventh and eighth anniversaries respectively of his victories at Worcester and

Dunbar – he died at Whitehall at the age of fifty-nine. He was given a magnificent funeral in Westminster Abbey, modelled on that of James I thirty-three years before. Although his office was not technically hereditary, he was succeeded by his third son, Richard; but 'Tumbledown Dick', as he soon came to be called, was a disaster, lacking as he did any of his father's intelligence, force of character or charisma. Neither did he have any power base, either in Parliament or in the army; and in May 1659 he resigned with every show of relief. General George Monck, the English Governor of Scotland, hurried down to London and held the fort until the King could be called back from exile and restored to his rightful throne.

But that was not quite the end of Oliver Cromwell; a final ignominy was still in store. In 1661 his body was exhumed from the abbey, and on 30 January – the anniversary of King Charles's execution – what was left of it was hanged in chains at Tyburn. It was thrown into a pit – all except the head, which was salvaged and displayed until 1685 on a stake outside Westminster Hall. After being taken down it changed hands several times, the last being as recently as 1960. Then it found its way to Sidney Sussex College, Cambridge, where its owner had studied in his youth and where, let us hope, it may remain.

41

Eyam
DERBYSHIRE

*H*istory offers us relatively few examples of communal, municipal heroism – heroism in the form of self-sacrifice, voluntarily undertaken by a single town or village, quite possibly at the cost of a large majority of its inhabitants. In the seventeenth century the little village of Eyam in Derbyshire had a population of only about 350; but its reaction to the arrival of the Great Plague in August 1665 has ever since been remembered as a lesson to the world.

Tradition has it that the plague was brought to Eyam in a flea-infested bale of cloth that was delivered to George Viccars, the local tailor. He was dead within a week, and several of his neighbours followed him to the grave. As soon as the epidemic was recognized, the two resident ministers of religion, the Reverend William Mompesson and the Puritan Thomas Stanley, called a meeting of the whole village to discuss what was to be done. Several measures were agreed, to take immediate effect: henceforth families were to bury their own dead; church services were to be held outdoors. But the one vital, heroic measure was simply this: that the entire village should quarantine itself, no one being allowed in or out of it until the sickness was past. Only thus could the villagers ensure – or hope to ensure – that the contagion would not spread to their surroundings.

For fourteen months the pestilence continued, the people of Eyam living daily with death and confidently expecting it. When at last the nightmare was over, the most probable of the several estimates available informs us that, out of the original 350 inhabitants, just 83 had survived. The so-called Riley graves can still be seen, testimony to the fate of a certain Elizabeth Hancock, who buried her husband and their six children in the space of eight days. She herself, almost miraculously, escaped unscathed.

Eyam, thanks to the nobility of its inhabitants, saw the only outbreak of the plague in the region; the worst of the suffering was, inevitably, in London. It was almost certainly caused by the same bacillus, *yersinia pestis*, that had been responsible for the Black Death between 1348 and 1350, which killed perhaps half the population of Europe, and was spread by fleas, travelling on the rats that infested merchant ships everywhere. There had been several minor epidemics since, one occurring in Holland as recently as 1663, serious enough for King Charles II to ban all trade with the Dutch; but the outbreak that began in London during the spring of 1665 was on a different scale to anything that had been encountered before. Not altogether surprisingly, the first cases were around the docks; but by the beginning of the summer – a summer, incidentally, that turned out to be one of the hottest in living memory – it had struck into the very heart of London. The King, his family and his court fled to Oxfordshire, while most of the merchants and the lawyers, the clergy and the physicians – who probably realized that they were powerless to stem the tide – sought refuge where they might; the roads leading out of the capital were clogged by the thousands desperate to escape.

To their eternal honour, however, the Lord Mayor, aldermen and the greater part of the other city authorities remained at their posts. So too, thank God, did Samuel Pepys, who gives us a first-hand account of it in his diary:

26 July: The Sicknesse is got into our parish this week; and is got indeed everywhere, so I begin to think of setting things in order, which I pray God enable me to put, both as to soul and body.

8 August: To Westminster Hall . . . hearing very sad stories of Mrs Michell's son's family. And poor Will that used to sell us ale at the Hall-door – his wife and three children dead, all I think in a day.

12 August: The people die so, that now it seems they are fain to carry the dead to be buried by daylight, the nights not sufficing to do it in. And my Lord Mayor commands people to be within at 9 at night, all (as they say) that the sick may have liberty to go abroad for ayre.

22 August: I walked to Greenwich, in my way seeing a coffin with a dead body therein, dead of the plague . . . which was carried out last night and the parish hath not appointed anybody to bury it – but only set a watch there day and night, that nobody should go thither or come thence, which is a most cruel thing – this disease making us more cruel to one another than we are to dogs.

31 August: Thus this month ends, with great sadness upon the public through the greatness of the plague, everywhere through the Kingdom almost. Every day sadder and sadder news of its increase . . . In the City died this week 7,496; and of them, 6,102 of the plague. But it is feared that the true number of the dead this week is near 10,000 – partly for the poor that cannot be taken notice of through the greatness of their number, and partly from the Quakers and others that will not have any bell ring for them.

After the plague itself, the greatest enemy was panic. There seems to have been a generally held view that any preventative measure, however illogical, was better than none at all, whereas in fact there were several that made the situation considerably worse. All the citizens were told to light their fires, and to keep them burning night and day – in a summer already sweltering. Still more disastrous was the order for the wholesale slaughter of dogs and cats – the only things that were keeping the rats in check.

Gradually, however, the toll of casualties began to fall; and by Christmas it was clear that the worst was over. In February 1666 the King returned to London. By then, however, the city had lost an estimated 100,000 people, some 20 per cent of its population. (By way of comparison, the Blitz in 1940 accounted for 43,000.) Nor were its tribulations over: for less than a year later, in September 1666, came the Great Fire. That, heaven knows, was another catastrophe; but at least it must have served to reassure such Londoners who were still alive that the Great Plague had been cauterized, and that the last of those revolting parasites had perished in the flames.

Coughton Court, Warwickshire.
It needed a brave man who, as a Roman Catholic from a long-established recusant family, dared build himself such a house at the beginning of the sixteenth century. But Sir George Throckmorton was such a man. It was at Coughton that the conspirators of the Gunpowder Plot (right) learned of its failure.

INfernall Fauks with Dæmoniack *heart*,
Being ready, *now*, to act *his hellish* part;
Booted *and* spur'd *with* Lanthorne *in his* hand,
And match *in*'s Pocket *at the* doore *doth stand*:
But *wife Lord* KNEVET *by Divine Direction*,
Him apprehends and findes the Plots *detection*.

Eyam, Derbyshire. The story of Eyam is still, I find, almost unbearably moving, particularly if you stand among those long-deserted graves. But I am haunted, too, by this tiny woodcut which seems to say more about the Great Plague than any other illustration I know.

Battlefield of Naseby, Northamptonshire. The typical civil war is composed of a whole series of small battles which are then unexpectedly interrupted by a much larger one that frequently decides the outcome of the war. In the Wars of the Roses it was Towton and Tewkesbury; in the Civil War it was Naseby. On that day, 14 June 1645, Charles's cause was lost.

Banqueting House, London. Why was the King's execution here rather than the Tower? Why choose a building whose prime purpose was celebratory and whose interior contained the most dazzling apotheosis of the King's own father that existed anywhere in England? The answer comes in a single word: drama. Here was, potentially, the greatest stage in London; where else should the greatest drama of the age be enacted?

Apple Tree at Woolsthorpe, Lincolnshire.
Perhaps it just happened to be lying there . . .

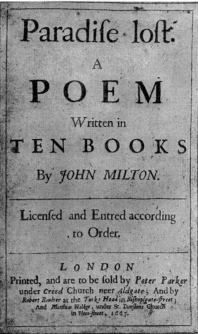

Milton's Cottage, Chalfont St Giles, Buckinghamshire. This cottage looks as if it might reasonably have seen the birth of a few sensitive lyrics; hardly of the mightiest, most majestic poem ever written, dealing with Revolution against God himself.

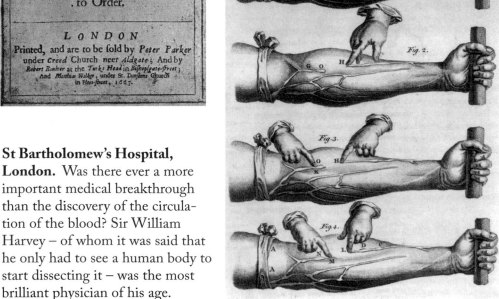

St Bartholomew's Hospital, London. Was there ever a more important medical breakthrough than the discovery of the circulation of the blood? Sir William Harvey – of whom it was said that he only had to see a human body to start dissecting it – was the most brilliant physician of his age.

The Monument. Despite being the highest stone column in the world, the Monument is now sadly hemmed in by other buildings. A climb to the top remains well worthwhile, however – even though the view of St Paul's is no longer quite what it might be.

Prime Meridian, Greenwich. It is not easy taking a photograph of a meridian, which is by definition invisible. We could more easily have included those Tompion clocks, or one of Harrison's incomparable marine chronometers, but this seems to me to breathe a certain abstract grandeur. And in the evening, the laser is magnificent.

Great Hall, Taunton Castle, Devon. In the years around 1700, refractory schoolchildren in the West Country were threatened that if they weren't careful Judge Jeffreys would be round to deal with them; the Monmouth Rebellion was even perpetuated in a card game depicting the fate of the rebels.

Severall of y̆ Rebells hang'd upon a Tree

The late D of M beheaded on Tower Hill 15 July 1685

Blenheim Palace, Oxfordshire. 'To enter the Great Hall of Blenheim', wrote Nigel Nicolson, 'is like a declaration of war.' No other palace in England implies so clearly that it is the residence of a great general, built for him by a grateful monarch as a reward for the destruction of the King's enemies.

The Duke of Marlborough at the Battle of Blenheim. Detail taken from one of a series of tapestries hanging at Blenheim Palace.

42

Milton's Cottage

CHALFONT ST GILES, BUCKINGHAMSHIRE

John Milton's cottage in the little Buckinghamshire village of Chalfont St Giles isn't much to look at today, and he lived in it for only a year – 1665 – when he moved his family to the country to escape the plague. We should all, however, be profoundly grateful for its existence, for two reasons. First, because there is no other surviving residence of his; second, it was here that he completed one of the world's most majestic masterpieces, *Paradise Lost*.

The seventeenth century was the golden age of English literature. Its first fifteen years saw the appearance of all Shakespeare's greatest plays except *Romeo and Juliet*; then in 1611 came the Authorized Version of the Bible, with the Book of Common Prayer some years later. It was the age of John Donne and the Metaphysical poets; and it was the age of John Milton. Milton began *Paradise Lost* in 1658, but its publication was delayed until after the Restoration, when he knew that the 'Good Old Cause', for which the Parliamentarian army had fought the Civil War, was lost for ever. The poem can be seen as one long lament: the Garden of Eden standing for the halcyon days of the Commonwealth, the Fall representing England's fall from grace under the restored monarchy. Well, perhaps it is: but it's the poetry that counts. What a beginning:

Of man's first disobedience, and the fruit
Of that forbidden Tree, whose mortal taste
Brought death into the world, and all our woe,
With loss of Eden, till one greater Man
Restore us, and regain the blissful seat . . .

Or that magical single line, perhaps my favourite in all English poetry:

Imparadis'd in one another's arms.

And, let's remember, Milton went totally blind in 1652, so all this was dictated to his three daughters, or to a succession of secretaries. He died in 1674, and was buried in the church of St Giles, Cripplegate; his funeral, we read, was attended by 'his learned and great Friends in London, not without a friendly concourse of the vulgar'.

'In England,' wrote Lord Macaulay, 'during the latter half of the seventeenth century, there were only two minds which possessed the imaginative faculty in a very eminent degree. One of these minds produced the *Paradise Lost*, the other *The Pilgrim's Progress*.' Born in Bedford in 1628, John Bunyan was twenty years younger than Milton. He too was a staunch upholder of the Protestant/Parliamentary cause, but there the similarity ended. Milton was a scholar and an intellectual who spoke seven languages; Bunyan was the son of an illiterate tinker – a profession which he himself adopted – and seems to have been very largely self-educated, though to his dying day he knew little except the Bible. And yet, somehow, he managed to write one of the most remarkable – and still immensely readable – religious allegories ever penned, which has kept its place as one of the sublime works of English literature for well over four centuries.

It is the story of a dream, in which the hero, Christian,

learns that his home will be destroyed by fire. On the advice of Evangelist, he flees from the City of Destruction, passing through such places as the Slough of Despond, the Valley of Humiliation, Vanity Fair and Doubting Castle, and meeting foul fiends like the Giant Despair. But the real pleasure of the book lies in the quiet simplicity of its language, the vividness of the characterization and – more surprisingly – a lovely gentle sense of humour rare indeed in religious works of the time.

In his youth, Bunyan tells us, he was a shameless debauchee: among the sins to which he confesses are profanity, dancing and bell-ringing. Then, one Sunday morning when he was once again risking eternal damnation by playing tip-cat, he heard a warning voice from heaven; thenceforth, religion dominated his life. He became an itinerant hot-gospeller – something a good deal more dangerous then than it is today. When the country returned to Anglicanism after the Restoration, all dissenting meeting-houses were closed and every citizen was obliged to attend his local parish church; all preaching was forbidden except by ordained ministers of the Church of England. In November 1660 Bunyan was arrested and imprisoned in Bedford Gaol. The authorities offered to release him if he would hold his peace, but he maintained that God's law had ordered him to continue. 'If you release me today,' he said, 'I will preach tomorrow.' The result was a three-month sentence, followed by another for six years, during which he produced his great work. He was not finally released until 1672, when the King issued his Declaration of Religious Indulgence.

To the modern mind, such an imprisonment was scandalous, reminiscent more of the gulags than of a civilized people. All that can be said is that it seemed very different in the seventeenth century. Indeed, there was a moment after the

Restoration when Milton was also in danger: his books were publicly burned, and many of the authorities were out for his blood. He was saved by the King himself, who refused to allow him to be put on trial for treason. 'He's old and blind, and full of fleas,' said Charles, 'so let him be.'

What conclusions are we to draw from this? Simply that if John Bunyan had not been incarcerated, we might never have had *The Pilgrim's Progress*; if John Milton had been, we should almost certainly have been deprived of *Paradise Lost*.

43

Apple Tree, Woolsthorpe Manor
LINCOLNSHIRE

Nature and nature's laws lay hid in night;
God said 'Let Newton be' and all was light.

Alexander Pope

*E*veryone knows the story of Sir Isaac Newton and the falling apple; the direct descendant of the tree from which it
fell – the most important apple tree since that in the Book of
Genesis – is still to be seen in the garden of Woolsthorpe
Manor, the modest seventeenth-century Lincolnshire farm-
stead where Newton himself first saw the light on Christmas
Day, 1642. He grew up to become far and away the most
influential scientific genius that England – many people would
say the world – has ever produced; he broke new ground in
virtually every branch of physics existing at that time: mathematics, where he first developed the infinitesimal calculus
(whatever that may be); optics, where he showed that light
could be refracted and decomposed into the colour spectrum,
thereby solving the mystery of the rainbow; mechanics, where
his three laws of motion made possible the Industrial
Revolution of the following century and where he defined his
most famous law – that of universal gravitation; and astronomy, where he applied his gravitational laws to investigate the
orbits of the planets and invented the first reflecting telescope.

Oddly enough, he was also fascinated by alchemy and the occult, and deeply religious, writing studies of the Bible and the early Fathers of the Church. He calculated the date of the Crucifixion to be 3 April AD 33 and was forever trying – unsuccessfully – to find secret messages in the Holy Writ. He saw no incompatibility between science and religion: 'Gravity,' he said, 'explains the motions of the planets, but it cannot explain who set the planets in motion. God governs all things and knows all that is or can be done.'

Newton was the most dazzling star of the Scientific Revolution, that thrilling period when all the various early doctrines – many of them had originated in Ancient Greece and become mummified in the Middle Ages – were swept away, together with all the religious inhibitions from which Galileo and his contemporaries had suffered so much. Though even in Galileo's day the process had begun: indeed, he was part of it. The starting date is often put as early as 1543, the publication year of both Copernicus's *On the Revolutions of the Heavenly Spheres* and Andreas Vesalius's *On the Fabric of the Human Body.* But it was only in the following century that it reached its apogee: in England alone we contributed a considerable number of hugely talented men who, even if they lacked the ultimate genius of Newton, pushed forward the boundaries of knowledge to an astonishing degree. Among them were the physicist Robert Boyle, who did much valuable work on the behaviour of air and gases (his epitaph describes him as 'Father of English Chemistry and seventh son of the Earl of Cork'); the astronomer John Flamsteed, who accurately calculated the eclipses of 1666 and 1668, was the first to gaze on the planet Uranus and gave his name both to an asteroid and a crater on the moon; and the clockmaker John Harrison, who was largely instrumental in making it possible to calculate longitude. This depended on knowing the precise time that the sun rises, reaches its zenith and sets again; but no one had yet succeeded in making a clock able to show this accurately through a long, rough sea voyage with dramatic variations of heat and humidity. This Harrison achieved, not once but several times.

We will come to Christopher Wren in the next piece, so we'll pass on directly to Robert Hooke; and Hooke somehow sums up the whole seventeenth-century revolution. He was, we know, Wren's colleague as an architect and surveyor, but he was much more than that: after a youthful period as an art student, studying with Samuel Cowper and Peter Lely – he remained all his life an exquisite draughtsman – he set out to study mathematics and mechanics; then, in 1655 at the age of twenty, he became Boyle's chief assistant, building, operating and demonstrating his master's *machina boyleana*, more familiarly described as an air pump. Next he turned his attention, like Harrison, to horology, in which he is credited with the invention of the anchor escapement and balance spring. As an anatomist, he explained the difference between veinous and arterial blood; as an entomologist, his hugely magnified drawings of insects are extraordinary. In 1660 he discovered the law of elasticity, and in that same year came a development that was to prove of immense value to British science: the foundation of the Royal Society of London for Improving Natural Knowledge or, as we know it, the Royal Society.

The society began as a group of a dozen scientists, which included all those mentioned above, and in 1662 it appointed Hooke to be its Curator of Experiments, a post that he was to hold for the next forty years. It suited him perfectly, leaving him time for his own work and at the same time keeping him in the scientific swim. There was only one problem: his character. He was described variously by his contemporaries as 'cantankerous, envious and vengeful', 'melancholy, mistrustful and jealous' and, in one instance, 'positively unscrupulous'.

During those forty years the society was riven with feuds and disputes, the most furious of all being Hooke's quarrel with Newton. This was not altogether surprising: Newton, who was the society's president, was an impossible man himself. He disliked Hooke intensely – that wasn't surprising either – and is said to have destroyed Hooke's only known portrait. During one public debate, after some none too gentle criticism from the latter, he took furious offence and walked out of the room. Newton also made an implacable enemy of Flamsteed, of whose *Historia Coelestis Britannica* he and Edmond Halley – who was to succeed Flamsteed as Astronomer Royal – in 1712 published a preliminary version without crediting him. Flamsteed bought as many copies of this pirated version as he could find and burned them publicly in front of the Royal Observatory.

But there: they were all great men; and the atmosphere of the Royal Society in those days, though seldom perhaps cordial, can never have been less than exciting as, bit by bit, the secrets of nature began to reveal themselves. They did so in many different ways; Newton's apple tree – his own personal Tree of Knowledge – is a case in point. As he himself wrote: 'I do not know what I may appear to the world, but to myself I seem to have been only like a boy playing on the sea-shore, and diverting myself in now and then finding a smoother pebble or a prettier shell than ordinary, whilst the great ocean of truth lay all undiscovered before me.'

44

St Paul's from the Monument
LONDON

*T*here are a million monuments in London of one kind or another, but there is only one Monument – that commemorating the Great Fire, which broke out at Thomas Farriner's bakery in Pudding Lane a little after midnight on Sunday, 2 September 1666 and raged for four days, spreading rapidly westward until the evening of Wednesday 6th. Fortunately it never reached Westminster Abbey or the Palace of Whitehall; but virtually the entire City was destroyed, including Old St Paul's Cathedral, 87 parish churches and upwards of 13,000 houses. The diarist John Evelyn wrote: 'I left it this afternoon burning, a resemblance of Sodome or the last day . . . The stones of Paules flew like grenados, the lead melting down the streetes in a stream, and the very pavements of them glowing with fiery rednesse, so as nor horse nor man was able to tread on them.' The death toll is unknown – relatively few of the casualties had been registered, and many of the bodies must have been totally incinerated in the intense heat – but in terms of sheer physical devastation it was by far the greatest disaster that London had yet suffered. (It has endured a still greater one since.)

But even disasters can have compensations of a kind. I have already mentioned how the fire cauterized the city after the Great Plague of the previous year, destroying the last of the dread bubonic bacteria; it also abolished the sprawling laby-rinth of mean, disease-ridden medieval alleys – some of which were so narrow that two men could scarcely walk side by side – clearing the way for the broader, straighter and far healthier thoroughfares that took their place.

The cathedral that the fire destroyed – the fourth on the site – had long been on the verge of collapse. For the past thirty years the central tower had been hidden under scaffolding simply to hold it up, and four months before the catastrophe Christopher Wren had already submitted plans for its recon-struction. But now something more radical still was required. In 1668 the dean wrote to Wren: 'What we are to do next is the present deliberation, in which you are so absolutely and indispensably necessary to us, that we can do nothing, resolve nothing, without you.' From that moment Wren, a man of thirty-six with no formal architectural training and only three buildings to his credit, was responsible for the new St Paul's. Forty years later, in 1708, the last stone was laid and the old man could gaze from his house across the river on his master-piece – surely the greatest building ever conceived by a single man in his own lifetime.

It is a curious fact that England's two superb baroque archi-tects had both taken up their profession as an afterthought. Sir John Vanbrugh had been an extremely successful play-wright and theatre owner, who accepted his first architectural commission – to build Castle Howard in Yorkshire – at the age of thirty-five. Wren had started life as a scientist, and had done much valuable work in a number of fields – they included optics, mechanics, meteorology and medicine – before becom-ing Professor of Astronomy at Oxford (where he was to build, *inter alia*, the Sheldonian and Tom Tower at Christ Church). In 1662 he was to become one of the founder members of the Royal Society. It was only in the following year, when he was thirty-one, that his uncle Matthew, then Bishop of Ely, asked him to design the chapel of Pembroke College, Cambridge – and his architectural career began.

He certainly made up for lost time. The list of buildings that he designed, or at least on which he was actively and seriously engaged, seems almost endless. Quite apart from his major commissions, like St Paul's and the Royal Hospitals at Chelsea and Greenwich, for example, or St James's Piccadilly, he was made responsible for the rebuilding of fifty-two London churches damaged or destroyed in the Great Fire. He had two others to help him – Robert Hooke and Edward Woodroffe – to whom he must have delegated much of the design and supervision; but he always seems to have retained ultimate control, and to have approved every design before it was put into effect.

St Paul's, however, remains his supreme achievement. Being a post-medieval building, it possesses disappointingly few treasures compared with our older cathedrals. There are, on the other hand, countless tombs and memorials, of which two should on no account be missed. The first is that of Wren himself, the first person to be buried in the cathedral. His tomb in the crypt bears the five-word inscription by his son that says it all: *Lector, si monumentum requiris, circumspice* – 'Reader, if you seek his monument, look around you.' The second is to the seventeenth-century poet and sometime Dean of St Paul's, John Donne. His tomb was lost in the Great Fire; but the statue that stood above it was miraculously saved. It must be one of the strangest of its kind in the world. Izaak Walton describes how Donne posed in his winding-sheet, 'with his eyes shut, and with so much of the sheet turned aside as might shew his lean, pale and death-like face'. Sir Henry Wotton, who knew Donne well, said of the statue: 'It seems to breathe faintly, and posterity shall look upon it as a kind of artificial miracle.' The same might well be said of St Paul's itself.

Finally, there is one thing that we should never forget. Neither St Paul's nor those fifty-two other churches would ever have existed had it not been for the Great Fire. One can't help feeling that its own Monument – this time with a capital M – designed, incidentally, by Wren and Hooke together and standing more than thirty feet higher than Nelson's Column – is richly deserved.

45

Prime Meridian
GREENWICH

*E*very day, hundreds – perhaps thousands – of tourists in Greenwich get themselves photographed standing on the Prime Meridian, with one foot in the western hemisphere and one in the eastern. This is a much more satisfactory operation than doing the same sort of thing on the Equator, because the Equator – where the sun shines directly overhead at midday – is a fact of nature. We all know where it is. Everywhere on it is like everywhere else – it needs no fixed point to measure from. The Prime Meridian, on the other hand, had to be invented; it might equally well have run through America or Asia. That it does not do so is very largely due to a splendid man, now unjustly forgotten, named Sir Jonas Moore. As Surveyor General to the Ordnance Office, it was he who in 1674 persuaded King Charles II that the Greenwich Observatory should be built, and that England's most distinguished astronomer John Flamsteed should be its first director, with the resounding title of Astronomer Royal. Flamsteed's instructions were spelt out at length; he was to 'apply himself with the most exact care and diligence to the rectifying of the tables of the motions of the heavens, and the places of the fixed stars, so as to find out the so much desired longitude of places for the perfecting of the art of navigation'.

The first of the Royal Observatory buildings, known as Flamsteed House, was designed by Sir Christopher Wren – probably with the assistance of Robert Hooke – and was the first purpose-built research facility in the country. It cost £520, which was £20 over budget. Moore, who was fortunately a rich man, provided all the principal equipment and key instruments at his own expense. He also donated two magnificent clocks, both built by Thomas Tompion, which were installed in the twenty-foot-high Octagon Room. They both had pendulums thirteen feet long, which made them correct to within seven seconds in twenty-four hours – a degree of accuracy unheard of in the seventeenth century.

From that time forth the Royal Observatory at Greenwich has been generally agreed as the site of the Prime Meridian, but its claim was formally accepted only towards the end of the nineteenth century. The acceptance came not a moment too soon. It is hard for us to realize today just how chaotic was the whole conception of time, even 150 years ago. In the early 1800s almost every town in the world still kept its own local time; there were no formal agreements about how time should be measured, when the day would begin or end, even the precise length of hours, minutes and seconds. It was the sudden expansion of the railways that woke people up to the fact that so unsatisfactory a state of affairs could not be allowed to continue. The result was the meeting of the representatives of twenty-five nations in Washington DC for the International Meridian Conference, 1884, when the claims of Greenwich as the site of the Prime Meridian and the base from which the world's mean time should be measured were finally accepted by a near-unanimous vote. The wisdom of the choice was obvious. The USA had already accepted Greenwich as the basis for its own time-zone system; moreover, three-quarters of the world's commerce depended on British naval charts which did the same. Even so, one nation – San Domingo – voted against, and two abstained: Brazil and – somehow predictably – France. The world's most important imaginary line is now marked by a stainless-steel strip running through the Royal Observatory courtyard and – more dramatically – by a powerful green laser beam shining northward across the night sky.

It has to be admitted, however, that the Royal Observatory today is not what it was. In 1947 the amount of atmospheric and light pollution persuaded the authorities to move it to Herstmonceux Castle in Sussex; in 1990 it moved again, this time to Cambridge; and in 1998, after over 300 years, it closed down altogether. Now part of the nearby National Maritime Museum, it has its own fascinating collection of astronomical and navigational equipment, including John Harrison's prize-winning longitude marine chronometer, which made possible the first accurate calculation of longitude; no fewer than four of his clocks are on display at Greenwich. So too is the Grubb refracting telescope of 1893, the largest of its kind in the United Kingdom. It would have been nice to have the latest and greatest, the Isaac Newton telescope built in 1967; but that has now been taken, very sensibly, to the Canary Islands. (I have always thought it remarkable that the vagaries of the English climate, even before the days of our appalling night pollution, have allowed our national astronomers to make any discoveries at all.)

We can't leave Greenwich without a mention of its magnificent architectural centrepiece, the Old Royal Naval College, designed by Wren but completed by Hawksmoor and Vanbrugh. These glorious buildings were intended not as a college but as a hospital – more accurately a residential home for old or injured sailors, like his one for soldiers in Chelsea. When it closed in 1869 it was converted into the navy's staff college, but now the navy too has left, to be supplanted by Greenwich University and Trinity College of Music. The whole site is now open to visitors; the Painted Hall and chapel in particular should not be missed.

So Greenwich must be seen as a whole – museum, observatory and college for a start, but it is even more than that. The entire place breathes history: the old royal palace of Placentia, long since gone but the birthplace of Henry VIII and his daughters, Bloody Mary and Elizabeth I; the old dockyards; and of course the clipper ships. *Cutty Sark* is moored in the river, as is *Gipsy Moth IV*, in which in 1967 Sir Francis Chichester was the first man to make a single-handed circumnavigation of the world by the old clipper route; on his arrival the Queen knighted him there and then, on the river steps of the college. Look from the Maritime Museum across to the college, and then up to Flamsteed House on its high hill; that's what Greenwich is all about: man's conquest of the sea, and his understanding of the stars.

46

Great Hall

*M*onarchy can be an admirable form of government, as long as the monarch dies with one legitimate, indisputable heir. If he doesn't, there can be trouble – as the Great Hall of Taunton Castle bears full witness.

And trouble, with the death of Charles II in February 1685, there certainly was. Charles had at least a dozen illegitimate children, by seven different mistresses – a fact that suggests that he didn't have much time for his queen, the Portuguese Catherine of Braganza, who died childless and largely ignored. Who, then, was to succeed him? Legally, his brother James, but James had a serious disadvantage: he was a Roman Catholic, and as soon as he reached the throne he began making hamfisted attempts to re-establish the rights of Catholics in England. Nobody liked him, nobody wanted him; anti-Catholic feeling still ran strong; and only three months after his accession came the first attempt to get rid of him. It was made by James, the eldest of Charles's sons, born in Rotterdam to his mistress Lucy Walter during his Commonwealth exile, who was by this time the staunchly Protestant Duke of Monmouth. (There was a strong contemporary suspicion that the King was in fact not his father, but that's another story.)

In May 1685 Monmouth sailed down the Channel from

Holland, landing with eighty-two supporters at Lyme Regis on the Dorset coast. There he quickly gathered a few hundred local men, armed for the most part with farm tools – they were called the Pitchfork Army – and marched north into Somerset. There were skirmishes at Bridport and Axminster with the Dorset Militia, ending with a good many of these latter changing sides and joining him; Monmouth was then crowned three times – at Chard, Taunton and Bridgewater, all improbable places for coronations. He marched on, but almost at once things started to go wrong. He had hoped to take Bristol, or failing that Bath; but both these cities were by now occupied by King James's troops. He had also been counting on support from local rebellions in Scotland, Cheshire and East Anglia; but the Scottish attempt was unsuccessful, and the other two had not materialized. Further significant advance seemed impossible, and by the end of June Monmouth had to accept that the enterprise had failed.

There was nothing for it but to turn back; but by now King James's army, led by the Earl of Feversham and John Churchill, the future Duke of Marlborough, was on his tail. On 1 July he reached Wells – where his army, by now thoroughly demoralized, severely damaged the glorious west front of the cathedral, stabling their horses in the nave – from which he was forced back further to the flat, marshy Somerset Levels. The levels had proved an admirable refuge for Alfred the Great, eight centuries before; for the Duke of Monmouth, they didn't do so well, for it was there, on the night of 6 July 1685 at the Battle of Sedgemoor, that his rebellion came to an end. His ramshackle force – you could hardly call it an army – was no match for the trained and disciplined troops, with at least 500 cavalry, lined up against them, and the result was a foregone conclusion. What happened afterwards was described by the Earl of Shaftesbury:

[Monmouth] rode, accompanied by Lord Grey, to Woodyates [near Ringwood in Hampshire], where they quitted their horses; and the Duke, having changed clothes with a peasant and being closely pursued, concealed himself in a ditch which was overgrown with fern and underwood. When his pursuers came up, an old woman gave information of her having seen him filling his pocket with peas. The place was immediately surrounded by soldiers, who passed the night there. As they were going away, one of them espied the skirt of the Duke's coat, and seized him. The Duke when taken was quite exhausted with fatigue and hunger, having had no food since the battle but the peas which he had gathered in the field.

The family of the woman who betrayed him were ever after holden in the greatest detestation, and are said to have fallen into decay, and to have never thriven afterwards.

The many others of Monmouth's men who fled and were subsequently captured were shot or hanged on makeshift gibbets at the roadside. He himself was brought to London and imprisoned in the Tower. There, despite last-minute claims of conversion to Catholicism, he was beheaded by the famous executioner Jack Ketch on 15 July 1685, only some six weeks after his ill-advised adventure had begun. Despite – or perhaps because of – Ketch's expertise, it took six or seven blows of the axe before the job was done.

But that was not the end of the King's revenge. Throughout the West Country, all who were suspected of having given support to the rebellion – which probably included a good many who weren't – were arrested, imprisoned and sent to trial; and a whole series of special courts, known with justification as the Bloody Assizes, were set up to deal with them. The task was given to a panel of six senior judges, led by the

Lord Chief Justice, the forty-year-old George Jeffreys. The trials began in Winchester on 26 August; the court then proceeded to Salisbury, Dorchester, Taunton and Wells. The largest and most important of these sessions was held in Taunton, on 18–19 September, in the Great Hall of the castle (now the home of the Somerset County Museum). There, out of more than 500 men and women in the dock, almost all were condemned to death; the rest received sentences of transportation to the West Indies. Similar results were reported from the other towns in which the court sat. In fact, many of the death sentences were later commuted to transportation – perhaps because the King received £12 for each prisoner transported. But what struck many of those present was the almost sadistic conduct of Jeffreys himself, who made no attempt to conceal his pleasure as he pronounced judgement, whether the unfortunate in the dock had pleaded guilty or not.

James had paid a high price for his throne; but, as we shall see, he was not to keep it for long.

47

Brixham Quay

DEVON

O n the quayside of Brixham harbour there stands a statue of William of Orange: a fine figure of a man, tall and stately, looking, despite his distinctly supercilious expression and the seagull almost invariably perched on his head, every inch a military leader – and indeed a king. In fact William was not a bit like that. He was, to say the least, unprepossessing, small and hunchbacked, looking more like Richard III than Henry V. But there: in monumental statuary a little artistic licence is, perhaps, all to the good.

William was the grandson of Charles I through his eldest daughter Mary, who had married his father the Stadtholder (don't ask: only the Dutch can understand) William II, Prince of Orange; with his uncle Charles II having left no legitimate offspring and his other uncle, Charles's brother James, being a Roman Catholic, he consequently had a strong claim to the English throne of his uncles. He landed at Brixham on 5 November 1688, at the invitation of a group of British statesmen, both Whigs and Tories, for whom the three-year reign of James II had continued long enough. James had proved even worse than had been expected. First there had been his unconcealed Catholicism. Not only had he awarded to Roman Catholics – who represented just 2 per cent of the population – several of the highest places in the government, the army and the universities; he had also accepted a Papal Nuncio from Rome, for the first time since the reign of Bloody Mary 130 years before. Moreover, he had tried to be an absolute ruler. He had prorogued Parliament before he had been a year on the throne and had never summoned it again, behaving, in fact, very much as his father had, with consequences that were still all too fresh in people's minds.

Then, on 10 June 1688, his queen, Mary of Modena, gave birth to a son. Here was a crisis indeed. Until then James's only children had been two daughters, of whom Mary, the elder and therefore the heir to the throne, was married to her cousin, the staunchly Protestant William of Orange (strengthening still further his claim to the throne). Thus Protestantism had been assured in the long term. But this son put a totally different complexion on things: if he were to succeed, England might be Catholic for all eternity. There were the inevitable rumours that the baby had been secretly brought in from outside and introduced into Mary's bed in a warming-pan; but such a story, it was realized, would not look too good in a court of law. There was no alternative. James must be deposed by force.

The King had already put down one rebellion; but Monmouth's had been a fairly amateurish affair, and anyhow he had been illegitimate. William, quite apart from having a far better claim, had more cogent reasons too: he suspected that James had concluded a secret pro-Catholic alliance with Holland's arch-enemy Louis XIV of France, and that the French would finance an English naval squadron in the Channel – a development that could in itself be fatal to Dutch interests. Fortunately for him, many of England's leading Protestant politicians felt much the same way; all William now asked was a formal invitation, which, on 18 June 1688, he received, signed by six noblemen and a bishop:

. . . the people are so generally dissatisfied with the present conduct of the government, in relation to their religion, liberties and properties (all of which have been greatly invaded), and they are in such expectation of their prospects being daily worse, that your Highness may be assured, there are nineteen parts of twenty of the people throughout the kingdom, who are desirous of a change; and who, we believe, would willingly contribute to it, if they had such a protection to countenance their rising, as would secure them from being destroyed.

It remained to raise an army, and the necessary finance. The city of Amsterdam had already guaranteed enough to hire 260 transports; more came from private sources, including the Jewish banking fraternity and – most surprising of all – Pope Innocent XI, whose detestation of Louis XIV overrode all religious considerations. Now William's preparations could carry on apace; and by the beginning of October he was ready. Maddeningly, a 'popish wind' from the southwest prevented his invasion fleet from leaving port for the best part of three weeks; but towards the end of the month it gave way to a 'Protestant' easterly, and he gave the order to sail.

The fleet was enormous: with 463 ships and carrying nearly 12,000 men, it was nearly three times the size of the Spanish Armada, which had set sail exactly 100 years before (and had taken ten times as long to assemble). Monmouth, with his pathetically inadequate force, had entered the Channel quietly and stealthily; William did so with colours flying, bands playing, troops drawn up on deck, guns firing salutes. Hoping that James's army might collapse and, if it didn't, to avoid the danger of being attacked before disembarkation was complete, he had chosen to land in Devon, at Torbay. He at first sailed past it, owing to fog; but this lifted just in time, and with another change of wind he was able to return, enter the bay and land his men and horses at Brixham without interference.

To resist him, the King had gathered at Salisbury an army of some 19,000, which he himself joined on 19 November; but it was no use. Every day brought more desertions; on 26 November, even his own younger daughter Anne – who had her own suspicions about her new brother – went over to William. Meanwhile anti-Catholic riots broke out all over southern England, and by the end of the month James knew that the game was up and, anxious lest he should follow his father to the scaffold, decided on flight. On the night of 9 December, the Queen and the baby Prince of Wales left for France, and the next day James followed them, dropping the Great Seal – without which, in theory, no parliament could be summoned – in the Thames on his way. He was captured in Kent but William, who had no desire to make his uncle a martyr, deliberately let him go again. The King's voluntary departure was considered an abdication; the throne was thus technically vacant; and William and his wife, cousin and co-ruler Mary, were only too happy to fill it.

The reign of William and Mary had begun.

48

Blenheim Palace
OXFORDSHIRE

UNDER THE AUSPICES OF A MUNIFICENT
SOVEREIGN THIS HOUSE WAS BUILT FOR
JOHN DUKE OF MARLBOROUGH AND HIS DUCHESS
SARAH, BY SIR J. VANBRUGH BETWEEN THE YEARS
1705 AND 1722. AND THE ROYAL MANOR OF
WOODSTOCK, TOGETHER WITH A GRANT OF
£240,000 TOWARDS THE BUILDING OF BLENHEIM,
WAS GIVEN BY HER MAJESTY QUEEN ANNE AND
CONFIRMED BY ACT OF PARLIAMENT.

(Plaque on the East Gate of Blenheim Palace)

'Queen Anne's dead!' used to be a common retort to any blatant statement of the obvious. The last Stuart Queen is surely the only English monarch famous for being no longer with us; one sometimes wonders whether she was ever really alive. Married to Prince George of Denmark – 'dull but pleasant, fat but faithful' – she had eighteen children, none of whom survived her: a fate that she unhesitatingly ascribed to divine punishment for her sins, chief of which, she believed, was her desertion of her father's cause – insofar as she had ever upheld it – at the time of the Glorious Revolution. She had done so, first, because despite being the daughter of James

II she had been baptized a Protestant, and was to remain fervently Protestant throughout her life; and, second, because she had allowed herself to be persuaded by her friends John and Sarah Churchill, later to become Duke and Duchess of Marlborough.

John Churchill was already well on the way to becoming the greatest general of his day – indeed, one of the greatest in English history. He was to spend much of Anne's reign abroad, commanding armies in what was known as the War of the Spanish Succession, a fourteen-year conflict fought to prevent the huge Spanish Empire (which included much of the Old World and the New) falling under the control of England's arch-enemy Louis XIV of France. His wife Sarah meanwhile remained at home, where she had long been the close confidante of the Queen, being appointed in swift succession to the posts of Groom of the Stole, Mistress of the Robes – the highest office at court that could be held by a woman – and Keeper of the Privy Purse. In these positions she wielded considerable power, acting as the Queen's private secretary and business manager and controlling all access to her.

The two had been friends since the 1680s, and their friendship had deepened during the previous reign. They now had pet names for each other: Sarah was 'Mrs Freeman', the Queen 'Mrs Morley', under which aliases they had kept up an almost continuous correspondence when apart. Anne's accession, however, put a new aspect on things. Sarah had never tried to flatter her – indeed, she had never needed to. She had always been known for her plain speaking, always telling her friend exactly what she thought; but when Anne succeeded, that old familiarity proved a little too much. Besides, with all the cares of state upon her shoulders, the Queen expected sympathy and compassion, which she seldom received. And there was another, more deeply rooted problem: the Churchills were Whigs, a party that Anne instinctively mistrusted; and as a convinced Tory she resented it when Sarah – her husband's advancement never far from her mind – tried to boss her around and tell her what to do, persistently pressing Whig ideas and Whig literature upon her and vehemently browbeating her if she resisted. In 1704 she quietly confided to Lord Godolphin that she had begun to wonder whether she and the Duchess would ever be true friends again.

Another of the Queen's complaints was that Sarah was spending increasing time away from the court, supervising work on the new estate at Woodstock in Oxfordshire that had been awarded to John after his victory at Blenheim in 1704. This, as Sarah should have seen, was seriously risking her own position. Anne desperately needed close feminine relationships; if the Duchess was no longer able to provide what was required, she would find someone who could, and that someone turned out to be Abigail, wife of one of the court gentlemen, Samuel Masham. Abigail was as unlike Sarah as it was possible to be – quiet and gentle, always sympathetic and not above a little subtle flattery – and the Queen took her to her heart.

Sarah's fury when she heard of the new favourite was terrible to behold. In July 1708 she came to court with a bawdy poem, accusing Anne and Abigail of a lesbian relationship; later she wrote to the Queen telling her that by her 'strange and unaccountable passion' for such a woman she had seriously damaged her own reputation. After the death of Anne's husband George of Denmark in that same year Sarah refused, out of sheer pique, to wear mourning. The final showdown came in 1710. Typically, Sarah demanded an explanation of the Queen's behaviour rather than offering one for her own; but Anne was impassive and unmoved, and quietly requested

Sarah to return the symbolic gold key that was the symbol of her authority. Marlborough himself tried to plead her cause, but in vain; the Queen ordered that royal subsidy for the building of Blenheim be stopped, and work on the great palace, which had begun in 1705, was immediately suspended. The Marlboroughs went into exile on the Continent, returning the day after the Queen's death, 2 August 1714.

The story of the building of Blenheim had been unhappy from the start. For its architect, the Duchess had always wanted Sir Christopher Wren; one evening at the theatre, however, the Duke had run into Sir John Vanbrugh – at that time a famous dramatist and quite untrained as an architect, though with one great house, Castle Howard, to his credit – and had commissioned him on the spot. Sarah had never concealed her annoyance, and had constantly criticized and argued, making Vanbrugh's life as difficult as she could until he resigned in despair and was accordingly banned from the site. The work was finally taken on by his assistant, Nicholas Hawksmoor, who brought it to its final completion in 1725. It is a pity indeed that the poor Queen never saw the magnificent pile that she had so generously endowed, but there – she was dead.

Georgian England

Introduction

*M*ost people see the period between the accession of
George I in 1714 and the death of George IV in
1830 as an age of elegance, occasionally lapsing – as in the
drawings of Hogarth, and even more those of Gillray and
Rowlandson – into its precise opposite, an almost shocking
earthiness and coarseness. This is true, as far as it goes; but the
period also saw the beginnings of striking religious and social
change. Under politicians like Sir Robert Peel and reformers
like William Wilberforce and Thomas Clarkson, active measures were taken towards the abolition of slavery. In religion,
the Church of Rome was no longer a bugbear; the struggle
now tended to be between Anglican orthodoxy and non-
conformism – Presbyterians, Congregationalists, Baptists,
Methodists and Quakers.

In the arts, England at last came into its own. Of the two
greatest painters of the previous century, Van Dyck had been
Flemish, Lely Dutch; now we could produce portraitists like
Reynolds, Gainsborough and Lawrence, landscape painters
like Constable and Turner; and we could honour them properly in the Royal Academy. In the world of architecture, the
baroque splendour of Wren, Hawksmoor and Vanbrugh was
no longer popular; the new Whig aristocracy preferred the
cool, clear, classical lines of the sixteenth-century Andrea

Palladio, as interpreted by a whole new generation of architects led by their fabulously rich patron Lord Burlington: Colen Campbell, William Kent, Matthew Brettingham and – a little later – Robert Adam, who paved the way for the neoclassical style that was to follow. In literature, the somewhat staid poetry of the eighteenth century gave way in the early nineteenth to the Romantics: the Lake poets Wordsworth and Coleridge, Keats and Shelley and of course the arch-Romantic of them all, Lord Byron. The contrast is even greater in the world of the novel, between Fielding and Defoe at the beginning of our period and the understated perfection of Jane Austen at the end. Nor should we forget the plays of Richard Brinsley Sheridan, the letters of Horace Walpole and the history of Edward Gibbon.

There was also the separate world of Bath, effectively the creation of its presiding genius, a professional gambler named Richard 'Beau' Nash. Bath had its own brilliant team of architects – notably the two John Woods, father and son, John Palmer and Thomas Baldwin. It has suffered one or two dreadful post-war blows; but it remains far and away the most attractive city in England, Georgian through and through.

Politically speaking, probably the most traumatic single event of the century was the loss of the American colonies after the War of Independence in 1776. At the time, many Englishmen saw this as the end of Britain as a great power; but the eighteenth was also the century of Clive of India, of General James Wolfe on the Heights of Abraham and of the astonishing achievements of Captain Cook, with his discoveries of Australia and New Zealand. The seeds of the British Empire were now well sown, to come to their full fruition in the next century. The French Revolution was followed by the English with increasing disgust, and also alarm; but the coming of Napoleon soon gave them more than enough to think about. The two great victories of Trafalgar (1805) and Waterloo (1815) were hailed as England's greatest since Agincourt, four centuries before.

Finally, and possibly most important of all, there was the Industrial Revolution. It began early in the eighteenth century, and steadily gathered momentum with each succeeding decade, culminating, perhaps, only with the Great Exhibition of 1851. And it was well named: the social and economic upheaval to which it gave birth totally transformed the country, both for better and for worse. England was never to be the same again.

The Georgian period ends, somewhat untidily, with the short and undistinguished reign of King William IV, who was obliged, on his totally unexpected succession, to leave his mistress, the celebrated musical comedy star Dorothy Jordan, and their ten children and marry Queen Adelaide of Saxe-Meiningen, who was generally considered the only woman in Europe more boring than himself.

49

Pump Room
BATH

B ath is a city of superlatives. First of all, it is the most
beautiful city in England. Next, it is the most appropriately named: had it not been for those extraordinary springs
which, every day since the world began, have hurled forth a
quarter of a million gallons of water heated to a constant 120
degrees Fahrenheit, the Romans would never have adopted it
as they did or adorned it with buildings of which enough have
survived to constitute the most important classical remains we
possess.

For all that, at the beginning of the eighteenth century
Bath was still an unassuming little town, its ruins unexca-
vated, unremarkable except for those springs. Then Queen
Anne went there to take the waters. High society followed,
and among the new arrivals was a professional gambler named
Richard Nash. Coming penniless from London in 1703, 'Beau'
Nash soon became Master of Ceremonies, and within a few
years had given his adopted home a social *cachet* that no other
English provincial city has ever enjoyed before or since. On
their arrival, distinguished visitors were welcomed by Nash
himself and by peals of bells from the abbey; visitors of whom
he was less certain would receive a courtesy call, during which
he quietly made sure of their suitability. Names and faces
were all registered in his infallible memory, so that he could

keep an eye on them at public functions and even fit them up with suitable dancing partners as required.

Those new arrivals soon found that while Bath society yielded nothing to that of the capital in its sophistication, it was in some ways refreshingly less exclusive. Nash, while he remained a crashing snob, realized that since his world was a lot smaller than London's, it needed a rather greater degree of social integration to make it work. This was by no means an easy thing to achieve, but he was remarkably successful; under his aegis, the smarter set met people, even danced with people, whom they would never have encountered at home, to the benefit of both sides. But this additional latitude did not mean any lack of discipline: indeed, quite the contrary. For half a century, the Beau ruled the city with a rod of iron. Being a prodigious dandy himself – hence his nickname – he was determined that sartorial standards should be maintained. Clothes to be worn in the public rooms were precisely regulated by decree; he even banned the calf-length boots fashionable for men at the time, insisting on normal shoes instead. Correct behaviour was demanded at all times; strong language in particular was forbidden. Offenders were asked to leave – and did so. Nash even laid down the pattern of daily life, always beginning with the required three glasses of spring water from the Pump Room.

The first Pump Room was opened in 1706, the joint brain-child of Nash and his doctor, William Oliver, inventor of both the Bath Bun and, for those who found this too fattening, the Bath Oliver biscuit. By the end of the century, however, the room could no longer contain the number of visitors; the present one, much enlarged, dates from 1796. Today, as one sits in prim gentility over coffee and tea-cakes while the Pump Room Trio – the longest-established resident ensemble in Europe – plays selections from *Bitter Sweet* or

Oklahoma!, the fashionable world described by Jane Austen seems far away; but we can still gaze down on the Roman Bath from the little arched recess where the spring water is dispensed, scarcely noticing as one sips it that, as Sam Weller correctly pointed out in the *Pickwick Papers*, it has 'a very strong flavour of warm flat-irons'.

At noon, in Nash's day, everyone crossed the square for a short service at the abbey. Next came dinner, a rest – oh, how they must have needed it – then drives and visits. These were followed by an evening at a concert, the twice-weekly ball or – most popular entertainment of all in the first half of the century – the card-tables in the Assembly Rooms. Here Nash, inveterate gambler as he was, came into his own. Never, it should be emphasized, did he take advantage of others at the tables; that was not his way. He had seen the dramas and tragedies that uncontrolled gambling could bring in its train, and he was determined that there should be no *mauvaises histoires* of that kind in Bath. Compulsive gamblers would be discreetly restrained from continuing to play, and he was constantly on the watch for card-sharpers.

Ironically – perhaps because there was no one to warn *him* – it was Nash who gambled away his fortune, to the point where he was obliged to move in with the last of his many mistresses, the irresistibly named Juliana Pobjoy. It was in her house – now Pobjoy's Restaurant – that he died on 3 February 1762. He was nearly eighty-seven, but such was Mrs Pobjoy's distress that she left her house to live in a tree. There she remained for the best part of fifteen years until 1777, when she returned home, following her Beau to the grave a few weeks later.

Jane Austen lived in Bath for five years, from 1801 to 1806, and hated it. In 1808 she wrote to her sister Cassandra: 'It will be two years tomorrow since we left Bath for Clifton, with what happy feelings of escape.' We, I suspect, should have felt very much the same way: apart from the inevitable secret assignations and clandestine love affairs, fashionable Bath life strikes us today as having been vacuous, vapid and quite shatteringly dull. And yet the city has retained all – or very nearly all – its astonishing Georgian beauty. When the guidebooks call Bath 'a monument to bygone elegance', they are wrong. Only the perishable has perished. The elegance remains.

50

Ironbridge
SHROPSHIRE

*T*he first iron bridge ever built, which spans the infant River Severn as it passes through a narrow gorge at the little village of Ironbridge (where else?) in Shropshire, was constructed in 1779 by the English ironmaster and Quaker Abraham Darby III; but it stands as a monument to the three generations of his remarkable family, and indeed to the whole Industrial Revolution in England. We tend, nowadays, to take the Industrial Revolution for granted, but we are wrong: from the very end of the seventeenth century and for the next 150 years its effect on virtually all classes in England and Wales would be little short of cataclysmic. Lives would be transformed – most of them (though by no means all), for the better.

The patriarch of the Darby family, Abraham Darby I, was born in 1678. His great achievement – to have developed a method of producing pig iron in a blast furnace fuelled by coke instead of by charcoal – may not sound terribly earth-shattering to most of us; in fact it was to transform the iron industry and, in the eighteenth century which was just beginning, to usher in a new Iron Age. Darby had started his professional life in a pottery, and it was perhaps understandable that the first iron he produced by his new process was used mostly for the production of cast-iron goods – kettles, saucepans and kitchen equipment in general. One of the principal disadvantages of iron was its weight; thanks to Darby's more refined techniques, however, he managed to turn out pots and pans that were thinner, lighter and considerably cheaper than those of any of his competitors. Another disadvantage was the relatively small quantity of the ore available in the British Isles. To meet the need, considerable amounts had been shipped from Sweden since the mid-seventeenth century; Russia, too, was to open up as a valuable source from the 1730s onward.

And then there was steam. The very first commercially viable steam engine – a combined vacuum and pressure water pump sold as 'the Miner's Friend' – was produced by Thomas Savery in 1698. It was used by several water works and a few mines but it can never have been called hugely successful, since it generated only a single horsepower and tended, on the least provocation, to explode. In 1712 Thomas Newcomen did a good deal better, with a far more sophisticated mechanism that proved invaluable for draining coal mines, thereby enabling them to be dug deeper than ever before.

But let us return for a moment to Abraham Darby. He was a Quaker, and what few people realize about the Industrial Revolution is the extent to which it was permeated by his co-religionists, the Society of Friends. This is not as surprising as it might appear. After the Restoration of the monarchy in 1660, several laws had been passed to prevent those religious groups outside the Church of England – groups that despised creeds and sacraments, Church hierarchies or worldly honours, preaching instead the equality of all men – from attaining positions of influence in the state. Thus, like other Dissenters, Quakers were not only banned from the universities; they were also debarred – this time by their own moral scruples – from all careers and professions for which taking an oath was a condition of entry. Their argument was that the swearing of oaths imposed a double standard of integrity; and they steadfastly refused to do anything of the kind.

With such a reduced field for their ambitions, it was only natural that they should enter the worlds of banking, industry and commerce. And having done so, their integrity, probity and capacity for hard work did the rest. Wherever they went, they inspired trust. As time went on, the Quaker phenomenon – for phenomenon it was – grew ever more noticeable: Huntsman's steel works in Sheffield; Lloyds and Barclays banks; Barclay Perkins breweries; Bryant & May's matches, Clark's shoes, Huntley & Palmer's and Carr's biscuits, Bradshaw's Railway Guide and the four principal chocolate manufacturers – Cadbury, Fry, Terry and Rowntree – all these, and many more, were Quaker industries: not bad for a group which in 1800 formed only 0.2 per cent of the population. The Roman Catholics, who suffered similar discrimination by the state but whose numbers amounted to some 8 per cent, had a neglible record in comparison.

There were, inevitably, those who disapproved of the whole thing: the Lake Poets, for example, tucked safely away in remote Cumbria (or Westmorland, as it then was), to say nothing of Keats, Byron and Shelley; or William Blake, with his nightmare visions of the 'dark, Satanic mills'. Mary Shelley also, perhaps: her novel *Frankenstein* could certainly be interpreted as a warning of the horrors of which the new scientific discoveries might be capable, if turned towards ignoble or perverted objectives. But these were in a minority; and even in the world of the arts there were those, notably the painter Wright of Derby, whose blast furnaces painted in heavy chiaroscuro reveal a romantic side to the revolution that few people knew existed.

Under Abraham Darby, his son and his grandson, the

villages of Coalbrookdale – Ironbridge did not yet exist – were buzzing with activity; nowadays, they are buzzing again, but with visitors not only to the bridge itself but to the *ten* different museums that have sprung up around it. And there is also

one major factory still *in situ* – and still firing, as it were, on all cylinders: the Aga-Rayburn foundry, manufacturers of the famous cookers. It stands on one of Abraham's original foundry sites, where he first smelted iron ore in 1709. How proud he would be.

51

Houghton Hall
NORFOLK

*H*oughton is Sir Robert Walpole; and Sir Robert Walpole is – or was – effectively our first Prime Minister. I say 'effectively' because the title as such was not recognized in his day. He was however indubitably first among his ministers, the leader of the Whig government of the time, the man who wielded supreme power in the country under the King; and the fact that the King, George I, had been brought over from Hanover and could speak barely a word of English increased his power still further.

Walpole's rise had been slow. He had first entered Parliament in 1701, the year before the accession of Queen Anne, and it was another twenty years before he was made First Lord of the Treasury – an office that all our Prime Ministers but two have held ever since* – and simultaneously Chancellor of the Exchequer and Leader of the House of Commons. Then and only then, in 1721, did his premiership begin. At that time the country had suffered one of the greatest financial disasters of its history: the so-called South Sea Bubble, a joint-stock company that in 1711 had been granted a monopoly to trade – principally in slaves – with the Spanish

---

* William Pitt, First Earl of Chatham, and the Marquess of Salisbury did not hold the office for most of their terms as Prime Minister.

colonies of South America, in exchange for attractive-sounding bonds. Such was the rush to invest that the share price went up in a single year from £100 to £1,000; but then in 1720 it crashed, with catastrophic results. Walpole saw the collapse coming and got out in time; most of his fellow investors, however, were not so lucky. Sir Isaac Newton (see the **Apple Tree, Woolsthorpe Manor**) is said to have lost over £20,000. As a result of the Bubble Walpole's two principal political rivals were eliminated, and he found himself the leading figure in the administration.

That administration was to continue for another twenty-one years. For all that time, Walpole's chief objective was peace. In 1722 he successfully put down a Jacobite plot (to restore the Stuarts to the throne) led by the Bishop of Rochester; in 1725 he concluded a non-aggression treaty with France and Prussia; and only six years later, in 1731, came the Treaty of Vienna, after which Austria rather than France became Britain's chief ally. And throughout this period Walpole, who concealed under his bluff, straightforward countryman's manner one of the subtlest political minds of any English Prime Minister, continued to increase his vast fortune.

As time went on, it was inevitable that he should become the butt of satirists; and it was his bad luck that he should have had as his contemporaries some of the sharpest wits that ever lived, among them Jonathan Swift, Alexander Pope and Samuel Johnson. He was also lampooned in John Gay's celebrated *Beggar's Opera*, which in 1728 took London by storm. Gradually the opposition to him grew. In 1736 there were all too understandable anti-Walpole demonstrations in London and elsewhere over his disastrous decision to raise the tax on gin. These were almost immediately followed by the so-called Porteous Riots in Edinburgh, after the King had seen fit to pardon a Captain Porteous, Captain of the Edinburgh City Guard, for having opened fire on a crowd of protesters; and the last six years of Walpole's administration saw him struggling to hold his own. Finally in 1742 he lost a vote of confidence in the House and handed the King – by this time George II – his resignation. In return, he was elevated to the peerage, becoming Earl of Orford. Three years later he was dead, in his sixty-ninth year. His title was to pass first to his son and grandson, then finally to his younger son Horace.

When he was at the height of his power, Walpole's influence was tremendous. His own party, the Whigs, ruled the country largely unopposed; their opponents, the Tories, their reputation stained by suspicions of Jacobitism, dwindled into comparative insignificance. His popularity was founded, he liked to think, on the fact that he was a man of the soil, a sensible, reasonable Norfolk country gentleman. Immovable principles, religious self-righteousness and all that mad, bigoted, baroque atmosphere of the seventeenth century could lead only to war and, ultimately, chaos. For him property, peace and pleasure were the foundations of a well-organized, satisfied society.

In a way, he was right; and since he saw nothing wrong in a man enriching himself it is hardly surprising that he himself did so, with remarkable success. His acquisition of No. 10 Downing Street was not, as has sometimes been asserted, an instance of this tendency; the house – it was originally three adjoining houses – was offered to him by George II and was accepted by him in his capacity as First Lord of the Treasury, a title still engraved on its letterbox. The fact remains that during his term of office he became an extremely rich man – rich enough to buy himself a superb art collection – most of which, alas, was sold off by his feckless grandson to Catherine the Great (much to the fury of his uncle Horace) and may now be seen in the Hermitage Museum in St Petersburg. He also completely rebuilt the family house in which he had been born, Houghton Hall.

To this day Houghton – which is open to the public – is one of the most glorious country houses of England. Certainly none of them speaks to us more dramatically of the wealth, power and splendour of the English aristocracy – even self-made – in its heyday, nearly 300 years ago.

52

New Room

BRISTOL

*T*he New Room is a misnomer. It isn't new at all; it's nearly 300 years old, and the oldest Methodist chapel in the world. Devoid as it is of the slightest vestige of decoration, with its unpolished wooden floor, its white-painted galleries along each side and its high pulpit centrally placed at the far end, it has a certain quiet, understated elegance. Wesley would not have approved of the nineteenth-century box pews – he wanted his buildings to look as unlike churches as possible. All he really wanted to do was to preach the word of God, as often as possible and to the greatest possible number of people; and the chapel, which he built for himself, perfectly suited his purpose.

The sheer energy of the man leaves one gasping. Getting up at four o'clock every morning, Wesley liked to preach his first sermon of the day at five, and at least two more before evening. Between sermons he would be travelling, usually on horseback, from one venue to the next. It has been calculated that during his long life – he was born in 1703 and died shortly before his eighty-eighth birthday – he must have clocked up an average of 8,000 miles a year, some 250,000 miles in all, and more than 40,000 sermons. Meanwhile he formed more and more Methodist societies, wrote copiously – the first edition of his prose works ran to no fewer than thirty-two volumes

– examined and commissioned preachers, superintended schools and orphanages and administered countless charities. He also tended and prescribed medicines for the sick, and pioneered electric shock treatment for mental illness. It is hardly surprising that his marriage proved a failure; the only wonder is that his unfortunate wife stuck with him for fifteen miserable years.

As a preacher, Wesley was undoubtedly fluent and persuasive – heaven knows he had had enough practice – but even he was overshadowed by his friend and colleague George Whitefield. Whitefield was a phenomenon, dubbed by the press as 'the marvel of the age' and described from the age of twenty-two as 'famous as any man in the English-speaking world'. He made seven trips to America, where he would have made Billy Graham sound like a beginner. Nobody had heard anything like him before, or ever would again. Frequently, while preaching 'The Great Awakening', he would burst into tears; occasionally he would break into a little dance. The volume and pitch of his voice varied from a whisper to a scream, both of which, it was said, were equally audible to his enormous congregations. 'I would give a hundred guineas,' said David Garrick, the greatest actor of his day, 'if I could say "Oh" like Mr Whitefield.'

But what were Wesley and Whitefield preaching about? What, exactly, *was* Methodism? The name itself was first applied derisively, by Oxford students who mocked Wesley and his friends for the methodical way in which they ordered their lives. What Methodism was *not* was a new faith; John and his hymn-writing brother Charles both remained clergymen of the established Church of England until their deaths. It was, as much as anything, a method of bringing new life into the Church, which since the beginning of the century had sunk into a state of apathy. The vast majority of the clergy came from the gentry, or even the aristocracy – often younger sons, whose elder brothers lived in the neighbouring manor house – and were steeped in the ideas of Newton and the Enlightenment. They mistrusted stories of miracles and divine revelation. They liked their religion to be decent and restrained; they deplored what they called 'enthusiasm' or any show of exaggerated piety or sanctimoniousness.

Wesley and his friends may or may not have been over-pious in their manner, but they believed fervently in their message and, with their passionate sermons, gave it all they had got. As travelling evangelists, often speaking out of doors, they appealed – as no gentlemanly vicar could hope to do – to the farm labourers and the populations of the rapidly growing industrial towns and cities, for which the old, long-outdated parish system had made no provision at all. Their sermons were not intellectual; their words were intended to go straight to the heart – which they did.

They were in no sense Puritans; music, for example, was important to them, and they wrote some of the greatest hymns in the language, which the Anglican Church is still proud to sing. They did however appeal directly to that strong instinct among the English middle classes for piety, strict morality and hard work. The consequence was, by the end of their mission, a network stretching right across England. They would divide themselves into groups, each group building its chapel or chapels and raising subscriptions to support those who minis-tered to it. Since relatively few of these were ordained ministers, Wesley would habitually appoint his own from the laity – often indeed from the working class, many members of which were now growing accustomed to public speaking. Towards the end of his life he even performed his own ordinations, particularly for those going on missionary work abroad.

It was these ordinations, as much as anything else, that

caused the final break from the Anglicans after Wesley's death in 1791. Soon it became mandatory that Methodist preachers and chapels should obtain licences before they could hold meetings. Gradually, too, polite society began to view them with suspicion as a potentially subversive body, deliberately arousing the working class and, by their exemplary lives of piety and self-denial, dangerously showing up the lethargy and lack of spiritual leadership in the established Church. These suspicions, as it turned out, were unfounded: the Church had survived much greater threats than the essentially peace-loving Methodists, and was far too deeply rooted in the heart of English society to sustain any lasting damage. However poor his record in regular church attendance, for as long as every right-thinking Englishman expected to be baptized, married and buried by a properly ordained Anglican priest, the Church of England would endure.

But so did the Methodists, and so did the New Room – still today looking much as it always did. And so did the other nonconformist religions – all those Christians (apart of course from the Roman Catholics) who after the Act of Uniformity in 1662 dissented from the beliefs of the established Church: principally, they were the Presbyterians, Congregationalists, Baptists and Unitarians. According to the religious census of 1851, together they numbered very nearly as many as the Anglicans. Today, the membership of all of them has probably dropped considerably; but all remain very much alive.

53

Brick Lane Mosque
LONDON

O nce holy, always holy: all archaeologists are aware of the curious process known as syncretism, by which a place sacred to one religion continues to be sacred to the religion that supersedes it. The Temple at Ephesus, for example, was first dedicated to a primitive goddess of fertility, then to the Greek goddess Artemis, then to the Roman Diana, the virgin huntress, and finally, with the coming of Christianity, to another virgin near-goddess, Mary, who is actually said to have settled there. Brick Lane, Spitalfields, isn't a bit like Ephesus, but No. 59 provides an even more striking example of the same phenomenon.

When this modest two-storey building with its outsize pediment was first built in 1743, it was intended as a Protestant chapel for the Huguenot weavers of Spitalfields. It performed this function, no doubt admirably, for over sixty years; but during that time the Huguenot community gradually dispersed and in 1809 the chapel was bought by the London Society for Promoting Christianity Amongst the Jews and taken over by the Wesleyans, who, ten years later, passed it on to their close brethren the Methodists. Then, in the later nineteenth century, the area welcomed a new body of immigrants, and the building transformed itself into the Machzike Adass, better known as the Spitalfields Great Synagogue.

Gradually, however, the Jews moved away, to be replaced by the present community of Bangladeshis; and the synagogue, having lost its worshippers, became a mosque. Alas, like most mosques in this country, it is not open to the infidel.

Its story thus accurately reflects the story of Spitalfields itself, and in some senses can stand for the story of immigration in England. Until the eighteenth century Spitalfields had little to differentiate it from its neighbouring parishes. It owes its subsequent distinction to the decision of Louis XIV in 1685 to revoke the Edict of Nantes, by which French Protestants were allowed to live and work peaceably in France. The revocation unleashed a whole new wave of persecutions, from which the Huguenots, as they were called, fled across the Channel. Many of them had been engaged in the silk industry, and these in particular settled in Spitalfields, just outside the bounds of the City of London, where they would be immune from the tiresomely restrictive regulations of the City guilds.

Within a few years the parish was transformed. Spitalfields had become silken, with a few quite grand mansions designed for the master weavers, several rows of quietly distinguished terrace houses for the remainder and no fewer than ten Protestant chapels. The number of these quite alarmed the Anglican authorities; and to assert the power and splendour of the good old C. of E. they commissioned from Nicholas Hawksmoor – the greatest architect of the day – the magnificent Christ Church, whose noble spire still dominates its surroundings.

But as the years went by the great looms began to clatter less smoothly. By the 1730s the Huguenots had been joined by numbers of Irish, and relations between the two groups were always distinctly strained. Soon after that, cheap imported French calicos became the fashion; small bands of weavers,

French and Irish, would go out into London and tear the dresses off the women wearing them. Angry demonstrations were frequent, and in 1769 there occurred the Spitalfields Riots, when an officer and a party of soldiers burst into an alehouse and tried to arrest a few weavers who were collecting funds for their clandestine and illegal trade union. In the ensuing fracas, two weavers were killed and four captured. On 6 December Jean Valline and John Doyle (the names are significant) were hanged in Bethnal Green in front of the Salmon and Ball pub, which still exists.

But no amount of rioting could stop the rot. The silk industry entered its long decline, dragging Spitalfields with it; and in 1860 a treaty with France, allowing the importation of cheaper French silks, administered the *coup de grâce*. The area became one of the seamiest in London, haunt of Jack the Ripper and a Dickensian rookery of robbers and prostitutes. Fortunately, towards the end of the century, the situation improved with the huge immigration of eastern European Jews, escaping the Polish and Russian pogroms. Many of them were tailors, and they settled in the area not only because, thanks to its reputation, houses were almost given away, but because of the huge picture windows installed by the weavers. For very nearly a century, from 1880 to around 1970, Spitalfields is said to have been the largest Jewish area in Europe, with over forty synagogues.

Then, as it tends to do, the pendulum swung again. The Jews prospered and performed their own mini-diaspora, seeking more salubrious homes in Golders Green and north London; and were replaced, during and after the 1970s, with the present community of immigrants from Bangladesh. They too tend to work in the textile industry, but also staff most of the country's 'Indian' restaurants; and they have made Brick Lane the curry capital of London – and, I sometimes feel, the world. Increasing numbers of Somalis, mostly engaged in trading, are now coming in to join them.

Finally, there has been a measure of gentrification. The lovely Georgian architecture remaining in Spitalfields has been recognized for what it is, and is being saved wherever possible. Perhaps the most remarkable instance of this is No.

18 Folgate Street, now known throughout the area as Dennis Severs's House. Severs was an American eccentric who bought the extremely dilapidated property in 1979 and restored the ten rooms as if they were actually being lived in from genera-tion to generation by a fictional Huguenot family. It is now open to the public. As Severs himself said, 'You either see it or you don't'; my advice is that you do. Returning to the present, Spitalfields has a thriving arts scene, and is the home of several celebrated artists. You may well see Gilbert and George strolling arm-in-arm down the street, or Tracey Emin in a nearby supermarket.

How can the whole story best be summed up? Soon, by the

fine old master weaver's mansion at No. 19 Princelet Street, which is being transformed into a museum and learning centre that is designed to reflect and interpret every religion and culture in Spitalfields' long history. It may well be open by the time you read this; if so, take full advantage.

54

Statue Gallery

NEWBY HALL, YORKSHIRE

*I*n their architecture, in the splendour of their contents, in their astonishing variety and in the immense period they cover – very nearly 1,000 years, from the eleventh century to the twentieth – English country houses are unequalled in any other part of Europe or the world; and Newby Hall is one of the loveliest. Every room is a delight; but I would draw your attention in particular to Robert Adam's Statue Gallery. It consists of two square rooms with a central rotunda; when Newby's owner William Weddell was showing his guests round it – usually in the evening, by candlelight – they must have felt themselves miraculously transported to some Ancient Roman temple, for around its walls is the finest collection of Roman statuary to be found anywhere in the country, mostly dating from the first century BC to the second century AD. Weddell had bought it *en bloc* from the English art dealer Thomas Jenkins in Rome, and had had it shipped, at considerable risk, in nineteen huge wooden crates to Yorkshire.

Weddell had been travelling, like so many rich young English and northern European *milords*, on what was known as the Grand Tour, which was considered, throughout the late seventeenth and eighteenth centuries, an integral part of a gentleman's education. The idea was that the travellers' eyes should be opened to the greater world beyond the Channel, and above all to the wonders and beauties of classical antiquity and the Renaissance. The tour might last anything between a few months and two or three years; often it might cover Spain and/or Germany, but the essentials were France – there to study the language and manners of French high society, indispensable if the young man had any ambitions towards diplomacy – and of course Italy. Most of those embarking on it took a tutor with them to supplement the probably unsatisfactory local guides, while the wealthier might travel with a valet or even a small retinue.

Once he had crossed the Alps – an experience in itself, which normally involved dismantling the coach and entrusting its integral parts, together with the party's always voluminous luggage, to a whole army of porters, mules and pack-horses – the Grand Tourist would probably spend a few days in Turin or Verona before making his way to Pisa and Florence, where, if he were a serious student, he might easily stay for three months or more. Only after he was thoroughly familiar with all the great monuments and works of art of the city would he pass on to the most important of all his destinations, Rome. Here, once he had seen everything worth seeing, he would have his portrait painted by Pompeo Batoni (or perhaps, if he chanced to be German, by Anton Raphael Mengs) leaning on a classical tomb or airily surveying the Colosseum. The more intrepid might make their way further south to Naples, perhaps to ascend Vesuvius with the Ambassador, Sir William Hamilton, or to admire the 'attitudes' of his wife Emma; a few, like Goethe, would get as far as Sicily before returning.

Such journeys would be hard, uncomfortable and occasionally even dangerous; but all inconveniences would be forgotten when, on the journey home, our young traveller reached Venice. Here was paradise indeed. Here the buildings were more beautiful, the gambling more unrestrained, the courtesans lovelier and more experienced than anywhere else on earth. Here carnival went on for a good six months a year; here, behind the obligatory mask, he could let his hair down while preserving his anonymity. The English would naturally call on their distinguished Consul, Joseph Smith, who just happened to be the agent of Canaletto. He would insist on taking them to see the master's studio, from which they would find it hard indeed to get away without a canvas or two; and so, finally, they would struggle once more back over the Alps and maybe through the Low Countries, with a couple of Canalettos and a mild dose of the clap to remind them of where they had spent the happiest months of their young lives.

Perhaps the nobleman who benefited most from the Grand Tour was Richard Boyle, third Earl of Burlington. He had succeeded to his title – and to untold wealth – in 1703 at the age of nine. Within a decade he had become England's leading patron of the arts, though for him patronage was not enough; he also became a practising architect. Burlington went on not one but two Grand Tours, the second one on purpose to study the work of his hero, Andrea Palladio. When he returned in 1719 he brought with him a whole sheaf of Palladio's drawings, an Italian edition of his *Four Books of Architecture* – and William Kent, who had been studying painting in Rome. They must have seemed an ill-assorted couple, the aloof, exquisite aristocrat and the bluff, barely literate Yorkshireman; but Burlington rightly sensed that Kent, with his astonishing flair for decoration and design, possessed all the ideas and imagination that he himself lacked. On their arrival in London Kent was installed at Burlington House, where he was to live for twenty-nine years until his death. Thanks to them, and to Burlington's close friend the architect

Colen Campbell, the Palladian style prevailed throughout the eighteenth century, not only in England but also in America; and still today it is by no means dead.

England's debt to the Grand Tour and to those who ventured on it is beyond computation. There must be many thousands of paintings, sculptures and other works of art in our country houses, museums and galleries that were acquired in this way, mostly from Italy, but also from France – including the glorious Gobelins tapestries at Newby – Flanders, the Netherlands, Germany and Spain. And these in turn must have inspired countless young artists who never had the good fortune or the money to see these countries for themselves. Travel, we have been told from childhood, broadens the mind, but that's only the beginning. It does much, much more than that – and we are all the beneficiaries.

55

Etruria Hall

STOKE-ON-TRENT, STAFFORDSHIRE

*J*osiah Wedgwood loved smashing pottery. He was a perfectionist: for him, nothing but the best was good enough. If he saw anything in his workshop – dish or plate, cup or saucer, sugar-basin or cream jug – that failed to meet his exacting standards, he would shatter it to smithereens with his stick, exclaiming, 'This will not do for Josiah Wedgwood!' Thanks to this splendid if alarming characteristic, and to his constant experimentation in ceramic techniques, he became one of the best – and best-known – manufacturers of china and porcelain in the world. For Josiah, however, even this wasn't enough: his dream, he said, was to be 'Vase Maker General to the Universe'.

It is perhaps surprising to read that, even in his youth and despite being born and bred in the industry, this master of the art of pottery had hardly ever thrown a pot himself. A bout of smallpox as a child had left him with a permanently weakened knee which, he claimed, made it impossible for him to operate the treadle of a potter's wheel. (Why he couldn't use the other leg was never satisfactorily explained.) Not that it mattered much; it simply meant that from an early age Wedgwood concentrated on design and technology. No one, even in the Staffordshire Potteries, knew more about the science that lay behind the art. He understood chemistry as well as any man alive, and was constantly on the lookout for fresh pigments and colours, new glazes and techniques, that might improve the quality and variety of his work. In his later years he publicly regretted what he considered his one failure: despite a lifetime of effort, he had never succeeded in finding the secret of the fine porcelain that only the Chinese could produce.

In 1764, he married his third cousin Sarah Wedgwood, who was a lot richer than he was; and with her generous dowry he was able two years later to open his new factory, which he named Etruria, having been much struck by the black Etruscan porcelain that was being discovered by archaeologists at that time. The factory was the most modern and the most enlightened of its day, Wedgwood having given real thought to the welfare of his employees, providing them with housing for themselves, a school for their children and even a health insurance scheme. His example would be followed many times in later years, notably by Cadburys at Bournville and Lever Brothers at Port Sunlight; but Josiah was, as in so many other fields, the pioneer.

In that same year, 1766, Wedgwood cut the first sod for the projected Trent–Mersey Canal for which, supported by his friends Erasmus Darwin, James Watt, Matthew Boulton and other members of the Lunar Society of Birmingham (see **Soho House**), he had headed the campaign. He needed that canal, desperately. Eighteenth-century roads were still terrible, rutted and rock-hard in summer, a morass of mud for the rest of the year; and all too many of his fragile goods would arrive at Chester, the nearest port, irreparably smashed. The canal, ninety-three miles long, with more than seventy locks and five tunnels, was completed just eleven years later and made transportation of his pottery safe for the first time. It is still in use today.

By the time Etruria was opened, Wedgwood was already

famous. Perhaps through the invention of his pearl-like 'creamware', he had caught the attention of George III and Queen Charlotte, who had ordered an elaborate tea service, including fruit basket and candlesticks, 'with a gold ground and raised flowers upon it in green'. On receipt of the order Wedgwood had set off for Kew Palace (q.v.) to discuss it in detail with the Queen; he had then returned to his factory and told his team to get to work. The commission proved an enormous success; the creamware was henceforth to be known as Queen's Ware, and he was accorded the title of 'Potter to Her Majesty' – the equivalent of what would now be a royal warrant.

Perhaps his greatest year was 1774 when he scored two major triumphs. First, after many years of experimentation, he managed to produce the first satisfactory examples of the matt-surfaced 'jasperware' for which his name is now principally known. Very shortly afterwards, he received an order from the Empress Catherine the Great. It was in fact, the second she had made; the first was for the relatively modest 'Husk' service in 1770, now on exhibition at Peterhof, just outside St Petersburg. Here, however, was something far more important: the 952–piece 'Frog Service', made especially for Catherine's palace of La Grenouillière (the Froggery). Each piece bears the emblem of a small, green frog, plus one – or sometimes two – British landscapes, 1,200 different scenes in all, ranging from Fingal's Cave, through English landscape gardens to the Coalbrookdale iron works. It can now be seen at the Hermitage in St Petersburg.

Once the jasperware had been introduced, Josiah could settle down to his great ambition, which was to produce ornamental vases 'that would captivate with the Elegance and simplicitie of the Ancients'. At the suggestion of his friend the sculptor John Flaxman, he spent years on attempts to copy

Houghton Hall, Norfolk. Sir Robert Walpole, our first Prime Minister, acting his favourite part of the bluff, rubicund country squire – far, far from the jiggery-pokery of the London political scene in which, of course, he wallowed up to the neck.

The New Room, Bristol. The whole point was that it should be utterly plain: nothing – not a vestige of decoration – to distract the worshipper from his God, or more accurately from the words of John Wesley, which emerged in a remorseless stream whenever there was anyone to listen.

Pump Room, Bath. Bath was a phenomenon. How did it really come about? And how can it possibly have been taken so seriously for so long? Did people really believe that their three daily glasses in the Pump Room did them any *good*?

The Statue Gallery, Newby Hall, Yorkshire. We must never knock the Grand Tour. These serious, spoilt young men – here caricatured by Rowlandson – provided a good half of the antique, classical and renaissance paintings and sculpture in English houses today. And they even had the portraitist Pompeo Batoni to show that they knew Rome like the back of their hand.

Captain Cook Memorial Museum, Whitby, Yorkshire. 'To go farther than any man has before me, but as far as I think it is possible for a man to go.' For Thomas Cook, what more was to be said?

Cromford Mill, Derbyshire. Is there any building in the country that more perfectly illustrates the Industrial Revolution? Or that celebrates more magnificently the greatest and most spectacularly successful of its giants?

Soho House, Birmingham. The Lunar Society had no resident painter to record its activities or transactions; but had it ever done so, Joseph Wright of Derby would have been its man. That dazzling chiaroscuro of his – every picture suggesting illumination by either a flame or a furnace – catches to perfection the sheer thrill of scientific discovery.

Etruria Hall, Stoke-on-Trent, Staffordshire. Here is Staffordshire pottery at its simplest: a creamware teapot of 1775–85, saved from Sir Josiah Wedgwood's shattering-stick and decorated only with a black-and-white transfer of an elegant tea-party scene.

Temple of Vaccinia, Gloucestershire. In James Gilray's 1809 cartoon
The Cow Pock or the Wonderful Effects of the New Innoculation,
Edward Jenner appears oblivious to the chaos he has unleashed.

Kew Palace, Surrey.
Domestication – that's what
Kew's all about. No English
king was ever more happily
married than George III –
and fifteen children should be
enough for anyone. (What?
Only a quartet?)

Caen Hill Locks, Devizes, Wiltshire. Pity the poor unsuspecting traveller on the Kennet and Avon Canal who rounds a bend and finds himself faced with that implacable flight of locks, each of which must be individually negotiated if he is ever to reach his destination. Many turn tail, and I don't blame them.

The Quarterdeck, HMS *Victory*, Portsmouth. In the days of my childhood, Benjamin West's great picture *Death of Nelson* was probably the most famous picture in England. There was a reproduction – usually of course the engraving – in every school and in the humblest of living rooms. No hero in all history expired more beautifully, or to greater effect.

Coke Monument, Holkham, Norfolk. Thomas Weaver's *Portrait of Thomas William Coke, Esq., inspecting some of his South Down Sheep with Mr Walton and the Holkham Shepherds* is one of the most purely satisfying paintings I know. Coke's astonishing Monument says the same thing again.

the exquisite Portland Vase, made probably during the life-time of Jesus Christ and now in the British Museum, before finally producing what he considered a satisfactory copy in 1789.

Meanwhile his business partner Thomas Bentley had died in 1780, and Josiah's health, though he was still only fifty, was beginning to fail. Continuing trouble with his knee had ended in an amputation, and he urgently needed someone to help him run the business. He therefore turned to his old friend Erasmus Darwin, and before long his oldest daughter Susannah married Erasmus's son Robert, who became a partner in the firm. Their son, the great Charles Darwin, would marry yet another Wedgwood, Josiah's granddaughter Emma.

Alas, the glorious Wedgwood story has ended in tragedy. In 2010, after the better part of 300 years, the firm of Waterford Wedgwood – as it had then become – was put into receivership, with debts that ran into millions. Poor Josiah must be spinning in his grave, as fast as a pot on a wheel. Such a disaster would never have happened, one feels, if he had still been around. As for Etruria itself, it must be admitted that it is a pale shadow of what it was in its heyday, though Josiah Wedgwood's house still stands, relatively unchanged, now part of a hotel. The locality is, however, still home to the Etruria Industrial Museum, and to the annual Canals Festival on the first weekend in June.

56

Captain Cook Memorial Museum
WHITBY, YORKSHIRE

Captain James Cook remains a curiously enigmatic figure. His letters and his logbooks reveal little about his personality, and none of his biographers, it seems to me, has really succeeded in bringing him to life. The picture that emerges is of a man totally devoid of dazzle or swashbuckle; a cool, nerveless, humourless character who is nevertheless a supreme expert in everything to which he sets his mind: not only in seamanship but in astronomy, navigation, mapmaking, surveying and several other sciences as well – in short, a superb professional. The Memorial Museum on the harbourside in Whitby is not, as many people assume, his birthplace, but is the house of Captain John Walker, a Quaker, with whom he lodged in 1746 as an eighteen-year-old apprentice.

John and his brother Henry were shipowners, whose ships did a thriving trade carrying coal between Whitby and London and across the North Sea to Flanders and the Netherlands. In 1749 Cook signed on as a seaman with the Walker ships, and continued until Walker offered him his first command. He refused. He had no intention of spending his life on the North Sea – a fairly inhospitable stretch of water at the best of times. On 7 June 1755 he joined the Royal Navy, and his real career began.

It was an exciting time. Britain was on the threshold of the Seven Years War, and within months of his enlistment, with the rank of master's mate on HMS *Eagle*, Cook was instrumental in the capture of one French ship and the sinking of another. During the next four years he was to serve in North American waters and then when peace returned he was ordered to make a thorough survey of the coast of Newfoundland and to produce the first large-scale and accurate chart. The result, which appeared in 1775, was a masterpiece. It brought him to the attention of the Admiralty, which woke up to the fact that here was an officer of rare ability; and it inspired in Cook the objective of his life: 'to go farther than any man has before me, but as far as I think it is possible for a man to go'.

Which is exactly what he did. He made three long-distance voyages. The first, in HMS *Endeavour*, sailed in August 1768 under the auspices of the Royal Society, its purpose to travel to the Pacific Ocean, there to record the transit of the planet Venus across the sun. On board were quantities of pigs and poultry, two greyhounds, a milking goat and ninety-four men, including one of the society's members, the botanist Joseph Banks. A friend wrote:

> No people went to sea better fitted out . . . nor more elegantly. They have got a fine library [and] all sorts of machines for catching and preserving insects; all kinds of nets, trawls, drags and hooks . . . they even have a telescope by which, put into the water, you can see the bottom at great depth. They have two painters and draughtsmen and several volunteers . . . This expedition would cost Mr Banks £10,000.

They touched at Madeira and Brazil – where Banks gave the first precise description of bougainvillea – before travelling round Cape Horn to Tahiti, where the transit was duly recorded, then on to New Zealand and the east coast of Australia. Sailing up the Queensland peninsula they passed through the Torres Strait to Java, and then across the Indian Ocean, round the Cape of Good Hope and so home, stopping at St Helena on the way. All points visited were of course meticulously surveyed and charted.

On their return in July 1771 Cook and Banks published their findings and were immediately hailed as heroes. Banks, who had clearly enjoyed himself, was ready to set off with Cook on his second voyage, but there wasn't enough room and he reluctantly decided to remain in England. That voyage began in the following year and was to continue until 1775. Once again it was commissioned by the Royal Society: Cook's instructions were to search for the mythical *Terra Australis*. Sailing in HMS *Resolution*, he took the eastward route, through the South Atlantic and past the Cape of Good Hope, crossing the Antarctic Circle on 17 January 1773. He surveyed, mapped and annexed South Georgia and came within a toucher of the coast of mainland Antarctica, but provisions were running short and he was obliged to head north to Tahiti for revictualling. After another fruitless search for his quarry, he returned via the Friendly Islands (Tonga), Easter Island and Cape Horn.

Cook was now forty-eight, an age when most seamen would have stepped down the gangplank for the last time, and the Admiralty offered him honorary retirement – but in vain: the call of the sea was too strong. And so in 1776 he sailed, once again in *Resolution*, on his third and last voyage. During his second, he had brought a young Tahitian, Omai, back to England, where Omai had been a huge social success and had his portrait painted by Sir Joshua Reynolds. The ostensible reason for the third was to return him to Tahiti; this purpose achieved, however, Cook sailed virtually due north, and then, having put in at Hawaii (which he named the Sandwich Islands), up the west coast of America in search of the famed Northwest Passage. He failed to find it, but it hardly mattered. He had explored and mapped the American and Canadian coast as far as the Bering Strait and determined the size and shape of Alaska, all of which proved of far greater importance.

In 1779 Cook sailed south again to Hawaii. After a month he intended to return to northern waters, but *Resolution*'s foremast broke and he had to delay his departure. And that was when the trouble started. Quarrels broke out; the Hawaiians turned hostile and drove Cook and his men to the beach. He was struck on the head and fell into the surf, where he was stabbed to death.

In my hearing, a US Senator from Hawaii once began a speech, 'I have always felt a close link with England, since my ancestors ate Captain Cook'; in fact they did nothing of the kind. They treated the body as if it were one of their own chiefs with various ceremonies of purification; it was then returned to his crew for formal burial at sea. The site where he was killed is marked by a white obelisk, and about twenty-five square feet chained off. This land was given by the US government to the United Kingdom and is technically British territory.

No other navigator has achieved half as much as James Cook. He mapped vast quantities of the Pacific for the first time. He made a huge contribution to the accurate calculation of longitude. Finally, he completed two circumnavigations of the globe without losing a single man through scurvy. You may think that the little memorial museum is an insufficient honour for such a hero; if so, you are not alone. The same thought occurred to Russell Grimwade of Melbourne, who in 1933 bought Cook's parents' cottage – which the great man would often have visited – in Great Ayton, transported it brick by brick in 253 cases to his home city, re-erected it and donated it to the fortunate people of Victoria.

57

Soho House

BIRMINGHAM, WEST MIDLANDS

Soho House, Birmingham, was the elegant home of Matthew Boulton FRS, industrialist and entrepreneur; but it was a lot more than that. It was the meeting place of the Lunar Society, and the Lunar Society has been described as 'the revolutionary committee of the Industrial Revolution'.

Let us consider Matthew Boulton first. Born in Birmingham in 1728, he inherited from his father a business manufacturing small metal products. (Birmingham being a long way from the sea, larger metal objects in those pre-canal days were virtually impossible to transport.) When Matthew took over, he greatly expanded the factory, giving it a more sophisticated output and specializing in such new techniques as ormolu and silver plate. His lifetime stroke of luck occurred, somewhat surprisingly, through a bad debt, incurred by the bankruptcy of a certain Dr John Roebuck. Roebuck happened to be the business partner of James Watt, inventor of the steam engine; and in settlement of the debt he handed over to Boulton his share of Watt's patent, together with the partnership. The result was the firm of Boulton & Watt, which in the last quarter of the eighteenth century manufactured and installed hundreds of Watt's steam engines in factories and mills all over England and beyond.

As an important sideline, Boulton also founded the Soho

Mint, which he equipped with eight steam-driven presses – guess where *those* came from – every minute turning out some eighty vastly improved and beautifully designed copper coins, including the large penny which continued to circulate with only minor variations until the 1971 decimalization. He also worked in close collaboration – or, sometimes, in close competition – with Josiah Wedgwood, making mounts out of ormolu or cut steel for many of Wedgwood's creations. 'It doubles my courage to have the first Manufacturer in England to encounter with,' wrote Wedgwood. 'I like the Man, I like his spirit.' The two became close friends; James Watt became a third.

Watt had probably the most enquiring mind of the three. No one of his day had a deeper understanding of physics and chemistry, or a greater ability to apply his scientific knowledge to practical purposes. Unfortunately he was a hopeless businessman, hating all bargaining and haggling, and his first partner Roebuck was very little better. But his partnership with Boulton, who took over the whole financial side of the enterprise, leaving him to concentrate on his inventions, changed his life. He was not only hugely admired by his colleagues, but was a brilliantly amusing conversationalist, and thus much sought after as a table companion at meetings of the Lunar Society, of which, like Boulton and Wedgwood, he was a founder member.

The society, which flourished between 1765 and 1809, was really a dining club of all the leading figures in the Midlands Enlightenment – scientists, intellectuals and industrialists. It owed its name to the fact that the members, who referred to themselves as *lunaticks*, met on the nearest Sunday to the full moon, when – in the absence of any street lighting – they would have less difficulty in getting home afterwards. As well as Boulton, Watt, Wedgwood and Roebuck, they also included the poet and physician Erasmus Darwin, the physicist Joseph

Priestley, the canal-maker James Brindley, the botanist Joseph
Banks and – as corresponding member – the all-rounder
Benjamin Franklin. Another member with strong American
connections was William Small, a Scotsman who had been
Professor of Natural Philosophy at the College of William
and Mary in Williamsburg, Virginia, and had there had a
lasting influence on his star pupil, Thomas Jefferson. When
Small died at the age of forty, Boulton wrote to Watt: 'My
loss is as inexpressible as it is irreparable. I am ready to burst.
I can't write more . . .' and then as a postscript: 'Acquaint Dr
Roebuck – I can't.'

Though Soho House was the favourite meeting place of the
society, it was not the only one. The members met sometimes
at Wedgwood's house at Etruria (q.v.), or at Darwin's in
Lichfield, or occasionally elsewhere. As far as we can tell, few
of them ever dreamed of visiting the capital – nor is there any
reason why they should have. These men were above all industrialists, and London was never an industrial city. Birmingham
was; in fact it could be said to have been born of industry. In
the Middle Ages an unremarkable little market town, it had
been transformed by the Industrial Revolution and was, at the
time of which we are speaking, the leading manufacturing city
in the world. It was the Silicon Valley of its day, the cutting
edge of modern applied science, the home – far more than
London was – of many of the outstanding scientific minds of
the later eighteenth century. The intellectual atmosphere that
these men together created has not been called the Midlands
Enlightenment for nothing. As Erasmus Darwin wrote,
apologizing for not being present at one of the Lunar Society
dinners:

I am sorry that the infernal Divinities, who visit mankind
with diseases and are therefore at perpetual war with doctors,

should have prevented my seeing all you great men at Soho today – Lord! What inventions, what wit, what rhetoric, metaphysical, mechanical & pyrotechnical will be on the wing, bandy'd like a shuttlecock from one to another of your troop of philosophers! While poor I, by myself I, imprison'd in a post chaise, am joggled & jostled & bump'd & bruised along the King's high road, to make war on a pox or a fever!

Those were the days. Soho House still stands today, much as it always was except that it now serves as a city museum. It is perfectly well looked after, but one feels it deserves something rather better; somebody should take it in hand.

58

Cromford Mill
DERBYSHIRE

The first great arkwright in history was, presumably, Noah; the second, unquestionably, was Richard, the one name that we associate more than any other with the Industrial Revolution. Born in Preston in 1732, the thirteenth child of poor parents, he was taught to read and write by his cousin and then apprenticed to a barber and wigmaker. It was not long before he made his first invention, a waterproof dye for use on the universally worn wigs of the time; soon afterwards, setting up on his own, Arkwright began travelling round the country in search of human hair, an occupation that often brought him into contact with weavers and spinners and others in the textile trade. Gradually, when the fashion for wigs declined, it was to textiles that he turned his attention, in particular to the all-important cotton industry.

Cotton on the bush looks like – and essentially is – little round blobs of cotton wool. Like real wool (see the **Wool Hall, Lavenham**) it needs carding, a process by which the fibres are untangled and combed out, much as might be done to the hair of a little boy just back from the rugby field. Until Arkwright's day, carding could be done only slowly and laboriously, by hand; but when he was thirty-five he teamed up with John Kay, a clockmaker, and moved to Nottingham where the two set up a small horse-driven factory. The following year he patented what he called his water-frame, using the power of a water mill to produce cotton thread thinner and stronger than ever before, and it was with this in mind that he came to Cromford. The site was ideal for his purpose, since it had a constant supply of warm water draining from lead mines nearby; so here it was that he built a five-storey mill.

From 1772 onward, he ran his mill day and night in two twelve-hour shifts, introducing in 1775 yet another even more remarkable machine: his so-called Carding Engine, which converted the raw cotton bolls into a continuous shank of cotton fibre all ready for spinning. From the start he employed a force of 200, far more than the little village could supply, so he imported workers and had adequate housing specially built for them around the mill – one of the first manufacturers to do so. He also built the Greyhound pub that still stands in the market square. Most of his employees were women and children, whom he accepted from the age of seven. These were given six hours' tuition a week in reading and writing, so that they could keep records of the work done – a task well beyond the powers of their illiterate parents. Life for these people was hard enough, though they reckoned themselves lucky in comparison with most of their working-class fellows; but Cromford was by no means one of the dark, Satanic mills evoked by William Blake. The building survives today, now beautifully restored by the Arkwright Society and a World Heritage site, with the words SIR RICHARD ARKWRIGHT & CO, ESTABLISHED 1769 proudly inscribed across the centre of the façade. Above it is a small cupola, which housed a bell used to summon the staff to work; but Arkwright was taking no chances: he shut the main gate – guarded by a huge and distinctly forbidding round tower – at 6 a.m. and 6 p.m. every day, and any worker who failed to arrive on time was docked two days' pay. In 1779 he went further still, installing just inside the gate a small cannon, permanently loaded with grapeshot, as a warning to any prospective troublemakers. (Another of his mills, in Birkacre, Lancashire, had just been burned to the ground during the anti-machinery riots.)

Cromford, however, went from strength to strength. By 1774, after only five years, it had trebled in size and number, employing 600 workers. Arkwright also expanded the business to several new locations, building more and more mills which proved less ill-starred than Birkacre. Only three years later he installed his first steam engine, though it was used not to drive the machinery directly, but to maintain the level of the millpond that drove the great waterwheel. But by then he had suffered, for the first time in his life, a major reverse. In 1775 he had applied for an all-embracing patent that, he hoped, would give him what would almost amount to a monopoly of the cotton industry; not surprisingly however, he had found Lancashire opinion implacably opposed to the idea. The case was brought to court and dragged on for years, but in 1785 the court decided against him, ruling that many of his patents had in fact been borrowed from the work of others. Most of them were withdrawn.

Like all cases of such a kind, it had proved hugely expensive; indeed, to most of Arkwright's competitors it would have been ruinous. But by now he was the richest man in England outside the aristocracy, and he hardly felt the loss. What did matter, of course, was the humiliation; but that too he managed to rise above – as, fortunately, did the government. Despite everything he was knighted in 1786 and in the following year was appointed High Sheriff of Derbyshire. By that time he was employing, directly or indirectly, some 30,000 people, either in his own factories or in others using his machinery. By that time too he had built himself a stately home, Willersley Castle, overlooking Cromford Mill, on land he had purchased from the uncle of Florence Nightingale. It was there that he died in 1792, leaving a fortune of half a million pounds, in the later eighteenth century an astronomical sum.

59

Temple of Vaccinia
GLOUCESTERSHIRE

The great Dr William Harvey's well-known dictum 'Don't think, try' must be one of the most dangerous pieces of advice ever offered to medical students. We know however that it was given to young Edward Jenner when he was studying at St George's Hospital, and can only assume that he was acting upon it when, on 14 May 1796, he deliberately made a small incision in each arm of his gardener's son, the eight-year-old James Phipps, and rubbed in the unattractive contents of a blister on the hand of Sarah Nelmes. Sarah was a milkmaid; she had caught the cowpox from a cow named Blossom, whose hide now adorns the wall of the library at St George's Medical School, since removed to Tooting. For a long time it had been noticed that people who had had the mild cowpox seemed immune to the dreaded smallpox; it was Jenner's aim to test this theory once and for all. Some time later he subjected James in much the same manner to smallpox itself; the boy remained in rude health. 'Vaccination' – Jenner's word – became first the fashion, then the norm, until it was finally made compulsory.

'The Temple of Vaccinia' was the name that the doctor playfully gave to the little thatched summerhouse in his garden at Berkeley, Gloucestershire. The main house, called the Chantry, was the scene of his experiment and his home for

nearly all the seventy-four years of his life, though his occupation as the local GP was later to be much interrupted by his
public duties – he became, among other things, Physician
Extraordinary to George IV – and the activities of the many
learned societies of which he was a member. For that tentative
vaccination of little James Phipps not only won fame and fortune for Edward Jenner; it also proved the first step in the
long eighteenth- and nineteenth-century crusade to transform the ever-growing towns and cities of England from the
stinking and fever-ridden hellholes that they were rapidly
becoming into places once again fit for healthy human beings
to live in.

The problem was partly the result of England's steadily
increasing population and partly that of the Industrial
Revolution, which had brought hundreds and thousands of
country-dwellers into the towns while barely attempting to
provide them with halfway acceptable accommodation.
Overcrowding was endemic, often with two and sometimes
even three families sharing a room. In some districts the
streets had no drainage and were little more than open sewers.
If they were unpaved – as most of them were – the filth in
them might be ankle-deep for weeks. Rivers, which had once
been the life blood of a city or town, were becoming mortal
threats. In Liverpool the River Aire, carrying all the refuse of
the city, would periodically flood; when it did, the ground
floors and basements of the low-lying houses would become
little better than cesspools. In London, the climax came with
the 'Great Stink' of 1858 when, during an unusually hot
summer, the Thames and its urban tributaries were flooded
with sewage; the smell became almost unbearable. People
refused to travel on the riverboats, and Parliament was able
to continue its work only by hanging huge cloths soaked in
chloride of lime over all the windows. In such conditions

disease – serious disease – was inevitable. Cholera, which had originally come from India, first struck in 1831, typhoid and influenza – also a potential killer – a few years later. In 1840 alone, scarlet fever was responsible for more than 20,000 deaths. The following year, the Registrar-General reported that while in Surrey the mean life expectancy was forty-five, in London it was only thirty-seven and in Liverpool twenty-six. The average age at death of 'labourers, mechanics and servants' was fifteen.

What was to be done? The first major activist to apply his mind and all his energies to the problem was Edwin Chadwick (1800–90). He began in 1832, with a thorough investigation into the workings of the Poor Laws, in the course of which he became convinced of the overriding importance of sanitation. Cleanliness, good drainage and proper ventilation were, he proclaimed, the key to good health and increased life expectancy. In 1842 he published, at his own expense, a report on *The Sanitary Condition of the Labouring Population*, which was taken very much to heart by the government of the day. In it he called for dramatic social improvements, including major work on the water supply and the sewage system, municipal rubbish removal and better ventilation in all new housing.

The second, still greater, public benefactor was Joseph William Bazalgette, the grandson of a Huguenot immigrant. In 1856, championed by his friend and fellow engineer Isambard Kingdom Brunel, he was appointed Chief Engineer of the Metropolitan Board of Works and immediately began to plan the complete remodelling and rebuilding of London's sewage system; and two years later – the year of the Great Stink – Parliament passed an enabling Act decreeing that the work, despite the enormous cost, should begin at once. It involved 1,100 miles of new underground main sewers, built of brick, to intercept the outflows, and another 1,100 miles of street sewers to deal with the raw sewage which was still flowing freely through the streets. Sewage treatment remained in the future; the outflows were directed along the river and finally dumped untreated, but a long way downstream, away from any centre of population.

When Bazalgette had eventually calculated the correct diameter for his sewage pipes, he doubled it. The result of his doing so is that those same pipes can even accommodate the needs of modern tower blocks – monstrosities of which he never dreamed. 'After all,' he said, 'we're only going to do this once, and there's always the unforeseen': a far wiser adage, one would think, than those three terrifying words that were drummed into the head of the young Edward Jenner 232 years ago.

60

Caen Hill Locks

DEVIZES, WILTSHIRE

*I*t's one of the most impressive sights that England has to
offer: that majestic flight of the Caen Hill Locks, sixteen
of them, climbing straight up a steep hillside near Devizes.
And even they are not the whole story; there are another thirteen, six at one end and seven at the other, before the Kennet
and Avon Canal – with an almost audible sigh of relief –
reaches flat country again. These locks carry the canal boats
and barges up a vertical height of 237 feet – Nelson's Column
is 170 feet – over a distance of just under two miles. They are
the work of one of several engineering geniuses who made our
Industrial Revolution the phenomenon it was: a Scotsman
called John Rennie, who specialized in canals and docks and
rose to a point of such distinction that he was buried in St
Paul's Cathedral.

There are 104 navigable canals in England, virtually all of
them built between 1700 and 1850; the Kennet and Avon
dates from the years around 1800. They revolutionized
transportation across the country. Eighteenth- and early
nineteenth-century roads were appalling, and in winter often
well-nigh impassable; even when they were at their best, they
were so rutted that the carriage of fragile goods was fraught
with danger. Of course there were always rivers; but rivers
seldom went where you wanted to go, and even when they did

they tended to choose a maddeningly circuitous route. The canals were relatively straight, as well as being smooth; they avoided the smaller towns and villages, and moreover there were no limitations as to weight; one horse tugging a barge along a canal could pull thirty tons, doing the work of ten or more on land. When the canal passed under a tunnel, the horse would be untethered and make his way round to the other end while the bargees would lie on their backs, propelling the barge with their feet on the tunnel roof; in many places their footmarks can still be seen today.

Economically, too, canals were a godsend. To take but one example: in the middle of the eighteenth century the Duke of Bridgewater, who owned several coal mines in the north of England, was looking for a cheap and reliable way of transporting his coal to the burgeoning city of Manchester, so he sent for the engineer James Brindley and ordered a canal. It was forty miles long, and needed an aqueduct to carry it over the River Irwell; nevertheless it was built in just nine months. It opened in 1761, and was hailed as the first major British canal. Within a year of its opening, the price of coal in Manchester had been reduced by over 60 per cent. Within five years, the duke had received all his money back.

He had also set the pattern for the future. After the success of the Bridgewater, canals sprang up thick and fast. Some were built by groups of industrialists, who needed them for their own purposes; many more were the brainchildren of speculators looking only for dividends. Huge sums were invested, and by the early nineteenth century the English canal network had expanded to nearly 4,000 miles; it was now possible to travel from one end of England to the other without setting foot on land.

At that time, the canals had only one serious disadvantage: they were hideously slow. Until the advent of motor traffic towards the end of the century, the speed of a barge was that of a heavily laden horse, perhaps one or two miles an hour; an extended journey might take many weeks. Thus it was that whole families took to living permanently on their barges – or narrowboats, as they came to be called – leading a totally nomadic life with no fixed home but the canal itself. Education for the children was inevitably a problem; but small elementary schools were set up at various centres through the network where they could look in from time to time for a few days. There was also a 'Boatmen's Floating Chapel', which operated under the aegis of St Thomas the Martyr, Oxford. In 1868 it unfortunately sank; but a replacement was soon found, dedicated to St Nicholas, which catered to the bargees' spiritual needs until 1892.

By that time, however, the canal business was already doomed. The railways, arriving in mid-century, could carry far more passengers and goods at far greater speeds, and by the end of the 1850s the amount of cargo entrusted to the waterways had fallen by 60 per cent. A few of the larger companies were able to survive, normally by carrying coal and timber to the factories and mills of the big industrial cities, but the development of the road haulage industry in the twentieth century dealt the canals a further blow, and more and more of them fell into disuse, eventually becoming abandoned and overgrown with, in some instances, even their outlines barely distinguishable. The Clean Air Act of 1956, which effectively dealt the deathblow to the coal industry, appeared to do much the same to the canals.

Nationalized – like the railways – in 1948, five years later they were entrusted to the newly created British Waterways Board (now British Waterways), which soon afterwards declared the cessation of all commercial traffic. By now, although the basic network remained more or less intact, it had shrunk to about 2,000 miles, only half what it had been in its heyday. But suddenly, just when all seemed lost, came salvation: tourism, in the form of canal holidays. The canals of England were no longer looked upon as a white elephant: they were a golden opportunity. Ambitious projects for canal-clearing were instituted, and there are today literally hundreds of narrowboat operators, hiring out their craft for weekends, weeks or even months to people who want to cruise through unspoilt England, far – for most of the time at any rate – from the railways and motorways and – except at Caen Hill – with only just enough locks to keep them occupied.

61

Kew Palace
SURREY

Kew isn't really a palace at all. It started life as a large, rather disturbingly red brick villa, built on the banks of the Thames by a successful Flemish merchant for his young wife in 1631; only a century or so later, in 1729, did it catch the fancy of King George II. He and Queen Caroline continued to live at Richmond Lodge at the southern end of the gardens; but with their eight children and their nursemaids space was becoming a little cramped, and they leased the nearby house at Kew for their three eldest daughters.

Considering that he reigned for thirty-three years, most people are a bit vague about George II. At least he was able to speak quite good English – his father George I, the German from Hanover who had succeeded the ultimately childless Queen Anne and with whom he got on extremely badly, could never string a sentence together – and he was the last King of England to lead an army in battle, at Dettingen in 1743. He dearly loved Caroline, who on her deathbed in 1737 implored him to marry again. Shaking his head sadly, he replied, 'No, I shall have mistresses.' 'Good God,' she whispered with her dying breath, '*ça n'empêche pas*' – 'that needn't stop you'.

George's relations with his eldest son, Frederick, Prince of Wales, were even worse than those with his father; but

Frederick was hit by a cricket ball and died before him. The result was that when George died in the loo in 1760 it was his grandson, George III, who succeeded and occupied the throne for the next sixty years. Though bilingual in German, which he presumably spoke at home with his wife Charlotte of Mecklenburg-Strelitz, he saw himself as an Englishman through and through and deliberately distanced himself from his Hanoverian relations. Unlike that of his father and grandfather, his sex life was irreproachable. He never took a mistress, and despite the fact that he and Charlotte had first met on their wedding day they enjoyed a sublimely happy marriage, resulting in nine sons and six daughters. There was no nonsense about leading his troops in battle; indeed, no king ever led a more unadventurous life. Dividing his time between Kew, Windsor and Buckingham House – later to be transformed into the palace we know today – he never in his life left southern England. Nor, as Horace Walpole reminds us, did he ever see the sea till he was thirty-four, when he and his family started taking a summer holiday in Weymouth.

There were two tragedies in George's life: the loss of the American colonies and, in his later years, his madness. From neither did he ever really recover. According to the Declaration of Independence, his was 'a history of repeated injuries and usurpations, all having in direct object the establishment of an absolute Tyranny over these States'; in fact it was nothing of the kind. George was a conscientious constitutional monarch who bowed to the opinions of his ministers even when he thought they were wrong; and when both Parliament and people were determined on war there was little he could have done to stop them, even had he wished to. John Adams, the first American Minister to London, presented his credentials on 1 June 1785 and reported the King's words to him:

I wish you, Sir, to believe and that it is understood in America that I have done nothing in the late contest but what I thought myself indispensably bound to do by the duty which I owed to my people. I will be very frank with you. I was the last to consent to separation; but the separation having been made, and having become inevitable, I have always said, and I say now, that I would be the first to meet the friendship of the United States as an independent power.

The second tragedy, George's madness, began in the summer of 1788. He went to Cheltenham Spa to recuperate – at just under 100 miles, it was the furthest he had ever been from London – but the celebrated waters did him no good and the insanity grew steadily worse. In February 1789 the government introduced a Regency Bill, authorizing the Prince of Wales to act as Prince Regent, but, just in time, before the bill had gone through the House of Lords, the King recovered. He kept his sanity through the French Revolution and – apart from two brief lapses in 1801 and 1804 – the rise of Napoleon; he remained in fairly good health until 1810 when, at the age of seventy-two, after the death of his favourite daughter Amelia, the darkness descended again – this time for good. For his last decade, while his son ruled as Prince Regent, he was permanently insane, living in seclusion at Windsor with Charlotte until she died in 1818. It is unlikely that he ever knew of her death.

If you go to Kew Palace today, the first thing you will see is a waxwork of George, from the waist up. Modelled from the life, it is the most uncannily lifelike of its kind that I have ever encountered anywhere; you can almost see him breathing. Look at him closely. It's a good, honest, open face, not particularly handsome nor perhaps outstandingly intelligent, but straightforward and trustworthy. He's in military uniform, but you can easily imagine him as 'Farmer George', which is what he was often nicknamed and what he liked to be, for he was passionately interested in farming and the huge advances that were made during his reign in agricultural science and technology. He understood tragedy, and loss, and bereavement; but thanks largely to his loving wife and children – deeply disappointing to him though several of the latter were – he was not, I think, unhappy. He worked hard, led an upright and sober life and did the very best he could; and when he died, though his mind may have been occluded, his conscience was clear.

62

Coke Monument

HOLKHAM, NORFOLK

*I*t comes as quite a surprise, this huge fluted Corinthian column, rocketing 120 feet from the wooded park up into the broad Norfolk sky; and the surprise increases as you approach. Columns are sophisticated things, more appropriate to great cities than to the countryside; but this one is crowned by an outsize wheatsheaf, while the four corners of the plinth, instead of the lions, unicorns or other heraldic beasts that one might have expected, carry a bull ('breeding in all its branches'), a flock of sheep ('small in size but great in value'), a plough and a seed-drill. Beneath these are four bas-reliefs of farm labourers performing their daily tasks. Clearly, the monument must commemorate a son of the soil; and so it does, for Thomas William Coke (pronounced 'Cook') was almost certainly the greatest single pioneer in the history of English agriculture.

Born in 1754, he had inherited the Holkham estate from his father at the age of twenty-two, together with the parliamentary seat for the Norfolk constituency. He was an MP for fifty of the next fifty-six years, during which he incurred the anger of George III for his enthusiastic support of America in the War of Independence; he never achieved ministerial status, but his political career was nevertheless distinguished enough to earn him, when he at last retired in 1832, the title of 'the greatest commoner in England'. Six times he was offered a peerage, and six times he refused; he accepted only on the seventh occasion, in 1837, when he was eighty-three. He lived for five more years, as Earl of Leicester, but found no pleasure in the House of Lords, which he described as 'the hospital for incurables'. He himself was unaffected by old age: he is recorded as having shot twenty-four deer with twenty-five cartridges when he was seventy-nine and, if that were not impressive enough, fathered a child three years later at the age of eighty-two.

Coke won his fame, however, not as a politician nor as a sportsman nor as a sexual athlete, but as leader of the Agricultural Revolution. Soon after the Norman Conquest, landlords had begun the nefarious practice of enclosure, and this had continued until around 1700, by which time – despite denunciations by the Church and totally ineffectual legislation in Parliament – most of the land had been enclosed and was under private ownership. Of course the peasant farmers received a degree of compensation, but many of them were none the less left half-starving. The lucky ones found work on the enclosed farms; those who failed to do so were obliged to emigrate to the colonies or seek employment in the rapidly increasing number of mills and factories that were springing up in the infancy of the Industrial Revolution.

Farming, meanwhile, was gradually becoming mechanized. The process began with one Jethro Tull, who in 1701 invented the first English seed drill; this made it possible for the first time to distribute seed evenly and efficiently across a field. The drill was followed by Joseph Foljambe's iron plough, which was lighter than those that had previously been in use and infinitely easier to steer and control. Then, in 1786, Andrew Meikle's threshing machine threw thousands more farm labourers out of a job. There was a major development, too, in the open-field system of crop rotation. No longer was it necessary to leave one of the three fields fallow; it was found that the judicious planting of certain crops – turnips mostly, but also clover and flax – made the land still more fertile than if it was left alone. An important innovation was also being introduced where sheep and cattle were concerned, in the form of selective breeding to improve the stock.

Thomas Coke, whose estate included fifty-four farms, was at the forefront of these last two reforms. In the former in particular, he was much influenced by the second Viscount Townshend – generally known as 'Turnip' Townshend – who in his father's time had owned a nearby estate similar to his own. Coke pioneered the use of new and more nutritious grasses, which enabled him to keep 2,400 sheep at Holkham in place of his father's 700, crossing the old Norfolk Horn breed with the fast-maturing – especially when fed on turnips – English Leicester strain. In cultivating his land, he used oxen for ploughing rather than horses, and was the first to dispense with the old wooden yoke, putting them into harness instead.

What was the result of all this? First of all, a vast improvement in the food supply. In 1720 an acre of wheat might produce nineteen bushels; by 1840 that figure had risen to thirty, sometimes even more. This led to a dramatic increase in population – which rose to 15 million – and in the demand for clothing, which in turn gave rise to new forms of employment such as cottage industries, a stepping stone to the Industrial Revolution. Most of the latter were run by women. In former days they had worked the fields with their husbands; unfortunately the new machinery not only tended to be too heavy for them to operate, but also reduced the number of workers required. If there had been no cottage industries available these unemployed women would probably have gone into domestic service, or have moved to the new industrial towns where, all too easily, they drifted into prostitution.

But we can't blame Coke and his fellow pioneers for this. Thanks to their researches, their experiments and their sheer hard work, they left English agriculture in a far better state than they found it. That magnificent monument bears the name of Thomas Coke; but in a very real sense it commemorates them all.

63

Dove Cottage
GRASMERE, CUMBRIA

Dove Cottage began life as a pub. The Dove and Olive – presumably a reference to Noah's Ark – was recorded as early as 1617, and finally closed in 1793. Just six years later, in 1799, the young William Wordsworth came upon it while on a walking tour of the Lake District with his friend Samuel Taylor Coleridge. For some time he had been looking for a small house in which he could settle down with his sister Dorothy. Dove Cottage looked ideal, so he made enquiries and found that it was available for rent at £5 a year. Then and there he took it, and moved in with Dorothy on 20 December. They were to stay there for the next nine years. It was far from comfortable: freezing cold in winter, to the point where the poet papered the whole of one room with newspaper in a vain attempt at insulation; no running water, the only loo a hut at the bottom of the garden. (Or perhaps just the bottom of the garden.)

And so it happened that this unassuming little dwelling saw the beginnings of Romantic poetry in England. It was here that Wordsworth wrote what is perhaps his most popular poem about the daffodils near Ullswater ('I wandered lonely as a cloud') and his magnificent ode 'Intimations of Immortality from Recollections of Early Childhood'; here too that he continued his work on *The Prelude*, begun in 1798 and the greatest autobiographical poem in English – or, so far as I am aware, in any other language.

A key moment in his life came in 1800, when he was joined in the Lake District by his old friend Samuel Taylor Coleridge, who took a house in nearby Keswick. The two men had travelled in Germany together and had already collaborated two years before in their joint work *Lyrical Ballads*, which had included Wordsworth's 'Tintern Abbey' and Coleridge's *Rime of the Ancient Mariner*; it had been hailed as a landmark of English Romanticism, the birth of a new age; and so it was. Another arrival at Keswick at about this time was Robert Southey with his wife Edith who chanced to be Coleridge's sister-in-law; and in 1808 the three were joined by a fourth, Thomas De Quincey. The principal quintet of 'The Lake Poets' – for we must not forget Dorothy – was now complete.

Here was a new poetry, based on instinct rather than reason, on country rather than town, on nature rather than on intellectual enlightenment; in short, against the remorseless progress of the Industrial Revolution; speaking, as Wordsworth himself put it, 'the real language of men . . . emotion recollected in tranquillity'. Now he and Coleridge were back together again, and in that same year of 1799 – presumably while Dove Cottage was being prepared for occupation – they fell in love with two sisters, the daughters of one Thomas Hutchinson: Coleridge with Sara, and Wordsworth with his old school friend Mary, whom he was to marry in 1802. Coleridge was to marry another Sara – Sara Fricker – with ultimately disastrous results; but William and Mary Wordsworth were to prove a very happy couple – despite the continued presence of Dorothy in the same distinctly overcrowded cottage – and over the following years were to produce five children.

In fact, Wordsworth had six altogether; in 1791, at the

impressionable age of twenty-one, he had visited France, now at the height of its revolution, and had become an enthusiastic supporter. ('Bliss was it in that dawn to be alive/ But to be young was very Heaven!') He had also had a passionate affair with the daughter of a French surgeon in Blois, a girl named Annette Vallon. (He tells the story in Book IX of *The Prelude*.) In 1792 Annette had presented him with a daughter, Caroline. At this point it seemed that he had every intention of marrying her; but the following year he returned to England alone. He saw neither of them again for ten

years; it was only in 1802, when he was getting ready to marry Mary, that he and his sister crossed to France and met Annette and Caroline at Calais. One evening during their stay he walked with his daughter along the beach, and was inspired to write his lovely sonnet 'It is a beauteous evening, calm and free'. He was to live another forty-eight years; but this was their last meeting.

By 1809, with eight full-time residents – and on occasion

more, when the Coleridges or the De Quinceys or the Southeys, or perhaps all of them, stayed the night – Dove Cottage was becoming still more overcrowded, and the Wordsworths began looking for roomier accommodation. Two other houses in Grasmere were tried, but both were found wanting; and in 1813 they moved into Rydal Mount, just outside Ambleside, a few miles to the south. Here Wordsworth lived another thirty-seven years until he died in 1850, and Mary another nine until her own death. But Dove Cottage did not disappear into obscurity. After the Wordsworths left De Quincey moved in, and lived there in a cloud of opium until 1820; he continued to rent it, largely as somewhere to store his books, until 1835.

After a succession of undistinguished tenants, the freehold of Dove Cottage was eventually acquired by the Wordsworth Trust in 1890 at a cost of £650. Very largely unchanged since Wordsworth's day, it is now open to the public, as is the little Wordsworth Museum next door, and the recently built Jerwood Centre, where we can admire the trust's impressive collection of Wordsworthiana. Alas, the Dove and Olive has gone for ever.

64

The Quarterdeck, HMS Victory
PORTSMOUTH, HAMPSHIRE

*H*MS *Victory* was launched on 7 May 1765, and is still in commission, serving now as the flagship of the Second Sea Lord but also open to the public as a perfectly fascinating museum. Having in 1805 been the flagship of the great Lord Nelson, killed on her quarterdeck on 21 October 1805 during the Battle of Trafalgar, she is probably the most famous ship in the world. It is sad in a way that she now suffers the indignity of being confined to permanent dry dock at Portsmouth – she would look a thousand times more beautiful and majestic at sea – but it certainly makes her a great deal easier to visit; and a visit is highly recommended.

Nelson had had an astonishing career. Soon after he joined the navy as an ordinary seaman in 1771 he was sent to join mercantile West Indiamen in the Caribbean. Over the next dozen years he saw service in the Arctic – coming within ten degrees of the North Pole – in India, and in Newfoundland and Quebec. Back in the West Indies in 1787, he married Fanny Nesbit, a young widow from Nevis – an action that he was later bitterly to regret. During the French Revolutionary Wars he was all over the Mediterranean and eastern Atlantic, losing the sight of his right eye at the siege of Calvi, Corsica, in 1794 and his right arm at Santa Cruz de Tenerife in 1797. In that same year he distinguished himself in the Battle of Cape

St Vincent off the south-western tip of Portugal, disobeying orders so as to get his ship into the front line, and then capturing two enemy vessels.

By this time the star of Napoleon had risen, and when in 1798 he launched his expedition to Egypt Nelson was given the task of intercepting his fleet. He failed to do so, but on finally arriving off the Egyptian coast he found thirteen French men-of-war anchored in Aboukir Bay, one of the mouths of the Nile. He knew that he could not reach them before nightfall, and most admirals would have decided to wait till morning; but Nelson decided on an immediate attack. By dawn all the French ships but four had been destroyed or captured, including their flagship, *L'Orient*. The Battle of the Nile, as it was called, was one of the greatest victories of Nelson's career. At a stroke he had not only destroyed the French fleet, but also severed Napoleon's line of communication with France, leaving his army marooned in Egypt and frustrating all his plans of conquest in the Middle East.

Nelson now sailed on to Naples, where the King and Queen gave him a hero's welcome. The French had already occupied Rome and were now on the very doorstep of Naples; Nelson's victory on the Nile gave the Neapolitans new hope. A great celebratory dinner was given in his honour, where he met the Ambassador, Sir William Hamilton, and his wife Emma. But over the next months the situation grew ever more threatening, and two days before Christmas 1798 Nelson carried the King and Queen, accompanied by the Hamiltons, to refuge in Sicily. There he moved in with the Hamiltons. He was physically exhausted, not having yet fully recovered from a head wound sustained during the battle; he was quarrelling with the Admiralty, and his relationship with his wife was giving him serious concern. He desperately needed emotional support, and Emma gave it to him. It was in Sicily that their celebrated affair began. For Nelson, it almost ended in disaster; his infatuation sadly sapped his morale, and he was very nearly relieved of his command. Fortunately for him, on the day after their daughter Horatia was born he was posted to the Baltic fleet.

In 1801 Nelson won another great victory, this time over the Danes at Copenhagen (don't ask – just take my word for it). He then returned to London and the Hamiltons, but in 1803 was summoned back to sea. He took part in the blockade of Toulon, later pursuing the French navy across the Atlantic and back, and finally meeting up with it – thirty-three ships of the line under Admiral Pierre-Charles Villeneuve – at Trafalgar. The famous signal 'England expects' was duly hoisted – Admiral Collingwood is said to have sniffed, 'I wish Nelson would stop signalling – we all know what to do' – and the two fleets joined. Soon *Victory*'s 104 guns were all firing full blast, and the French cannonballs were hurtling back with devastating effect. Around 1.15 p.m. Nelson was hit by a lead ball, which cut an artery in his lung and lodged in his spine. Two hours later, Villeneuve surrendered, and Captain Thomas Hardy was able to go below, to report to the dying man that twelve or fourteen of the enemy ships were taken, and that not one British vessel had been lost. Nelson died soon after four.

As the news spread around the fleet, many of the exhausted sailors burst into tears. Nelson may have been vain, moody and something of an exhibitionist; but he possessed the 'Nelson touch' – a combination of confidence, courage and that extraordinary charisma of his that made him worshipped by his men. His leadership was based not on authority but on love; and no commander in history, perhaps, has been loved more. There was, as always, a negative side. His treatment of his wife and his affair with Emma earned him the implacable disapproval of the Admiralty and indeed of polite society;

there were also certain aspects of his actions in Naples – notably his complicity in the execution of young Francesco Caracciolo, whom he had hanged from the yardarm of HMS *Minerva* – that were bitterly attacked in Parliament by Charles James Fox; but as time went on these matters were forgotten. When the news of his death reached London *The Times* wrote: 'We do not know whether we should mourn or rejoice. The country has gained the most splendid and decisive Victory that has ever graced the naval annals of England; but it has been dearly purchased.' King George III, however, had no such doubts. 'We have lost,' he said, as the tears poured down his cheeks, 'more than we have gained.'

We had indeed. Nelson's body was returned to England preserved in a cask of brandy, and buried – after a magnificent funeral – in St Paul's Cathedral; and his memorials – the 170-foot column crowned by his statue and standing in the centre of the vast open space named after his greatest victory, his flagship in Portsmouth and a thousand pubs up and down the country – are on a scale infinitely more impressive than those awarded to any other Englishman.

65

Wilberforce House Museum
HULL, YORKSHIRE

*T*here is a delightful story – one of Byron's favourites, I'm told – of how the playwright Sheridan, dead drunk, was found lying in the gutter by the watch. Asked for his name, he opened one eye and mumbled the words 'William Wilberforce'. It was, in its way, a tribute: Wilberforce was famous across England and beyond for his piety, saintliness and moral rectitude, as well as for the dogged persistence with which he gave his life to good causes – above all the abolition of the slave trade, for which he was largely responsible. Wilberforce House in Hull is his birthplace, and has now been converted into a museum of slavery and its abolition.

Oddly enough, unlike virtually all the other tub-thumping evangelicals of the day, Wilberforce was also wonderful company: the novelist Madame de Staël described him as the 'wittiest man in England' and the Prince of Wales said he would go anywhere to hear him sing. Under Secretary for the colonies Sir James Stephen wrote:

> He was the most 'amusable' man I ever met ... Instead of having to think what subjects will interest him, it is perfectly impossible to hit on one that does not. I never saw anyone who touched on life at so many points; and this is the more

remarkable in a man who is supposed to live absorbed in the contemplation of a future state.

His early youth had been the mildly dissipated one expected of any eighteenth-century English gentleman, though it had not prevented him from entering Parliament in 1780 at the age of twenty-one as member for his home town, Kingston upon Hull (to give it its full, though seldom-used name). He soon proved himself a brilliant speaker in support of his close friend William Pitt, and a dazzling political career was confidently predicted; but in 1784 he had embarked on a tour of Europe during which he had undergone a radical spiritual conversion, resolving to spend the rest of his life in the service of God. At about this time he had met the Reverend James Ramsay, who had been a clergyman in the West Indies and had subsequently written *An Essay on the Treatment and Conversion of African Slaves in the British Sugar Colonies*, in which he graphically described the depraved lifestyles of the slave owners and the brutal treatment endured by the slaves. Wilberforce did not immediately follow up this first meeting; but then, in 1787, he met Thomas Clarkson, and his life was changed.

Clarkson – who subsequently had the distinction of being the addressee of Wordsworth's worst sonnet, beginning 'Clarkson! It was an obstinate Hill to climb' – introduced Wilberforce to his own active anti-slavery group; and so began a collaboration that would last for the next half-century. As well as writing innumerable essays and pamphlets and lecturing throughout the country, Clarkson was an indefatigable collector of evidence. During his research he interviewed 20,000 sailors who had crewed the slave ships, and amassed a huge collection of handcuffs, shackles, branding irons and thumbscrews which he put frequently on exhibition.

Wilberforce, meanwhile, with Pitt's encouragement, concentrated on furthering the cause in Parliament.

The first meeting of the newly founded Society for Effecting the Abolition of the Slave Trade was held on 22 May 1787. It was composed of Quakers and Anglicans together, and boasted one of the earliest ever campaign logos, designed by Josiah Wedgwood and depicting a Negro kneeling on one knee with the inscription *Am I not a Man and a Brother?*. The society lobbied tirelessly, producing pamphlets, holding public meetings and conferences, organizing boycotts and petitions. Wilberforce played an enthusiastic part in all these activities, but his principal objective was to keep the issue constantly in the parliamentary eye. In April 1791, in a speech that lasted a little under four hours, he introduced the first bill to abolish the trade; alas, it was ill-timed, the French Revolution having dramatically increased the forces of reaction, and he was defeated by 163 to 88. He refused, however, to be discouraged, and the next sixteen years saw annual bills on the subject, all suffering various degrees of failure. Finally in 1807 the Prime Minister, Lord Grenville, introduced an Abolition Bill in the House of Lords, where it received a large majority. At last, it seemed, there might be success – and there was, by an overwhelming 283 to 16. The whole House rose in tribute to Wilberforce, who acknowledged the cheering as tears streamed down his face.

On 25 March 1807 the Slave Trade Act received royal assent and became law. As the historian William Lecky wrote: 'the unweary, unostentatious and inglorious crusade of England against slavery may probably be regarded as among the three or four perfectly virtuous pages comprised in the history of nations.' But the work was not over. The slave trade had been abolished, but slavery itself still continued. Wilberforce now gave his attention to innumerable other causes – improving working conditions for textile workers and chimney sweeps, prison reform, capital punishment, animal welfare, even duelling (he was horrified when Pitt fought a duel in 1798, particularly as it happened to be on a Sunday) – but slavery always remained his primary concern; he could never rest, he said, until that odious institution had been totally abolished once and for all. He made his last anti-slavery speech at Maidstone in April 1833. In May the government introduced a Bill for the Abolition of Slavery, effectively eliminating it throughout the British Empire. On 26 July, by now bedridden, he heard from his friend Zachary Macaulay that the bill had passed its second reading and that its success was now assured. 'Thank God,' Wilberforce murmured, 'that I should have lived to witness the day.' Three days later he was dead.

66

Peterloo Plaque

MANCHESTER

S t Peter's Field was Manchester's Tiananmen Square. Alas, it no longer exists. Even in 1819 it was only temporary – a vast open space, recently cleared to allow for the new buildings that were being planned to occupy the site. Among these was the Free Trade Hall. This too has been transformed, most recently into the Radisson Hotel; but it was deemed the most suitable place to erect the traditional blue plaque, in this case commemorating one of the most shameful events in English history. The inscription on that blue plaque, however, was – rightly – thought to be a wishy-washy understatement, referring as it did only to the 'dispersal' of the unarmed protesters; in 2007 it was replaced by a red one describing Peterloo as what it really was: a massacre.

During the years immediately after Waterloo, the cities of the north were suffering acute economic depression. In the textile industry alone, weavers who at the beginning of the century earned fifteen shillings for a six-day week were now lucky to be paid five. Their situation was made still worse by the first of the Corn Laws, passed in 1815, which imposed tariffs on imported grain, forcing people to buy the more expensive – and greatly inferior – local produce. Nor was there any possibility of appeal, since not only was the franchise restricted to male landowners, but the whole of Lancashire –

which included Manchester, Salford, Blackburn, Oldham and Rochdale, together numbering almost a million – was represented by just two MPs. (Another two represented Old Sarum in Wiltshire (q.v.), in which there was only one voter.) In such circumstances it was hardly surprising that there were vociferous calls for reform. In the summer of 1819 Joseph Johnson, Secretary of the Manchester Patriotic Union, wrote to the radical agitator Henry Hunt, inviting him to speak at an important meeting planned for 2 August. 'Nothing but ruin and starvation stare one in the face,' he explained, 'the state of this district is truly dreadful, and I believe nothing but the greatest exertions can prevent an insurrection. Oh that you in London were prepared for it.'

Somehow, this letter was intercepted and brought to the attention of the government. Perhaps it panicked at the word 'insurrection'; it was a pity that it failed to notice the word 'prevent'. The 15th Hussars were ordered immediately to Manchester. Ironically enough, the organizers were taking enormous pains in the other direction, determined that those taking part should be clean and sober, dressed in their best, and should carry no 'weapons of offence or defence'. They were to march into Manchester from all over the county and beyond – there was a sizable contingent from Stockport in Cheshire – and they came in their thousands, probably 60,000–80,000 (the Cavalier army at Naseby numbered about 12,000) and almost certainly more than had ever been gathered together in one place in England before, all packed into an area of some 14,000 square yards. So dense was the throng that, in the words of one eye-witness, 'their hats seemed to touch'.

The date chosen for the demonstration was Monday, 19 August. Henry Hunt, in his famous white top hat, arrived at about one o'clock, and made his way to the two wagons that did duty as the hustings. The Hussars, supported by the Manchester and Salford Yeomanry, were standing by. They should have been commanded by General Sir John Byng, but he had a couple of horses entered in the York races that afternoon and had therefore delegated his authority to his deputy, Lieutenant Colonel Guy L'Estrange. The civil authorities were represented by William Hulton, chairman of the local magistrates. Hulton had the jitters from the start. Seeing the enthusiastic reception that was being given to Hunt, he ordered his immediate arrest, together with that of Joseph Johnson and two others; and when the Chief Constable pointed out the difficulty of carrying out this order in the immense crowd, he instantly called up the troops, 'since the magistrates consider the Civil Power wholly inadequate to preserve the peace'. Within minutes sixty mounted members of the Yeomanry had arrived, several of them, according to some reports, far from sober.

But the task was no easier for the soldiers, drunk or not, than for the local constabulary. In the words of another eye-witness:

> The cavalry were in confusion: they obviously could not, with all the weight of man and horse, penetrate that compact mass of human beings, and their sabres were plied to hew a way through naked held-up hands and defenceless heads; and then chopped limbs and wound-gaping skulls were seen; and groans and cries were mingled with the din of that horrid confusion.

When L'Estrange and his Hussars arrived just before two, Hulton was on the edge of hysteria. 'Good God, Sir,' he shouted, 'don't you see they're attacking the Yeomanry? Disperse the meeting!' At this the Hussars charged from the eastern end into the crowd while the Cheshire Yeomanry charged from the south, all with sabres drawn. Fifteen minutes later the field was empty, except for the dead, the wounded and those tending them. Surprisingly, there seem to have been not more than eleven killed outright; but several more were to die later of their wounds, and those injured, many of them seriously, amounted to 600 or 700. One of the fatalities, John Lees, had fought at Waterloo, just four years earlier. Shortly before his death on 9 September he confided to a friend, 'At Waterloo there was man to man, but there it was downright murder.'

The name 'Peterloo' was coined by the *Manchester Observer*, but was somehow inevitable. The atrocity continued to be denied by the establishment. On 27 August the Home Secretary, Lord Sidmouth, conveyed to the magistrates the thanks of the Prince Regent for their action in 'the preservation of the public peace'. In March 1820 Hunt, Johnson and eight others were tried for sedition, five being found guilty; Hunt – who had done nothing but accept an invitation – was sentenced to thirty months' imprisonment. Two years later, a test case was brought against four members of the Manchester Yeomanry; all were acquitted.

One favourable consequence of the massacre was the founding of the *Manchester Guardian* in 1821. Apart from that, however, we so far have no commemoration but the red plaque, and it is good news indeed that there is a vigorous campaign now in progress to erect in the city a fitting memorial, not 'of a meaningless, abstract nature' but 'prominent, explanatory and respectful'. I intend to contribute.

67

Brighton Pavilion

EAST SUSSEX

There never was an individual less regretted by his fellow-creatures than this deceased king. What eye has wept for him? What heart has heaved one throb of unmercenary sorrow? If he ever had a friend – a devoted friend in any rank of life – we protest that the name of him or her has never reached us.

So wrote *The Times* in its obituary for King George IV after his death in June 1830, in his sixty-eighth year. Many of its readers considered this something of an under-statement; one of his own senior aides had confided to his diary: 'a more contemptible, cowardly, selfish, unfeeling dog does not exist.' He was drunken, dissipated and dropsical, criminally irresponsible and insanely extravagant: in 1795 his debts amounted to the equivalent of £50 million in today's money, almost all of it spent on himself and his innumerable mistresses. To quote *The Times* once again, he would always prefer 'a girl and a bottle to politics and a sermon'. By the age of thirty-five he already weighed seventeen and a half stone, and in 1824 he would have measured fifty inches around the waist – if he had had one.

But George wasn't all bad. He was probably the country's most cultivated ruler since Charles I, two centuries before.

Fluent in French, German and Italian, he was a munificent patron of the arts, and an elegant and witty conversationalist; and all this, together with his style and manners, earned him the title of 'the First Gentleman of England'. The Duke of Wellington, the last of his Prime Ministers, described him as 'the most extraordinary compound of talent, wit, buffoonery, obstinacy and good feeling – in short a medley of the most opposite qualities, with a great preponderance of good – that I ever saw in any character in my life'. He was largely instrumental in the founding of the National Gallery and of King's College, London. He commissioned Sir Jeffry Wyatville to remodel Windsor Castle. He left England a lot more beautiful than he found it. Finally, he was responsible for Brighton Pavilion.

And Brighton Pavilion is perhaps the most improbable building in England. Those wild, bulbous, Indo-Saracenic domes, those curious spires intended to suggest Crusaders' tents, all suddenly rising from the middle of an otherwise sedate Georgian seaside town, are surprising enough; but they are positively restrained in comparison with the elaboration and exuberance within. The pavilion had begun life as a relatively modest farmhouse, which George had rented largely to get away from London with his long-time mistress – whom he later secretly married – Mrs Fitzherbert. Gradually he bought more and more of the surrounding land, and eventually in 1815, as Prince Regent, called in the brilliant designer and architect John Nash, to whom we owe the building as it looks today, the King's most splendid – and somehow not inappropriate – memorial. He made the little town fashionable, popularized sea-bathing as his father had done in Weymouth, installed a German band and gave lavish banquets in the pavilion, with a team of French chefs – notably the great Carême – who used such delicacies as cocks' testicles and calves' udders to make the food almost as exotic as the surroundings.

He had nearly become Prince Regent after George III's first bout of madness in 1788, but the patient had recovered before the necessary legislation could be passed. When in 1810 the King finally and permanently lost his sanity, Parliament went to work again; this time it finished the job with the Regency Act 1811 and, for the first time in English history, a son reigned in the place of his still-living father. He remained, however, sublimely uninterested in politics, and was only too delighted to leave the government in the hands of his Prime Ministers: Spencer Perceval, who was assassinated in 1812, Lord Liverpool, George Canning, Lord Goderich and finally, in 1828, the Duke of Wellington.

The prince had first fallen in love with Maria Fitzherbert when he was twenty-one. Being six years older, twice widowed, a commoner and a Roman Catholic, she could hardly have been more unsuitable. Thanks to the Act of Settlement 1701 which barred any spouse of a Catholic from succession to the throne, and to the Royal Marriages Act 1772 which forbade him to marry without his father George III's consent, the marriage had no legal validity; but Mrs Fitzherbert, for whom the law of the Church would always outweigh the law of the state, always believed that it did. She was consequently far from pleased when in 1795 her 'husband' married his cousin, Princess Caroline of Brunswick. No bridegroom was ever more reluctant, but the marriage was a necessary condition for the King's assistance with his son's ever-increasing debts. The pair detested each other from the start, and after the birth of their daughter Charlotte the following year were, to their mutual relief, legally separated; but when George succeeded his father in 1820 this did not stop Caroline – who was by this time living openly with her Italian manservant – from returning to London from her exile and claiming the crown of the Queen Consort. On coronation day she tried to enter Westminster Abbey by at least three doors, but was always refused admittance. Shouting and screaming, she then made her way to Westminster Hall, where she found her passage blocked by guards with fixed bayonets, and had the doors slammed in her face. At last, having made a thorough exhibition of herself, she was bundled back into her carriage and driven away. She never recovered from her humiliation, and died three weeks later.

George himself lived on till 1830. His only legitimate child, Princess Charlotte, had died in 1817 after giving birth to a stillborn son. George III's second son, Frederick, Duke of York, had died in 1827, so the throne now passed to the third son, William, Duke of Clarence, who now became King William IV. William is best known for having lived for twenty years with the most dazzling musical comedy actress of her day, Dorothy Jordan. The pair had ten children, all of whom proved astonishingly fertile. They consequently have hundreds of descendants. David Cameron is one; I, more humbly, claim to be another.

68

Old Sarum

WILTSHIRE

Old Sarum may be of some minor interest archaeologically: it was an Iron Age hill fort and is the ancestor of Salisbury, to whose present site, a couple of miles away, its population wisely moved in the thirteenth century. For us, however, its interest lies in the fact that since the reign of Edward II in the fourteenth century it regularly elected two members to Parliament, despite the fact that after about 1600 it had only three houses and no resident voters at all. In 1831 the total electorate numbered eleven, all of whom were landowners who lived elsewhere. Of all England's fifty-six 'rotten boroughs' (there was also a single one in Scotland) that were disenfranchised by the Reform Act of 1832, Old Sarum was the rottenest.

Most of these boroughs had been flourishing towns when they gained the right to return their two members; for various reasons, however, they had become depopulated – or even, like Old Sarum, deserted. Another constituency, Dunwich on the Suffolk coast, retained its rights even though it boasted only forty-four houses and thirty-two voters, all the rest of the town having slipped away into the North Sea. The trouble was that the regulating system remained somehow set in concrete and took no account of these changing populations, so that gradually over the centuries parliamentary representation became more and more unfair – the more so since the rottener the borough, the easier and cheaper it was to buy its handful of voters. And the unfairness was still more evident – and perhaps more serious – in the great new cities of the north. The whole of Lancashire for example, with a population nearing a million and the teeming city of Manchester at its heart, was, like its neighbour Yorkshire, a single constituency until 1832, represented – like Dunwich or Old Sarum – by just two members. It is worth noting that of those fifty-six rotten boroughs, fifty were in the south of England.

Then there were the 'pocket boroughs'. These were not so rotten as the rotten boroughs, but they were quite rotten enough. They were the constituencies said to be in the pocket of their patrons, usually members of the nobility whose wealth and prestige gave them power to direct the voting. If a member for such a borough were to vote (as they very seldom did) against the wishes of his patron, he could not hope for re-election. The Duke of Norfolk is said to have possessed eleven of these boroughs, the Earl of Lonsdale nine.

That year of 1832 – the year of the great Reform Act – was one of the greatest years in our parliamentary history. About the pocket boroughs the Act failed to do very much; but it finally disenfranchised the rotten boroughs and gave proper representation to the large cities that had been spawned by the Industrial Revolution; it also increased the size of the electorate by some 75 per cent. It did however make one serious mistake, which may not even have been entirely deliberate, by referring to the enfranchised voters as 'male persons'; this was the first statutory bar in history to women's voting, which had previously been at least theoretically permitted.

There had of course been several previous attempts at parliamentary reform. Oliver Cromwell had done his best, but all his changes had been countermanded on principle by Charles

II. In the eighteenth century William Pitt had proposed a number of very moderate measures, but they had all been rejected – George III was always against any kind of change – and then as the century reached its end the horrors of the French Revolution had caused a further swing to the right. It was on the death of George IV in 1830 that the reform movement became unstoppable. As a result of the Duke of Wellington's outspoken opposition to it, he was forced to resign the prime ministership; but his successor Lord Grey vowed to carry out all the reforms he believed necessary. When he was unable to get his first bill through Parliament, he decided to request a dissolution and to take the appeal to the people.

At the election of 1831, the reforming Whig Party was rewarded with an overwhelming majority; the stick-in-the-mud Tories were left with little more than their rotten and pocket boroughs, and the bill went easily through the House of Commons, with most of its Tory opponents abstaining. Alas, it failed in the Lords, largely thanks to the twenty-two bishops present, twenty-one of whom voted against it. But this time public patience had been stretched too far. That same evening riots broke out across the country. In Bristol, both the Bishop's Palace and the Lord Mayor's Mansion were burned to ashes; in Nottingham, they set fire to the castle; at Derby, they broke into the jail and liberated several of the prisoners.

And so Lord Grey tried again. The only way through, he realized, was to create a pack of new reformist peers. But King William IV – who probably disliked the whole idea of reform just as much as his father – refused to do so. Grey was beaten, and resigned; back came the Duke of Wellington, who brought with him chaos. By this time he was so unpopular that there was a run on the banks, accompanied by calls for the abolition of the nobility and even of the monarchy. The duke failed to form a government; back came Grey; and this time at last the King, now properly scared, consented to swamp the Upper House with Whigs. In fact, he never did so. Instead, he circulated a letter around all the Tory peers asking them to withdraw their opposition, warning them of the consequences. They obeyed, and the swamping was avoided. On 7 June 1832 the bill received the royal assent.

It was, of course, not the whole story. There were to be two more Reform Acts, one in 1867, the third in 1884, before suffrage could claim to be anything like universal, and even then it was confined to only half the population. (Women had to wait until 1918 – but that's another story.) Still, it was the first step, as well as being by far the most controversial; and, as Madame du Deffand the French *femme de lettres* and friend of Horace Walpole said when told the story of St Denis walking two miles with his head under his arm, *C'est le premier pas qui coûte* – it's the first step that counts.

69

Tolpuddle Martyrs' Tree

TOLPUDDLE, DORSET

The story of the martyrs of Tolpuddle is not, perhaps, quite as shocking as that of Peterloo, but it runs it close; and the presence of the original sycamore tree under which George and James Loveless, Thomas and John Standfield, James Hammett and James Brine met together in 1832 to plan their perfectly peaceful action somehow gives it additional poignancy.

The offence with which the six men were charged was the swearing of an oath as members of the Friendly Society of Agricultural Labourers, which they themselves had founded. They had done so in desperation. Increasing mechanization was beginning to have its effect, unemployment was on the rise and the landowners of the south-west, as yet virtually untouched by the Industrial Revolution, did not have to compete with the higher wages paid to workers elsewhere. Gradually their earnings had been reduced, from the ten shillings a week on which a labourer's family could just about get by, down to eight, then seven, and finally six. At which point the six members of the society, led by a local Methodist preacher named George Loveless, put their foot down: they would not work for less than ten, and that was that.

It is difficult nowadays to understand what immense courage was needed to make such a decision. Friendly societies were the ancestors of modern trades unions, and in those days were viewed by the establishment with the deepest suspicion. The French Revolution of only forty years before was still remembered with horror. That was what happened when the working class was not kept in its place; never must it be allowed to repeat itself in England. And so it was that in 1834 a local squire by the name of James Frampton wrote to Lord Melbourne, the Prime Minister, to complain, referring him to an almost forgotten law passed in 1797 against the swearing of clandestine oaths. The six were arrested, imprisoned and sent to trial. Of this trial George Loveless wrote:

> . . . the whole proceedings were characterised by a shameful disregard of justice and decency . . . The Grand Jury appeared to rack heaven and earth to get some clue against us, but in vain; our characters were investigated from our infancy to the then present moment; our masters were inquired of to know if we were not idle, or attended public-houses . . . and much as they were opposed to us, they had common honesty enough to declare that we were good labouring servants, and that they had never heard of any complaint against us; and when nothing whatever could be raked together, the unjust and cruel judge, John Williams, ordered us to be tried for mutiny and conspiracy, under an Act 37 Geo. III, Cap. 123, for the suppression of mutiny amongst the marines and seamen, several years ago.

The sentences were for seven years' transportation to Australia. The men were taken to two prison hulks lying off Portsmouth, whence they sailed for Van Diemen's Land, better known to us as Tasmania.

Transportation was a nightmare. Some 600 men, shackled and in leg-irons, would be crammed into the three-decker ships and confined in dark and airless holds for six or eight weeks or even more, suffering appalling heat in equatorial waters and defenceless against the regular epidemics of cholera, dysentery and smallpox. Many died on the way; the survivors often found themselves wishing they were back on the ships. James Brine later testified:

> . . . having walked so far without shoes, my feet were so cut and sore that I could not put them to the spade. I got a piece of iron hoop and wrapped it round my foot to tread upon, and for six months . . . I went without shoes, clothes or bedding, and lay on the bare ground at night . . . Having told my master that I was very ill, I asked him if he would be so good as to give me something to cover me at night, if it were only a piece of horse-cloth. 'No,' said he . . . 'I understand it was your intention to have murdered, burnt and destroyed every thing before you, and you are sent over here to be severely punished, and no mercy shall be shown you.'

Meanwhile in England, details of the trial had become known. Indignation was mounting. As the news spread, protest marches were organized; as early as 21 April 1834, a crowd estimated at 100,000 gathered at Copenhagen Fields near King's Cross, after which a petition was carried to the Home Secretary, Lord Melbourne. He refused to accept it, but the agitation for the men's release continued. More petitions flowed in, with a total of over 800,000 signatures, and in June 1835 Melbourne's successor, Lord John Russell, granted conditional pardons. But these failed to satisfy the martyrs' parliamentary champion Thomas Wakley MP. He continued the struggle until at last, in March 1836, the government agreed that the men should be given a full and free pardon, and gave orders to bring them home.

Back in Tolpuddle, however, life for them was still difficult; they had too many enemies. Five of the six soon moved to

Essex, where a committee from among their supporters had bought them farm leases; but they could still never forget the injustice they had suffered, and enthusiastically supported the new Chartist movement for political reform. As a result, history began to repeat itself: the Essex squirearchy reacted much as Squire Frampton had. Before long five of the six had once again been transported – but voluntarily this time – to Canada, where they settled peacefully in London, Ontario.

The sixth, James Hammett, had always been the odd man out. He alone was not a Methodist, never wrote about his experiences and had a criminal record. (As a boy, he had stolen a few pieces of iron.) He died in 1891, having previously moved into Dorchester Workhouse so as not to be a burden on his family. He was buried in his parish churchyard where his grave may still be seen, but orders are said to have been given that there were to be no speeches at the graveside. After all, somebody might have made an incendiary speech – and that, in Tolpuddle, would never do.

70

Copenhagen's Grave
STRATFIELD SAYE HOUSE, HAMPSHIRE

God's humbler instrument, though meaner clay,
Should share the glory of that glorious day.

Not many horses get an incised gravestone; but Copenhagen certainly deserved his. He carried the Duke of Wellington all through the Peninsular campaign, and then all day at Waterloo, when the duke was in the saddle for eighteen hours. For any horse, that should have been enough; but the moment he dismounted Copenhagen lashed out and broke free; it took his groom half an hour to catch him. He retired to the Wellington estate at Stratfield Saye, where the duke and his children continued to ride him for many years, eventually dying in 1836 at the age of twenty-eight, and being buried with full military honours. His grave is now shaded by a turkey oak, which grew from an acorn planted by the duke's housekeeper, the wonderfully named Mrs Apostles, in 1848.

Wellington himself died at Walmer Castle in Kent in 1852, at the age of eighty-three. He had had an astonishing career. Born in 1769 as Arthur Wesley – a name he later changed to Wellesley – and brought up in Ireland, he was sent to Eton, which he hated. (His famous remark about Waterloo being won on its playing fields is almost certainly mythical, particularly since Eton had no playing fields in his day.) Joining the army at eighteen, he never looked back: Ireland, Flanders and then seven years in India, where he rose to the rank of major-general. On his way back to England in 1805, his ship stopped at the island of St Helena, where he stayed at Longwood House, the future place of exile of his last defeated enemy. There followed a couple of years in England and Ireland, where he made his highly unsatisfactory marriage; very soon after came the war in the Iberian Peninsula.

This was the six-year Napoleonic War, in which Napoleon Bonaparte personally participated for some two and a half months; for the rest of the time he was busy elsewhere. By 1807, when his army invaded Spain and Portugal, he was master of virtually all Europe; but just a few months later he made a disastrous mistake by dethroning King Charles IV of Spain and making his brother Joseph king in his stead. Immediately, the Spaniards revolted. This led to the so-called Guerrilla War, which turned into the full-blown Peninsular War. The Emperor's other blunder, a few years later, was to launch his Russian campaign, removing – and subsequently freezing to death – many thousands of soldiers whose presence was desperately needed in the peninsula. Wellesley, aided by the Portuguese, drove the remainder steadily back. The last battle, at Bayonne on 14 April 1814, was actually fought after Napoleon's abdication; he arrived in his first place of exile, the island of Elba, a month later.

His escape from Elba the following February signalled the last chapter of Napoleon's extraordinary career, which ended on Sunday, 18 June on the field of Waterloo. That battle lasted from about noon until 10 or 11 p.m.; as Wellington – he had by now received his dukedom – later remarked, it had been 'a damned close-run thing', and might easily have gone the other way had it not been for the arrival of the Prussians under their Marshal Blücher shortly before nightfall. Even as it was, it had proved to be something of a Pyrrhic victory: Wellington lost some 15,000 men, Blücher some 7,000; Napoleon 25,000 plus another 8,000 taken prisoner. But it had achieved its objective – Napoleon Bonaparte was finished.

Little more than a week before the battle, the Congress of Vienna had held its last session. It had opened the previous September, five months after Napoleon's abdication, and had suffered an awkward moment when the news arrived of his escape from Elba; but it had continued to sit – casting a wary eye to the west all the time – and its final settlement was to prove the most comprehensive treaty that Europe had ever seen. Tsar Alexander I was there in person; the Austrian Emperor was represented by his First Minister Prince Metternich, King George III by Lord Castlereagh. The later admission of Bourbon France to the table brought the most brilliant of them all, Prince Talleyrand. The numbers were swelled by countless international noblemen and their ladies, all come to enjoy the most brilliant social season that the Continent had to offer. The Congress's deliberations were encapsulated in the Treaty of Paris, signed in November 1815; and with it, the map of Europe was redrawn.

It was Waterloo, and Waterloo only, that had made it possible. That one battle had decided the future fate of Europe and, through Europe, of the rest of the world. Had Napoleon been victorious, had the map not been redrawn, we – together with much of the Continent – might well have been speaking French today. The threat he posed to England, though far less evil, was comparable to the threat posed by Nazi Germany in 1940: that this country might have been reduced to a minor province in a vast military empire. The Second World War, however, was won through any number of different factors; Napoleon's ultimate defeat was brought about in a single battle, on a single day. That is why Waterloo was one of the dozen most important battles of all history.

The Duke of Wellington, who won it (whatever the Prussians may say) was then only forty-six, and still had a long and distinguished career ahead of him. He now returned to politics, was appointed Master-General of the Ordnance and, in 1827, Commander-in-Chief of the British Army. After that no one was surprised that in the following year he became Prime Minister. And when he did so, and when he rode up Downing Street to No. 10 with his seals of office, it was Copenhagen, once again, who carried him.

71

Box Tunnel
WILTSHIRE

The story of the railways is one of the great romances of English history, and Isambard Kingdom Brunel one of the first of its heroes. As Chief Engineer of the Great Western, he set the standards for what railways ought to be, minimizing curves and gradients, building bridges at Windsor, Maidenhead, Saltash and Bridgewater, and tunnels like that at Box in Wiltshire, dead straight and almost two miles long, which when built was the longest railway tunnel in the world. Most tunnels simply have entrances; Box has portals, the western one built in magnificent classical style – the more remarkable in that nobody ever sees it except the engine-drivers. There is a story that Brunel designed the tunnel so that on his birthday, 9 April, the rising sun is visible from this portal down the length of the tunnel; but no one seems quite sure whether this is true, and would-be photographers are discouraged from confirming it for fear, as P.G. Wodehouse might have said, of receiving the 6.54 in the small of the back.

The world's first public steam railway was, as everyone knows, the Stockton–Darlington, which opened in 1825; the second was the Liverpool–Manchester, pulled by George Stephenson's *Rocket*, which was launched five years later. Among the passengers on the inaugural trip on 25 August was the actress Fanny Kemble, who wrote to a friend:

Wilberforce House Museum, Hull, Yorkshire. Wilberforce was only twenty-nine when this splendid portrait was painted by John Rising. What I love about the man is that everybody else loved him too: he was light in the hand, without a suspicion of sanctimoniousness, and extremely funny.

The anti-slavery medallion issued by Wedgwood in 1787.

Tolpuddle Martyrs' Tree, Tolpuddle, Dorset.
Tolpuddle was another of those nightmare atrocities in which we seemed to specialize in the early nineteenth century; what a relief that this time we have such a beautiful and peaceful place in which to remember it.

The Peterloo Plaque, Manchester. Why is Peterloo so little and so inadequately remembered? Have we tried to sweep it under the carpet? Did England ever see a more shameful peacetime atrocity than this?

Old Sarum, Wiltshire. *Political Amusements for Young Gentlemen, or the Old Brentford Shuttlecock*, by James Gilray. The unfortunate shuttlecock is the head of John Horne Tooke, whom Lord Camelford – patron of the borough of Old Sarum (seven members) selected to represent it.

Copenhagen's Grave, Stratfield Saye, Hampshire. Copenhagen was not the easiest of horses, but not many, perhaps, could have carried the Duke of Wellington for eighteen hours uninterruptedly at Waterloo or given his children and grand-children rides for many years afterwards. If any horse deserved a gravestone, he did.

Mary Seacole Plaque, Soho Square, London. Here, then, was an historic meeting. Alexis Soyer, formerly chef at the Reform Club, now in charge of the Crimean Commissariat, meets Mary Seacole, the Jamaican nurse who established a hotel to house and tend Crimean troops. How Miss Nightingale – who rather loved Soyer but despised Mrs Seacole – would have hated it . . .

Deene Park, Northamptonshire. Tennyson's famous Valley of Death in the Crimea. Few photographs are more outwardly boring than this one – until you notice the cannonballs. They were probably hardly cold when Roger Fenton, the first official war photographer, immortalized them. But, you notice, no bodies: Fenton was a sanitiser.

Cragside, Northumberland. Lord and Lady Armstrong settle down for dinner, some considerable distance below two of Mr Swan's 'incandescent lamps'. The apparatus on the nearer one suggests that it was capable of being lowered nearer the table – but perhaps they weren't quite sure of it yet.

The Study, Down House, Kent. Interior decoration was never the forte of the Darwins. On the other hand, as Sir Kenneth Clark once pointed out, nobody has ever had great thoughts in an enormous room; from the study of Down House, Darwin's great thoughts ranged to the very borders of the universe.

North Pier, Blackpool. It is impossible nowadays to imagine the excitement that must have been felt by the labouring masses of the north on their first visit to Blackpool. There was the initial thrill of the railway; of the first-ever view of the sea and the first head-on encounter with it; and, not least, that for the first time in your life you were there to enjoy yourself, and for no other purpose.

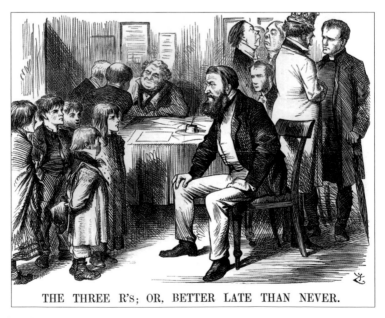

THE THREE R's; OR, BETTER LATE THAN NEVER.

Stanley Grove School, Manchester. *Punch* cartoon from 1870 depicting William Forster speaking to 'pupils'. His Elementary Education Act resulted in the building of several thousand schools which provided education for every child between the ages of five and twelve.

Wightwick Manor, Wolverhampton. This is the Great Parlour, looking towards the Minstrels' Gallery, which was added in 1893. The idea is that of a fifteenth-century Great Hall, converted to a late Victorian living room. A lot of the oak panelling is Jacobean, carved and painted with much exuberance.

Osborne House, Isle of Wight. Happy family domesticity all over again – just like we had for Victoria's grandfather George III. But it too was to be overshadowed, not by disease but by forty years of widowhood.

EX LIBRIS

RUDYARD KIPLING

19 09

Bateman's, East Sussex. Rudyard Kipling's father, John Lockwood Kipling, was President of the Mayo School of Arts, Lahore, and subsequently Curator of the Lahore Museum. The bookplate he designed for his son is now proudly displayed in the study at Bateman's: an easily recognisable Kipling, happily and comfortably ensconced under the howdah, the hookah-wallah looking marginally less secure behind.

The snorting little animal, which I felt inclined to pat, was harnessed to our carriage, and Mr Stephenson having taken me on the bench of the engine with him, we started at about ten miles an hour . . .

The engine having received its supply of water, the carriage was placed behind it, for it cannot turn, and was set off at its utmost speed, thirty-five miles an hour, swifter than a bird flies (for they have tried the experiment with a snipe). You cannot conceive what the sensation of cutting the air was . . . I stood up, and with my bonnet off 'drank the air before me'. The wind, which was strong, or perhaps the force of our thrusting against it, absolutely weighed my eyelids down. When I closed my eyes this sensation of flying was quite delightful, and strange beyond description; yet, strange as it was, I had a perfect sense of security, and not the slightest fear.

Just three weeks later there occurred the first famous railway accident, when William Huskisson MP was run over by the *Rocket* in the presence of the Duke of Wellington; but it took more than that to halt the march of the railways. By 1845 over 1,000 projects had been proposed; in the following year no fewer than 272 Acts went through Parliament setting up new railway companies. Already, however, the vexed question of class was raising its hideous head. The following is taken from *Nineteenth-Century Railway Carriages* by Hamilton Ellis:

The attitude of many companies was that summed up in the amiable pronouncement made by Charles Saunders, secretary of the Great Western, before a Parliamentary Committee in July 1839, that perhaps the company would arrange later on to convey the very lowest orders of passengers, once a day at a very low speed in carriages of an inferior description, at a very low price, perhaps at night.

In these early years a serious problem arose: there was no general agreement about the width of the gauge, and because none of the companies in those days envisaged using each other's rails, they didn't seem to think it mattered. Much of the fault was Brunel's; he was convinced that a broad gauge of 7 feet ¼ inch between the rails would be safer and more comfortable for the passengers than the standard, much narrower gauge of 4 feet 8½ inches. Besides, he pointed out, the broad gauge would allow for larger carriages and a far greater capacity for freight. He therefore unhesitatingly adopted it for the Great Western. There can be little doubt that he was right; but it made construction – especially of the tunnels – a good deal more expensive and, since nearly all the other railways in the course of construction had plumped for the standard gauge, confusion was bound to occur. After Brunel's death in 1859 – he was only fifty-three – the GWR caved in and, at near-ruinous cost, relaid all its tracks.

By this time the railway mania was dying down; there was nowhere else to go. By 1850 – just twenty years after the Liverpool–Manchester opening – it was possible to travel by train from London to Scotland. The vast majority of our towns and cities, and even a good number of our villages, had at least one rail connection, sometimes two or three; and the plethora of small companies was seen to be wildly uneconomic. Share prices levelled out, then fell dramatically. Many unwise investors lost all they had and fell into bankruptcy. By the end of the 1850s, most of the small companies had merged, or been taken over by the larger ones; and soon only a few of the giants remained.

And life in England was never the same again. Some saw it as a loss. As John Ruskin put it:

The very quietness of nature is gradually withdrawn from us; thousands who once in their necessarily prolonged travel were subjected to an influence, by the silent sky and slumbering field . . . now bear with them even there the ceaseless fever of their life, and along the iron veins that traverse the frame of our country, beat and flow the fiery pulses of its exertion, hotter and faster every hour. All vitality is concentrated through these throbbing arteries into the central cities. The country is passed over like a green sea by narrow bridges and we are thrown back in continually closer crowds upon the city gates.

For others, the railways spelt liberation. Families could be reunited, business made infinitely easier, excursions planned, holidays enjoyed, the country for the first time opened up. In the 1950s and 1960s, when most people had become car owners, it seemed that their day might have passed; today, with concern about global warming and pollution by fossil fuels – to say nothing of the introduction of Eurostar – we may be standing on the threshold of the second Age of the Railways. Since for me they have always been by far the most comfortable and civilized form of transport, I certainly hope so.

Victorian England

Introduction

*T*his is the only section of our book dedicated to a single reign; but that reign was the longest in English history and developed such a strong and individual character of its own that it could not possibly be combined with any other.

We tend to think of the Victorian age as a long period of peace, broken only by the Crimean War in the middle and the Boer War at the end. We are wrong: in virtually every year of Victoria's reign there was fighting going on somewhere – in Afghanistan, in Zululand, in India, in the Sudan, indeed in almost every corner of the rapidly growing empire. It was none the less a period of considerable prosperity, thanks in large measure to the Industrial Revolution which, at least during the first half, was still very much in progress. Communications took a huge leap forward – first with the canals and almost immediately afterwards with the railways, which between *c.*1840 and *c.*1860 transformed the country. Meanwhile the population rose from nearly 15 million in 1841 to 32½ million in 1901.

That rise in population, however, brought much destitution in its train. High unemployment kept wages down to a bare subsistence level; overcrowding was unspeakable. In London and the big industrial cities large houses were turned into tenements. A contemporary described the scene as 'Hideous slums, some of them acres wide, some no more than crannies of obscure misery, make up a substantial part of the metropolis . . . In big, once handsome houses, thirty or more people of all ages may inhabit a single room.'

There were several consequences to this misery. One was child labour, in factories or in mines – crawling through tunnels too low and narrow for adults – or very often as chimney sweeps. Many other children drifted into prostitution, one of the greatest banes of Victorian England; in 1857 the police estimated that there were some 8,600 child prostitutes in London alone.

In architecture, the Gothic Revival ruled – best exemplified by St Pancras railway station and hotel, and by A.W. Pugin's extraordinary detailing of the new Houses of Parliament, rebuilt after the fire that destroyed its predecessor in 1834. The dazzling exception was Paxton's Crystal Palace, home of the Great Exhibition, bitterly condemned by John Ruskin – who in matters of architecture was almost invariably wrong – as 'the very model of mechanical dehumanisation'. Painting was dominated by the Pre-Raphaelites and their followers (though the actual Brotherhood was of remarkably short duration). Music, with the important exception of the Gilbert and Sullivan operettas, was dominated by foreigners, preferably German ones – Queen Victoria infinitely preferred Mendelssohn to Mozart. Our best showing by far was in literature. Among the novelists, Dickens, George Eliot, Thackeray, the Brontës and Trollope are only the beginning. Among the poets, Tennyson and Browning together lead the field, but Arnold, Swinburne, Hardy and Meredith and several others must be considered worthy runners-up.

And, presiding over all, Queen Victoria herself: a tiny black ball of bombazine, instinctive rather than intelligent, passionately emotional in her love for her husband, for her Prime

Ministers Lord Melbourne and Benjamin Disraeli, for her groom and ghillie John Brown and, at the end of her life, for 'the Munshi', her deeply dishonest, turbanned body-servant who stood behind her and gave her remarkably unsuccessful lessons in Urdu; she was self-confident enough to give vehement and thrice-underlined advice to her ministers on all the political issues of the day and yet to retire into complete seclusion for some three years after her widowhood, effectively abrogating almost all her royal responsibilities. Thanks to her numerous progeny and their marriages she became, as it were, the matriarch of Europe, to whom virtually all the royal houses of Europe claimed parentage; and when she died in 1901 at the age of eighty-one the whole Continent went into mourning.

72

Albert Memorial

LONDON

*A*lbert of Saxe-Coburg-Gotha, Queen Victoria's Prince Consort, died a fortnight before Christmas in 1861, at the tragically early age of forty-two. He had been an admirable husband, giving the Queen no fewer than nine children – she was pregnant within two months of their marriage – and had made a huge contribution, in many different fields, to the life of his adopted country. Above all he is remembered for the Great Exhibition of 1851, which was his brainchild and owed its immense success largely to his persistence, enthusiasm and sheer hard work. And that is why Sir Gilbert Scott's superb memorial is built on the site that it occupied in Hyde Park, and why Albert's golden statue, beneath its glorious Gothic canopy, is holding a copy of the exhibition catalogue on his knee.

Its full name was the Great Exhibition of the Works of Industry of all Nations, but its real purpose was to demonstrate both the huge achievement of the Industrial Revolution and the infinite superiority of British industrial manufactures to those of other countries. It heralded a new age, an age of iron and steel, of chemistry and physics, of mechanics and engineering. Technology, it seemed to say, was the key to a happier and more prosperous future for Britain and the world. Well, perhaps it was; but not everyone thought the Great Exhibition a good idea; King Ernest Augustus I of Hanover, the Queen's uncle and, despite his position and title, more English than the English, heartily disapproved:

> The folly and absurdity of the Queen in allowing this trumpery must strike every sensible and well-thinking mind, and I am astonished the ministers themselves do not insist on her at least going to Osborne during the Exhibition, as no human being can possibly answer for what may occur on the occasion. The idea . . . must shock every honest and well-meaning Englishman. But it seems everything is conspiring to lower us in the eyes of Europe.

But where and in what way could such an exhibition be housed? Several designs were proposed, all for various reasons rejected. One year before it was due to open, the organizing committee were growing distinctly panicky. Then, at the last moment, appeared the Duke of Devonshire's builder of greenhouses, Joseph Paxton. His plans for the greatest and grandest greenhouse of them all were finally approved in August 1850; and just nine months later, on 1 May 1851, the Great Exhibition opened. Perhaps the Crystal Palace, as it came to be called, was the most dazzling exhibit of them all: made entirely of huge sheets of plate glass, held in place by 202 miles of cast-iron sash bars, it was over 600 yards long and over 150 wide – an area about six times the size of St Paul's Cathedral – and it rose high enough to contain full-grown trees. As to its contents, an astonished Charlotte Brontë wrote: 'Its grandeur does not consist in one thing, but in the unique assemblage of all things. Whatever human industry has created you find there, it seems as if only magic could have gathered this mass of wealth from all the ends of the earth.'

There were in fact some 13,000 exhibits, coming from as far away as China. The imperial colonies of India, Canada, Australia and New Zealand were well represented, as well as several European countries and the United States, which sent over a gigantic reaping machine. The French in particular won an embarrassing number of awards, as was ruefully recorded in the British press. Visitors could watch with fascination the machines in motion, the thrust of pistons, the spinning of flywheels; they could follow the whole process of cotton production from the carding and spinning to the clattering of the monster mechanical looms and the finished textiles. They could admire all the state-of-the-art scientific instruments: barometers and microscopes, air pumps and electric telegraphs. Other crowd-pullers were the Koh-i-noor diamond, at that time the largest ever discovered, the celebrated Tempest Prognosticator, a barometer that used live leeches, a voting machine that counted votes automatically – we still count them by hand over a century and a half later – and, in the Retiring Rooms, England's first public conveniences, open to all at the cost of one penny.

When the Exhibition closed on 15 October, it had been visited by 6 million people, equivalent to a third of the entire population of Great Britain. Admission prices were deliberately reduced as the season wore on, from three guineas (about £275 in today's money) for the first day – ladies paid only two – to one shilling (say £4.30) in the high summer and autumn. The result was a clear profit of £186,000 (now some £16.2 million). Much of this was used for the funding of the Victoria & Albert Museum, the Natural History Museum and the Science Museum, all built next to the Imperial Institute in South Kensington, soon to be nicknamed – and with excellent reason – Albertopolis; the remainder was used to establish a trust to provide grants and scholarships for industrial research, which continue to this day. Paxton's great glass building was transported to Sydenham in south London, where it remained until it was tragically destroyed by fire in 1936.

The Albert Memorial, declared open by the Queen – still in heaviest mourning – in July 1872, was financed entirely by public subscription. It is an art gallery in itself. Around its vast plinth are 169 sculptures of painters, poets, sculptors, composers and architects, together with allegories of Agriculture, Commerce, Engineering and Manufacturing; other groups represent four of the five continents and, in the canopy, four statues standing for the arts, eight personifying the practical arts and sciences, eight more of the moral and Christian virtues and, to top the whole thing off, some gilded angels and a gold cross.

When I was a boy everybody used to laugh at the Albert Memorial, holding it to be the height of Victorian kitsch; now, painstakingly restored and with the prince himself gloriously regilded, the English have, I believe, at last taken it – and him – to their hearts.

73

Deene Park
NORTHAMPTONSHIRE

*M*ost monuments date from later than the event they are commemorating: Deene Park is an exception to the rule. It is a lovely, rambling old Tudor house, still lived in by the family – the Brudenells – who have owned it for half a millennium. But it is also, in a very real sense, a monument to the Crimean War, having been the property of James Brudenell, seventh Earl of Cardigan, who, on 25 October 1854 at the Battle of Balaclava, led the insane, disastrous and quite undeservedly celebrated charge of the Light Brigade. We are reminded of it at every step. There is a wonderful painting of Lord Cardigan recounting the story of the charge to a Prince Consort desperately trying to conceal his boredom; Queen Victoria, it is said, had herself painted out when she heard of one or two of His Lordship's other adventures, notably one with a Miss Adelaide Horsey de Horsey, whom he subsequently married. In her old age she would appear in the ballroom wearing her husband's uniform and mounted on his charger, Ronald, by this time safely stuffed. Ronald had survived Balaclava, but this last *épreuve* was apparently too much for him, even in his present condition; he wasted away, and now only his head remains, still to be seen in the Hall, at the foot of the stairs.

Cardigan was, by all accounts, a nightmare. In his childhood he had suffered a bad fall from another horse, and his parents had feared that his serious head injuries might have harmed his intellect; in his later life, many believed them to have been right. He grew up as the sort of nobleman who gives the English aristocracy a bad name: insufferably arrogant and conceited, overbearing and an inveterate bully. In the Crimea, where conditions for the soldiers were appalling and thousands died of cholera and dysentery, he lived comfortably on his yacht, the *Dryad*, safely anchored in Balaclava harbour. At the onset of winter, with food and fodder running dangerously short, he refused to bring any supplies up from the coast to his men, despite having more than enough horses to do so. Many animals perished as a result.

The famous charge, in which his brigade lost 107 lives out of 674, was the result of a mistake. As Tennyson pithily put it, someone had blundered; and that someone, it must be said, was not Lord Cardigan. Nor, for all his faults, did the man lack courage. The fateful order from his immediate superior (and brother-in-law) Lord Lucan had been brought by a Captain Nolan, whom both Lucan and Cardigan subsequently blamed for getting it wrong; but as Nolan was killed a few minutes later we shall never know for sure. Anyhow, Cardigan leapt on to Ronald, brandished his sabre and charged off, reaching the Russian guns unscathed. Then, 'disdaining,' as he later testified, 'to fight the enemy among private soldiers', he returned at a gallop, which he slowed to a walk when he realized that people were looking. Once back in England he was to describe his own gallantry in terms that were not so much exaggerated as palpably untrue; his statement that he had shared the privations of his men by living 'the whole time in a common tent' was only one of his many whoppers. As a recent biographer wrote: 'a more misleading account of his own exploits could hardly have been given'.

The Crimean War was fought in order to check Russian territorial ambitions at the expense of the gradually disintegrating Ottoman Empire; but its cause was far less important than its consequences, the most important being the radical reform of the army, which the war had shown up to be a byword for inefficiency and ignorance. It had not seen any important action since Waterloo – the Commander-in-Chief, the aged Lord Raglan, caused much embarrassment by continuing to refer to the enemy as 'the French', who were now fighting on the same side – and its ideas of modern warfare were by now hopelessly out of date. When it went on manoeuvres in 1853, it did so for the first time since Waterloo. Commissions were still bought and sold – in 1832 Lord Cardigan had paid £35,000 for his regiment of Hussars – and officers never underwent more than the minimum of rudimentary training. After all, if Marlborough's and Wellington's officers had got on well enough without it, so surely could they. They were gentlemen and sportsmen, handy with a firearm and good fellows in a scrap. What more could anyone ask?

The Commissariat Department, responsible for transport and supplies, was another bad joke. Provisions often arrived late – sometimes after the army had left – and were frequently not distributed till they were rotten. Often, too, those in charge stuck rigidly to peacetime regulations, refusing, for example, to issue nails in quantities of less than a ton. Pairs of boots were issued with two left feet, and hardly anyone had any maps. All these deficiencies, and countless others, were revealed by *The Times* war correspondent, William Howard Russell, who for the first time in any war sent back regular first-hand despatches from the front line – despatches that were entrusted to the newly invented electric telegraph, thanks to which they could reach London in hours, rather than weeks. It was largely as a result of these – in which their author pulled no punches – that the government of Lord Aberdeen was swept away in 1855 and, a year or two later, the Secretary of State for War Edward Cardwell embarked on an unprecedented programme of military reform, one that was in time to make the army thoroughly professional – and proud of it.

Russell's journalism was supplemented by the work of one Roger Fenton who, inspired by the examples of early photography that he had seen at the Great Exhibition, had studied the new techniques in Paris and completed a long photographic tour of Russia before embarking, at the request of the Prince Consort, with technical assistant, manservant and large four-wheel wagon to carry his equipment, for the Crimea. There, despite the cripplingly hot summer temperatures, an accident that broke several ribs and a nasty bout of cholera, he managed to produce over 350 large-format negatives, 312 of which he exhibited soon after his return to London. They did not have the ultimate impact of Russell's despatches: Fenton photographed no wounded soldiers, no sick or dying, and certainly no corpses; and his necessarily long exposures limited him to posed pictures or landscapes. Nevertheless, he brought the battlefields to life; thanks to the two men, the Crimean War is more vivid in our minds than any previous engagement could ever have been.

74

Mary Seacole Plaque
SOHO SQUARE, LONDON

*T*he plaque on the wall of No. 14 Soho Square that commemorates Mary Seacole is actually the third to have
been put up – the site of the first two was twice redeveloped
– but she had no monument at all until 1985, over a century
after her death. In any case she deserves not just a plaque (or
even three plaques) but a statue – and a big one, for her
achievement was heroic. Mary was a Creole, born of a black
mother and a Scottish father. She had had long experience of
nursing through epidemics of cholera and yellow fever in
Panama and Cuba, as well as in her native Jamaica. She was
thus already forty-nine when, on the outbreak of the Crimean
War, she came to London at her own expense, went to the
War Office and offered her services as a nurse, 'knowing,' as
she wrote later in her autobiography, 'that I was well fitted for
the work, and would be the right woman in the right place'.
The War Office, however, simply ignored her. She tried
several other government offices and finally the organization
then being set up by Florence Nightingale; they all turned her
down flat. But it took more than that to discourage Mary
Seacole. Once again at her own expense, she collected a store
of food, medicines and some basic medical equipment, and
boarded a ship for Constantinople.

On her arrival she immediately crossed the Bosphorus to

the Nightingale hospital at Scutari. There once again she offered her services; and once again her offer was rejected. The prim and aristocratic Miss Nightingale in her sober black outfit clearly took one look at the ever-smiling Mrs Seacole, a riot of Caribbean colour in her bright yellow dress, blue bonnet and red ribbons, and was horrified. It is doubtful that Mary minded very much; she must have seen within five minutes that the two could never get on together. Anyway Scutari didn't particularly interest her; she was bound for the battle-field. A week later she was at Balaclava. By this time she had spent nearly all her money; somehow, she was going to have to earn her living. And so, with driftwood, old packing-cases, a few sheets of iron and various doors and window-frames salvaged from one of the local villages, this extraordinary woman began building; and in March 1855, at a place she called Spring Hill some three miles along the road from Balaclava to Sebastopol, she proudly opened the British Hotel.

It was, inevitably, a fairly ramshackle affair. At one end was a shop stocked with provisions brought in from London and Constantinople, at which she sold 'anything from a needle to an anchor'; at the other a kitchen and dining room, providing food and drink for convalescing army officers and passing travellers. There were also two sleeping huts and an enclosed stable yard. The mornings were given over to running the establishment and dispensing first aid to the increasing numbers of sick and wounded who came to seek her services; in the afternoons, whenever the occasion demanded, she would load up two mules, one with her bags of provisions, the other with her medical equipment, and make her way to the battle-field, where she would tend the wounded – sometimes enemy Russians as well as British and French – on the spot. After the fall of Sebastopol in September 1855, she was the first woman to enter the town. She emerged carrying a ten-foot-long painting of the Madonna.

Before long she became a familiar and much-loved figure. 'Mrs Seacole,' reported the *Times* correspondent, William Howard Russell, 'doctors and cures all manner of men with extraordinary success. She is always in attendance near the battle-field to aid the wounded, and has earned many a poor fellow's blessings.' 'Mother Seacole', the soldiers called her, or 'the black Nightingale', though the two were as chalk and cheese: Miss Nightingale, respected but remote, four days' sail away, waiting for her patients to be brought to her; Mrs Seacole, cheery and colourful, expertly caring for them where they fell.

And there is no doubt that Miss Nightingale – I wish people had called her 'the White Seacole' – disapproved. The British Hotel charged for its services, supplied copious quantities of alcohol and was open to all passers-by. In a letter to her brother-in-law Sir Harry Verney, Miss Nightingale said that Seacole was 'a woman of bad character' who 'kept a bad house' – in those days a synonym for a brothel. 'She was very kind to the men &, *what is more* [my italics], to the Officers . . . & made many drunk.' When she sent a number of her nurses to help at the Land Transport Hospital, dangerously near the British Hotel, she made every effort to ensure that they should stay well away.

The standard of the British Hotel's cuisine, though it may hardly have merited a Michelin star, had at least briefly received the attention of one of the great cooks of Europe. Alexis Soyer, after years as chef at some of England's greatest country houses and later at the Reform Club, had written to *The Times* saying that in view of the appalling reports of the Army Commissariat he would be happy to assume overall responsibility for the catering, which he promised to transform

– 'and if we are reduced to eating rats, I am sure I can make them extremely palatable'. He, like Mary, had paid his own passage to the Crimea, where he had proved as good as his word – though rats never quite made the menu. He and Mary took an instant liking to each other; he described her as 'an old dame of jovial appearance, but a few shades darker than the white lily'.

At the end of the war, Mary Seacole could barely afford her fare back to England, and soon after her return she was declared bankrupt. Fortunately, and thanks largely to Queen Victoria's step-nephew Count Victor Gleichen, who had known her in the Crimea, a great gala banquet and concert, with eleven military bands, was held on her behalf, and she was quickly discharged; she then settled down to write her autobiography, *The Wonderful Adventures of Mrs. Seacole in Many Lands*. After a return to Jamaica, she was back in England in 1870, aged sixty-five, applying to nurse victims of the Franco-Prussian War; but Miss Nightingale soon scotched that. Mary ended up a few years later as masseuse to the Princess of Wales; still, one feels, she would have been happier at Balaclava.

75

Study

DOWN HOUSE, KENT

When Charles Darwin and his wife (and cousin) Emma Wedgwood bought Down House in 1842, his brother Erasmus remarked wittily that it should be called 'Down-in-the-Mouth', a joke that enjoyed only moderate success; but Charles and Emma made extensive alterations, and although the house will never be an architectural jewel – and their interior decoration leaves a good deal to be desired – it now looks, at least from the outside, cheerful enough. And anyway, beauty is not the point. Down House is where the Darwins lived for forty years, where they had the last seven of their ten children, and where Charles wrote his masterwork, *On the Origin of Species*.

But that was not until 1859, when he was fifty. By then he had been an active biologist for over thirty years, his first major discovery having been made as early as 1827, when he established that the black spores found in oyster shells were the eggs of a skate leech (a fact which I personally would never have suspected). His big opportunity came in 1831 when he was proposed as a suitable 'gentleman naturalist' to accompany Captain Robert FitzRoy on an expedition to chart the coastline of South America in HMS *Beagle*. The voyage, scheduled to last for two years, lasted for nearly five. Darwin, who suffered appallingly from seasickness, left FitzRoy to do his charting and himself spent as much time as possible ashore, looking for beetles, fossils and the inhabitants of rock pools and sending them – I'm not quite sure how – back to Cambridge for more expert examination.

The expedition continued via the Falklands and the Galapagos, where Darwin not only discovered his four famously different finches with differently adapted beaks, but mockingbirds that varied subtly from island to island – as indeed did the shells of the giant tortoises, which by now formed a regular part of the diet on board (and did little to diminish his seasickness). At this stage of his life he was no ornithologist, but he added the birds to his collection of specimens, the size of which was beginning to give Captain FitzRoy cause for serious concern. On they went to Cape Town, then across the Atlantic again to Brazil, and so back via Tenerife to Falmouth, where they arrived on 2 October 1836, four years and nine months after their departure.

Within a few weeks Darwin found himself a celebrity. A whole regiment of geologists, biologists, zoologists, entomologists, ornithologists and palaeontologists were set to work on his collection, while the dinosaur fossils were entrusted to the great Richard Owen and the Royal College of Surgeons. He wrote up his *Journal* and prepared a multi-volume *Zoology of the Voyage of HMS Beagle*; meanwhile he pressed on with his researches on the great theory that was beginning to take shape in his mind. By this time, too, he was contemplating marriage, drawing up a list of pros and cons. Among the cons were 'less money for books' and 'terrible loss of time'; among the pros 'Better than a dog anyhow'. The pros won, and he and Emma married in January 1839.

Six years later, just after the move to Down House, Darwin published – anonymously – his *Vestiges of the Natural History of Creation*. It aroused great controversy but, surprisingly, proved a bestseller – a *succès de scandale* that gave him much encouragement for what was to follow. *On the Origin of Species* finally appeared on 22 November 1859. The whole stock of 1,250 copies was sold out on the day of publication. Darwin had, as he explained to his friend and rival Alfred Russel Wallace, deliberately avoided the vexed question of human origins, as being 'surrounded with prejudices'; he limited himself to the prophecy that 'light would be thrown on the origin of man and his history'. That, however, was enough. The very first review picked up the 'men from monkeys' theme, and already the knives were out. The scientific establishment, including Darwin's friend Owen, dismissed the theory out of hand; from the Church of England there were differing opinions: the Reverend Charles Kingsley saw natural selection as 'a noble conception of Deity', but many of his colleagues were less happy. Darwin's precarious health hardly ever allowed him to take part personally in public discussions; his principal champion was Thomas Henry Huxley, 'Darwin's Bulldog', who in the famous Oxford debate on evolution on 30 June 1860 memorably defended his friend against the Bishop of Oxford, 'Soapy Sam' Wilberforce. The bishop was unwise enough to enquire whether Huxley was descended from an ape on his mother's or his father's side, at which Huxley retorted that he would rather be descended from an ape than from a man who misused his great gifts to suppress debate.

On the Origin of Species marked the apogee of Darwin's career – but by no means the end of it. Other books followed: *Fertilisation of Orchids*; *The Variation of Animals and Plants under Domestication*; *The Descent of Man, and Selection in Relation to Sex* – in which he stated categorically that humans were animals. Thereafter came *Insectivorous Plants*; *The Effects of Cross and Self Fertilisation in the Vegetable Kingdom.* His last book was *The Formation of Vegetable Mould through the Action of Worms*. It had, I suspect, a limited sale.

As for his religious views, Darwin had studied divinity and always described himself as an agnostic rather than an atheist; but though he remained on excellent terms with the local vicar and played an active part in the life of the parish, when his family went to church on Sundays he preferred to go for a walk. A book published in 1915 – thirty-three years after his death – maintained that he had reverted to Christianity on his deathbed, but this was firmly denied by his children, two of whom were with him when he died. To his daughter Henrietta and his son Francis he said, on 19 April 1882, 'It's almost worth while to be sick, to be nursed by you.' They were, as far as we know, his last words.

76

HMS Warrior

PORTSMOUTH, HAMPSHIRE

*D*espite her name, HMS *Warrior* never saw a battle. There was one rather exciting moment when in 1878 it looked as though Russia might be about to attack Constantinople; the ship was hastily mobilized and sent off to the Bosphorus. But the Russians thought better of it and called the whole thing off, and not one of *Warrior*'s twenty-six muzzle-loading sixty-eight-pounder guns, nor of her fourteen RBL guns – the latter provided by William Armstrong (see **Cragside**) – ever fired a shot in anger.

And a good job too. Historically, however, this magnificent vessel is a good deal more important than many that did; for *Warrior* was the first iron-hulled, armour-plated warship ever built for the Royal Navy. She owed her existence to that good old Anglo-French rivalry that had been going on ever since the Hundred Years War and probably longer: Naval Intelligence – such as it was in those days – had learned of a French secret weapon already a-building, a steamship called *La Gloire* – another misnomer, since her construction was shrouded in deepest secrecy – whose wooden hull was plated with thick iron armour. Such a piece of Gallic effrontery could not be tolerated: *Warrior* was planned to be very nearly twice the length of *La Gloire* and to move far faster through the water: 13 knots under sail, 14.5 knots under steam, and 17.5

knots under both combined. Construction, to be sure, did not go without a hitch: none the less, the ship was completed within two years. When she was eventually launched on 29 December 1860 it was the coldest winter for half a century and she froze to the slipway; it took six tugs to free her and drag her down into the Thames. She had cost £357,291 – about £24 million today.

Warrior and *La Gloire* together had started something. Within two years, Italy, Austria, Spain and Russia had all ordered ironclads. Soon, too, the German Empire had entered the lists – Kaiser Wilhelm II was determined to wrest the mastery of the seas from Britain – and this led to the great naval arms race of the early twentieth century, in the years preceding the First World War. In 1906 Admiral Sir John ('Jackie') Fisher had pushed through plans for HMS *Dreadnought*, which was to change the whole course of battleship construction, making all previous warships obsolete. 'Germany keeps her whole fleet always concentrated within a few hours of England,' he had told the Prince of Wales. 'We must therefore keep a fleet twice as powerful within a few hours of Germany.' His basic idea was an 'all-big-gun' armament of ten twelve-inch guns, arranged in five turrets distributed the length of the ship, which gave her twice the broadside fire of her closest competitors; furthermore her steam turbine engines could drive her forward at 21 knots, making her by far the fastest capital ship afloat. The design was such a success that the navy instantly ordered six more.

The result of all these preparations was that both the British and the German navies entered the First World War in 1914 superbly equipped to blast the hell out of each other. Disappointingly for both sides, they never did so. There was no Trafalgar, no decisive clash of modern battle fleets as they had hoped. The nearest they came to it was at Jutland in 1916, where there was certainly a clash – but no decision. Naval historians are still debating the outcome of the battle. Our losses in shipping tonnage were almost twice as great as Germany's, and we sacrificed more than twice the number of men (6,094 to 2,551); on the other hand, we remained in undisputed control of the North Sea, and we were still capable of blocking the German High Seas Fleet from operating meaningfully in the North Atlantic. At the end of the battle, too, the Germans fled back into harbour, leaving us commanding the site. Moreover, in spite of our losses, we had maintained our numerical superiority; we had twenty-three dreadnoughts and four battle-cruisers still able to fight, while the Germans were now down to ten. A month after the battle, our Grand Fleet was stronger than it had been before it. The Germans, by contrast, apart from two tentative and abortive sorties towards the end of the year, confined themselves to the Baltic for the rest of the war.

With the renewed outbreak of hostilities in 1939, it was soon clear that those great and noble battleships had had their day. In the First World War they had been the very embodiment of sea power; but as early as 1914 Admiral Sir Percy Scott had predicted that they would rapidly be made irrelevant by aeroplanes. By 1918 torpedoes could already be launched from the air and the next quarter-century was to prove the admiral all too right. In the 1920s General Billy Mitchell of the US Army Air Corps told Congress that '1,000 bombardment airplanes can be built and operated for about the price of one battleship, and that a squadron of these could sink that battleship'. Now it was realized that future wars were to be decided in the air, and that there could be only one naval vessel of the future: the aircraft carrier.

The age of the battleship had in fact lasted for just half a century, during which Britain fought only one major naval battle, and that an indecisive one. The old *Warrior* was lucky indeed not to be scrapped – though she suffered an arguably worse humiliation when in 1929 she was towed to Pembroke Dock and transformed into a floating oil jetty known as *Oil Fuel Hulk C77*. There she lay for fifty years, refuelling some 5,000 ships between 1929 and 1979, during which time all our other surviving ironclads and battleships went for scrap.

The ship was saved by the Maritime Trust, established in 1969 for that very purpose. Refitted, restored – and, it must be admitted, partly recreated – she is now a museum ship at Portsmouth, where she is in constant demand for business meetings and wedding receptions, birthday parties and bar mitzvahs.

77

Cragside
NORTHUMBERLAND

*W*illiam, the first Lord Armstrong, was England's Alfred Nobel: an armaments manufacturer who had strong feelings of philanthropy and did his best – with how much success we cannot say – to leave the world a better place than he found it. 'If I thought,' he is quoted as saying, 'that war would be fomented, or the interests of humanity suffer, by what I have done, I would greatly regret it.' But 'it is our province, as engineers, to make the forces of matter obedient to the will of man' – what a wonderful phrase – 'and those who use the means we supply must be responsible for their legitimate application.' Believing this, he cheerfully sold his Armstrong Gun in large quantities to both sides of the American Civil War – and both sides were happy to buy it.

On the credit side, he gave his first country house of Jesmond Dene and its long wooded valley, together with Armstrong Bridge and Armstrong Park, to the people of Newcastle; he founded what is now Newcastle University; he gave today's equivalent of well over half a million pounds to the Hancock Natural History Museum in Newcastle; and a few months after his death – in 1900, two days after Christmas, at the age of ninety – his heir, almost certainly on his instructions, gave £100,000 (nowadays more than £8 million) for the building of the New Victoria Infirmary in Newcastle.

Armstrong was elected President of the Institution of Civil Engineers – the members of which proudly bore the word MICE after their name – in 1881. He had, incidentally, been elected member of the Royal Society at the age of thirty-six, while still a practising lawyer.

And he built Cragside. This started life as a modest two-storey country lodge, but, by the time Armstrong and his architect Norman Shaw had finished with it, it looked more like a creation of King Ludwig of Bavaria. I suppose it is more Tudorish than anything else – timber framing in the upper floors, tall chimneys, mullioned windows – but it is hard indeed to describe adequately. He surrounded it with a 1,700-acre forested park, in which he planted 7 million – yes, 7 million – trees, adding five artificial lakes and thirty-one miles of carriage drives. But what is really important about Cragside is its interior; because here Armstrong the inventor and engineer let himself go. In 1868 he installed one of his own hydraulic engines, with which he powered his laundry equipment, a primitive sort of telephone, a passenger lift, a Turkish bath and even a rôtisserie. Two years later he used the water from one of his lakes to drive a Siemens dynamo and thus to create the world's first hydroelectric power station. The electricity it generated he used to power a huge arc lamp in the gallery, but this lasted only two years; it was then replaced with Joseph Swan's 'incandescent lamps'. Swan himself considered this 'the first proper installation' of his electric lighting anywhere.

Before electricity – though only for thirty or forty years in most private houses – there was gas. It had been used for street lighting since the early nineteenth century, but only after it was installed in the Palace of Westminster in 1859 did it become popular. And even then there were disadvantages. You could light only one gas lamp at a time. The gas could burn only upwards, so that all the fittings and incandescent mantles directed the light towards the ceiling. (Mantles that burned downwards came in as late as 1897.) It also generated a good deal of heat and soot. What has to be admitted is that it gave a lovely light. I well remember, in my early childhood, the lamplighter with his long pole, lighting each Bloomsbury streetlamp individually; and to my great delight there are plenty of gas lights still working in London – in Green Park, Covent Garden, St James's Square and in front of Buckingham Palace, just for a start.

With electricity all that was changed. Now, for the first time, it was possible to illuminate an entire room by the operation of a single switch, directing the beam at whatever angle you liked. There was little heat, and no pollution. When on 28 December 1881 the entire Savoy Theatre was illuminated by electricity for the first time, its owner Rupert D'Oyly Carte smashed a lighted bulb in front of his audience to prove its safety; fire insurance premiums plummeted. When Oxford University set as the theme for the Newdigate Poetry Prize 'The Benefits of the Electric Light', Hilaire Belloc composed a mock ode:

> *Whatever be its nature, this is clear:*
> *The rapid current checked in its career,*
> *Baulked in its race and halted in its course*
> *Transforms to heat and light its latent force:*
> *It needs no pedant in the lecturer's chair*
> *To prove that light and heat are present there.*
> *The pear-shaped vacuum globe, I understand,*
> *Is far too hot to fondle with the hand,*
> *While, as is patent to the meanest sight,*
> *The carbon filament is very bright . . .*
> *For instance: if you want to read in bed*
> *No candle burns beside your curtain's head,*

Far from some distant corner of the room
The incandescent lamp dispels the gloom,
And with the largest print need hardly try
The powers of any young and vigorous eye.

With all his hydraulic machinery, it was little surprise that Armstrong had a piped – and pumped – water supply, with comfortable – or fairly comfortable – bathtubs and proper flushing loos. These last were not, as we all love to think, the invention of the great Thomas Crapper, though he did invent the floating ballcock, together with 'Crapper's Valveless Water Waste Preventer, One Movable Part Only'. Whether or not he provided the equipment for Cragside is uncertain, but in the 1880s he certainly installed thirty items for the future King Edward VII at Sandringham – all, I am happy to report, with cedarwood seats.

With the energy crisis so much in people's minds today, it is interesting to see what Armstrong thought about it because, once more, he had ideas far ahead of his time. Already a century and a half ago, in 1863, he was warning everyone that coal was a limited commodity – besides which it 'was used wastefully and extravagantly in all its applications' – and that within two centuries England would cease to produce it. He also thought a lot about the potential of solar power, calculating that the solar energy received by a single acre in tropical areas 'would exert the amazing power of 4,000 horses acting for nearly nine hours every day'. In short, he used his undoubted genius to improve the creature comforts of our daily lives without damaging the world around us. All the power that was used at Cragside for so many different purposes was drawn from his own lakes, dams and aqueducts. 'Sustainability' was a word unknown in his day; but no one understood better than Lord Armstrong what it meant.

78

Stanley Grove School
MANCHESTER

*I*n the whole history of Victorian education, the year 1870 blazes like a beacon; for this was the year of the most idealistic and ambitious – and to its opponents, by far the most dangerous – piece of legislation that could be imagined: the Elementary Education Act, whose object was to provide, for the first time, universal elementary education for every child in the country between the ages of five and twelve. (It was generally known as Forster's Law, having been drafted by a Liberal MP named William Edward Forster, who had started life as a Quaker, but had been expelled from the brotherhood after he married the daughter of Dr Thomas Arnold.) As a direct result, the next thirty-odd years saw the building of several thousand new schools – they were known as Board Schools, since they were administered by School Boards elected by the local rate-payers – and of these there could be no more perfect example than the magnificent red-brick pile of Stanley Grove, the thirty-ninth (and almost certainly the last) to be built in Manchester.

Until the later nineteenth century, the Church of England had been responsible for most schools in the country. The earliest 'grammar schools' had been founded in the Middle Ages, so called because they taught Latin grammar and very little else; they were in theory open to all, with poor children receiving their education at the expense of those who could pay. In fact, poor children were seldom so lucky: their labour was needed at home. The truth was that until well after the Industrial Revolution the whole idea of schools for the working class was deeply mistrusted: it didn't do to give the poor ideas above their station. If you taught them to think, they might well become dissatisfied with their lives and even start a revolution; after all, you had only to look at what had happened in France. In the mid nineteenth century, however, this view came to be reversed. The seething masses in the new factory towns, godless and brutalized, were already dangerous; somehow they had to be controlled, and education seemed to be the best – if not the only – way of doing so.

But how to do it? And what sort of education? There were several varieties: the 'dame schools' for example, usually kept by one or two elderly ladies in their own homes. Occasionally these ladies would be themselves barely literate, in which case they provided little more than day care; mostly, however, they were able at least to give their charges an adequate foundation in the three Rs. Then there were the 'ragged schools', charitable institutions founded by true philanthropists – often pretty ragged themselves – who took their pupils directly off the streets. One of the first and most celebrated was John Pounds, a crippled Portsmouth cobbler, who began teaching in 1818 in his own home, bribing children to join him with the promise of a potato. He was widely imitated, to the point where in 1844 Lord Shaftesbury founded the Ragged School Union, and in the next eight years 200 free schools were established in Britain. In the next forty, these were to educate some 300,000 children.

Gradually, then, things were improving; but it was still very much a matter of hit or miss – and there were more misses than hits. There was also open opposition. Factory owners tended to protest when deprived of the cheap labour they had come to expect. Churchmen were horrified by the specific provision in the Act that religious instruction in the new Board Schools must be non-denominational; in many indeed there was no scriptural teaching at all. Many country children still lived several miles from the nearest school; and for this reason – as well as the number of new schools that had to be built – Forster's Law could not immediately be put into effect. In 1880, however, education – at least up to the age of ten – became compulsory everywhere in both England and Wales, and in the following year elementary schooling became free in both Board and the Church schools.

Secondary education, however, had somehow to be paid for until 1944, when the so-called Butler Act (named after the then Minister of Education R.A. Butler) once again radically changed the system and brought in free secondary education for all. There were now to be three different types of secondary school: grammar, secondary technical and secondary modern. Theoretically, the eleven-plus exam decided which; in fact, nearly everyone went to a secondary modern – including far more girls than ever before. It also opened up secondary education – and often higher education afterwards – to the working class, unfortunately awakening bitter class divisions. All in all, the system was only a partial success: nobody liked the eleven-plus, and secondary technicals never really got off the ground. And so, just after the war, came the first experiments with comprehensives – schools that took in all-comers, without regard to their aptitude or academic level.

It comes as something of a surprise to learn that the earliest comprehensives were modelled on the old grammar schools, with mortarboards and gowns and strict classroom discipline. Needless to say, this didn't last long. Under Anthony Crosland, Education Secretary in the 1964–70 Labour government, there was an explosion of comprehensives all over the country, all the local authorities being instructed to plan for conversion. Crosland's successor, Margaret Thatcher, who detested the idea, did her best to put this programme into reverse; but it had gone too far. Nowadays comprehensives account for some 90 per cent of secondary school pupils and in Wales 100 per cent.

There has, however, been one radical change. Since 1988, parents may choose their children's school – a privilege that has led to competition among state schools, the less popular ones being forced either to improve or to close down. And of course, the school buildings themselves are changing. After the churches and country houses, they represent the largest and most distinguished body of Victorian architecture still in existence. Relatively few still serve their original purpose, but the large majority continue to serve their community in one capacity or another. As for Stanley Grove itself, it now possesses a huge modern wing; its appearance has not been improved, but when we remember that the alternative was probably demolition we can hardly complain.

79

North Pier

BLACKPOOL, LANCASHIRE

> *There's a famous sea-side place called Blackpool,*
> *That's noted for fresh air and fun,*
> *And Mr and Mrs Ramsbottom*
> *Went there with young Albert, their son.*

So recited Stanley Holloway, on one of the earliest 78 r.p.m. records that I possessed as a child. The Ramsbottoms were unimpressed:

> *They didn't think much to the ocean,*
> *The waves they were piddlin' and small,*
> *There were no wrecks, and nobody drownded,*
> *Fact, nothin' to look at at all.*

But not everybody agreed with the Ramsbottoms: Blackpool, and in particular its North Pier – the oldest of the three, less than a quarter of a mile from the railway station – opened a new era, indeed a new world, for the labouring masses of northern England. The first generations of the Industrial Revolution never had a holiday longer than Sunday; there was nowhere for them to go, no means of getting there and no way of paying for it; but then, in the 1830s and 1840s, came the railway, and the railway introduced cheap excursion fares, and their lives – or those of many thousands of them – were changed. For the first time they saw the sea; and the sea was so wonderful that they wanted to go as far as they safely could into it – hence the pier.

By the better off, who had already discovered the delights of the seaside half a century before, the sudden advent of hordes of day-trippers was not well received. Already in 1851 a Preston newspaper had warned that 'unless immediate steps are taken, Blackpool as a resort for respectable visitors will be ruined', and in the south, nearer London, the problem was worse still. Brighton, which remembered the days of George IV and Beau Brummell, was horrified to receive, in a single week of May 1850, no fewer than 73,000 visitors; it eventually managed to persuade the railway to change its fare structures and price most of them out.

But meanwhile more and more resorts were establishing themselves, and such is the sheer quantity and splendour of England's beaches that there was room for everybody. The cheap boarding-houses were often a nightmare: the unfortunate lodgers were forced out of the house (and often into the pouring rain) at 9.30 a.m. and not allowed back till the evening meal at five or six. None the less, they didn't seem to mind: conditions were probably a lot worse at home – and anyway, they were on holiday.

You went to the seaside not only for the sheer fun of it, but also for your health. Doctors had decided that bathing in salt sea water was far better for the constitution than any number of inland spas, however medicinal; and at a time when people were seriously concerned – and rightly so – with the dangers of pulmonary disease, the fresh sea air was tempting indeed. Many sought the coast on their retirement and never returned to their former homes. But the water and the fresh air were not enough; if a resort was to be a success, it must have 'attractions', and these varied according to the people it wished to attract. Some towns stressed the gaudier aspects of seaside life: the pier, usually with a small theatre at the far end in which the great names of the music halls and, in more recent times, stars of the calibre of Gracie Fields and George Formby appeared during the summer season; the amusement arcades, equipped with plenty of slot machines and 'What the Butler Saw' peep-shows; the donkey rides and Punch-and-Judies on the beach; the illuminations, the jellied eels and toffee apples (to be succeeded in our own day by the ultimate nadir of British cuisine, candy floss); the rollercoasters and round-abouts and, in Blackpool, the Tower. Others – Southport, for example, Weymouth and Scarborough – were somewhat more sedate, with parks, petunia-strewn municipal gardens, promenades, bandstands and perhaps even an art exhibition or two.

The Victorians in particular loved the seaside. Just look at them all in William Powell Frith's glorious picture, *Ramsgate Sands* – now in the Royal Collection – painted in the 1850s. They weren't very good at dressing – or undressing – for it, but you can instantly see how much it meant to them. In their literature, too, it is inescapable: Charles Dickens, for instance, in *David Copperfield*, Lewis Carroll in *The Walrus and the Carpenter* and *The Mock Turtle's Story*; even Charles Kingsley in the now unreadable *Water-Babies*. The Victorians, I suspect, were more responsible than anyone else for the seaside as it has come down to us. They set the style, which continued essentially unchanged up to the Second World War; and though they might have been shocked by 1930s swimwear, let alone the postcards of Donald McGill, they would still have recognized the old formula.

What they would not have recognized is seaside life as we know it today: in the Balearics, the Caribbean or the Maldives, the bikinis, the snorkels, the Ambre Solaire, the living *in* the water rather than looking at it or paddling in it. Certainly they missed a lot; on the other hand they didn't know that they were missing it, and it's an open question whether they were as happy at their seaside as we are nowadays at ours. The English have always loved the sea, but they have never taken it for granted: it's too beautiful, and too dangerous. And if you want to enjoy the beauty and avoid the dangers – well, there's always the end of the pier, where you can sit back and listen to the band playing

> *Oh I do like to be beside the seaside,*
>   *I do like to be beside the sea!*
> *I do like to stroll along the prom, prom, prom*
>   *While the brass band plays tiddley-om-pom-pom . . .*
> *So just let me be beside the seaside,*
>   *I'll be beside myself with glee,*
>   *And there's lots of girls beside*
>   *That I should like to be beside*
>   *Beside the seaside, beside the sea!*

80

Osborne House
ISLE OF WIGHT

Queen Victoria and Prince Albert decided to build their new country house at Osborne on the Isle of Wight because the view of the Solent reminded Albert – I can't think why – of the Bay of Naples. I suspect that the Queen never really loved it as she did dear Balmoral; but Scotland is beyond the bounds of this book, and Osborne is, after all, where she died. Moreover, with its astonishing Durbar Room – done up in a gloriously over-the-top Indian style by one Bhai Ram Singh, assisted by John Lockwood Kipling, Rudyard's father – and Her Majesty's distinctly macabre collection of the limbs of the royal infants, modelled in marble, it admirably encapsulates both her imperial and her domestic aspects. Best of all, there is the Queen's own bathing machine from which, on 30 July 1874 at the age of fifty-five, she for the first time in her life cautiously lowered herself into the sea.

But Victoria was more than a queen-empress: she was an institution and an icon. Her reign of sixty-three years and seven months was longer than that of any of her predecessors and since all her nine children and twenty-six of her forty-two grandchildren married into royal and noble families across the Continent, she became known as 'the grandmother of Europe', which in a very real sense she was. She has given her name not only to the later two-thirds of the nineteenth century, but also to a taste and style of architecture, costume and interior decor-ation and, more significantly, to a moral prudishness that in extreme cases even caused people to conceal the legs of their pianos.

Her very succession had been improbable – the result of three of her uncles dying without legitimate issue. The ten illegitimate children of her uncle King William IV by the leading musical-comedy actress of her day had scandalized her mother, the Duchess of Kent, and was probably the cause of her rigorously strict upbringing (and perhaps of later Victorian morality). She shared a bedroom with the duchess – whom she not surprisingly loathed – until the day of her accession, after which she would often refuse to meet her. It was an early example of that almost childish stubbornness that she never lost and was to be the despair of her future Prime Ministers.

Of those Prime Ministers – there were nine altogether, covering twenty administrations – the first, Lord Melbourne, became to her the father that she had never had; for the first three years of her reign she depended on him absolutely. After their marriage on 10 February 1840 – 'the happiest day of our life' – Prince Albert took over this role and retained it till his death in 1861, by which time the Queen, to put it mildly, knew her own mind. She disliked Melbourne's successor, Sir Robert Peel, though nowhere near so much as Lord Palmerston, who took over the government in 1855. She had dire – and well-founded – suspicions of his private life, and mistrusted the apparent levity with which he conducted affairs of state; most of all she deplored his habit of negotiating with foreign gov-ernments without keeping her informed. Mr Gladstone she disliked most of all. Not only did he persist in addressing her 'as if I were a public meeting', he had the misfortune of twice succeeding Benjamin Disraeli.

Disraeli was a hard act to follow. In Victoria's view, he was exactly what a Prime Minister should be. First of all, he treated her as she felt a queen should be treated. 'Everyone likes flattery,' he said, 'and when you come to royalty you should lay it on with a trowel.' His references to 'our faery Queen' were thought by some to be going a little far, even for Disraeli, though Victoria contentedly lapped them up; but 'we authors, ma'am' – he had been responsible for a distinguished body of novels, while the Queen had published only *A Journal of our Life in the Highlands* – was a perfect example of the technique, as was his arranging in May 1876 that she should be made Empress of India. The title was not inappropriate, since by this time the British Empire was reaching its apogee; the 'queen-empress' role was insistently stressed in 1887 and 1897, at both her golden and her diamond jubilees.

Even on these joyful occasions, however, the Queen remained firmly in her customary deep mourning; she never properly recovered from Albert's death, for several years refusing to appear in public and never setting foot in London if she could help it. This persistent seclusion on the part of 'the widow of Windsor' was seen in some quarters as a dereliction of duty and an encouragement to the embryonic republican movement; but as the years went by and the seemingly indestructible old lady became gradually more visible, so her popularity increased. And – although she would never have admitted it – she probably also grew happier. During the 1860s and 1870s she became increasingly reliant on her Scottish ghillie, John Brown, to the point where there were rumours of an affair, and even a secret marriage; after Brown's death in 1883 she was with difficulty dissuaded from writing his biography. She had already confided in a letter: 'Perhaps never in history was there so strong and true an attachment, so warm and loving a friendship between sovereign and servant . . . The Queen feels that life for the second time is becoming so trying and sad to bear, deprived of all she so needs . . . The blow has fallen too heavily not to be very heavily felt.'

'For the second time' certainly suggests that this was indeed true love; and the Queen's insistence on being buried with a lock of Brown's hair, his photograph and several of his letters (the photograph was discreetly concealed in the bouquet she held in her left hand) surely leaves us in little doubt that her interest in John Brown's body was not appreciably less than that which she had felt for her husband's.

All through her widowhood, she had spent Christmas at Osborne, and – although John Brown was of course in constant attendance – Osborne was Albert. He had designed it, he had loved it, and after his death the entire house had remained as he had left it; even his clothes were still on their hangers. Victoria was there as usual in 1900; but by now she was failing fast. On Tuesday, 22 January 1901, at half past six in the evening, she died of a stroke, aged eighty-one; and her world died with her.

81

Wightwick Manor

WOLVERHAMPTON, STAFFORDSHIRE

Osborne tells you all about Queen Victoria; but if you want to understand Victorian artistic taste, off you go to Wolverhampton and thence to Wightwick Manor – which, you may be grateful to learn before you get there, is pronounced 'Wittick'. This timber-framed, mock-Tudor manor house was built by Theodore Mander, a local manufacturer of paints and varnishes who was also a dedicated follower of John Ruskin, William Morris and their friends. Having married an American lady happily named Flora Paint, he bought the Wightwick estate in 1887 and settled down to creating a shrine to the Pre-Raphaelites and of the Arts and Crafts movement that followed them. His collection was much increased by his son and daughter-in-law, and is now immaculately preserved by the National Trust.

The towering giant who cast his shadow over Victorian aesthetics from the 1840s on was John Ruskin. He wrote profusely about every aspect of art, from architecture to zoological drawing; the official edition of his collected works runs to thirty-nine heavy volumes. His literary style – if you like purple passages – is superb; but though few writers have ever been able to produce more magnificent single paragraphs or to encapsulate more brilliantly some lapidary truth – 'A single villa,' he wrote, 'can mar a landscape, and dethrone a dynasty of hills' – he is also capable of writing turgid nonsense by the ream. His masterpiece, *The Stones of Venice*, contains much breathtakingly beautiful prose, but is for most people quite unreadable except in abridged versions. He analyses, for example, the exterior decoration of the Doge's Palace in remorseless detail, with whole chapters dedicated to such matters as the development of the cusp; but there is barely a reference to the building as a three-dimensional enclosure of space, a total inability to see the wood for the trees. And it has always struck me as significant that the author of *The Seven Lamps of Architecture* should have bought his own house, at Coniston in the Lake District, sight unseen.

Ruskin had married the beautiful Effie Gray, but had been unwilling or unable to consummate the marriage; it was annulled after she had eloped with one of his principal friends and protégés, John Everett Millais, by whom she was to have eight children. Millais was one of the founders, with William Holman Hunt and Dante Gabriel Rossetti, of the Pre-Raphaelite Brotherhood; he was also by far its most talented member. The Brotherhood considered itself avant-garde, though it seems hard to apply such a description to a group who wanted to revert to the style and technique of the fifteenth century, with its brilliant colours and meticulous painting of nature, every flower, fern and frond lovingly delineated. Above all, it fervently believed that true art must be idealistic and spiritual – as opposed to the dreadful down-to-earth materialism of those so-called Impressionists across the Channel. For five months in 1850 it published a literary magazine, which might have lasted longer if it had not been called the *Germ*; but the whole movement soon disintegrated, with Millais changing his style and Rossetti going into business with his friends Edward Burne-Jones and William Morris.

William Morris was a visionary. Artist, writer, textile and

wallpaper designer, printer and socialist, he was as a youth deeply influenced by Ruskin's hatred of the all-too-prevalent tawdriness in art and architecture. What was vitally necessary was a return to old-fashioned craftsmanship, using hand tools rather than modern machinery, with artisans being raised to the status of artists. From this philosophy there sprang in about 1880 the Arts and Crafts movement, of which Morris was the leading light. It embraced every aspect of interior decoration, not only Morris's specialities of wallpaper and textiles but also furniture, lace-making, bookbinding, leather-work, carpets, decorative tiles and stained glass. It was in many ways a conscious reaction to the Great Exhibition of 1851, which had emphasized the importance of heavy machinery in manufacture. The Exhibition had looked forward to the future; Arts and Crafts looked back to the past, and in particular to the Middle Ages. This fascination with the medieval it had inherited from the Pre-Raphaelites and had also absorbed from the prevailing Gothic Revival, which extended roughly between 1830 and 1880. As Morris himself put it: 'Because craftsmen took pleasure in their work, the Middle Ages was a period of greatness in the art of the common people . . . The treasures of our museums now are only the common utensils used in households of that age, when hundreds of medieval churches – each one a masterpiece – were built by unsophisticated peasants.'

The Middle Ages also suggested the institution of the guild, a society of free craftsmen. In 1884 was founded the Art Workers Guild, which still exists today, as does the Society of Designer Craftsmen. Four years later C.R. Ashbee set up the Guild and School of Handicraft in London's East End. All these organizations, and many others like them, were the off-spring of Morris, who was – even more than Ruskin himself – the driving force behind English creative artistry in the latter half of the nineteenth century. And all this is illustrated, as nowhere else, at Wightwick Manor. Here are the William Morris wallpapers, textiles and carpets; here are tiles by William de Morgan, stained glass by Charles Kempe – names largely forgotten now but hugely important in their time – paintings and drawings by Millais, Holman Hunt, G.F. Watts, Ford Madox Brown and Edward Burne-Jones, whose *Love Among the Ruins* dominates the Great Parlour. Their late Victorian style may not be our taste today, but it is no longer mocked, as it was some fifty or sixty years ago. Any visit to Wightwick will be well rewarded indeed.

82

Sir Richard Burton's Tomb
MORTLAKE, SURREY

*I*t is not easy to find but is well worth seeking out, for it must be the strangest tomb in England. Tucked away in a corner of Mortlake Cemetery – it is actually in the church-yard of St Mary Magdalen's – is a sandstone reproduction of a tent, its walls rippling as if caught by the desert breeze. Oddly enough, it's not really a desert tent at all – no Bedouin would be seen dead in it – and it has a rather large crucifix over what would have been the entrance if it had had one. Within it lie the bodies of Sir Richard Burton – surely the most extraordinary figure in the history of the English explor-ation in Africa – and of his wife Isabel. If you want to see inside you must go round to the back, climb a little iron ladder and peer through a glass window. There are the two coffins, with a distinctly oleaginous religious painting above Isabel's and various pieces of oriental bric-à-brac lying higgledy-piggledy over the floor.

Burton deserves better – perhaps an obelisk like the one commemorating his fellow traveller (and arch-enemy) John Hanning Speke in Kensington Gardens. During his eleven years with the Indian army he proved a spectacular linguist; by his death he spoke twenty-nine languages. He performed many undercover operations for General Sir Charles Napier, commander-in-chief of the British Army in India, including the investigation of a male brothel in Karachi, on which he wrote a detailed and distressingly vivid report which got him into trouble later. Then in 1853 he was the first British non-Muslim to visit Mecca and Medina (having previously had himself circumcised to improve his disguise). There followed expeditions to Ethiopia – he was the first European to enter Harar – and Somalia. It was while he was in Aden that he met Speke, and prepared to embark on a journey with him and two other young officers into the interior of Africa; but before they could leave they were attacked by a band of 200 Somalis. One of the officers was killed; Speke was captured and was wounded eleven times before he managed to escape. Burton too escaped, but only after being transfixed by a javelin, the point of which entered through his right cheek and emerged from his left. Not surprisingly, the expedition was called off.

In 1857 Burton and Speke set off from Zanzibar on their grand expedition to find the great lakes of Central Africa, hoping that they might also stumble on the source of the Nile. The journey was a nightmare: unreliable bearers, stolen provisions and equipment and, worst of all, diseases. Speke was blind for much of the journey, and couldn't see Lake Tanganyika when he got there; Burton, too sick to walk, had to travel by litter and eventually was obliged to go home. Speke went on alone, and – his blindness gone – was rewarded by the sight of Lake Victoria, which he firmly believed was the source of the Nile.

From the start, the two detested each other. Speke was the typical imperialist army officer, despising the fuzzy-wuzzies and speaking no language but his own; Burton was – well, Burton. Their subsequent extremely public quarrel – during which Speke accused Burton of trying to poison him – was a huge embarrassment to the Royal Geographical Society, which had financed the expedition. Indeed, it may well have culminated in Speke's suicide, though this has never been proved. Both, however, were superbly intrepid men.

David Livingstone, by contrast, was a missionary. Travelling at the same time as the other two, he was the first European to see the Victoria Falls, which he renamed after his queen, and one of the first to cross the African continent from west to east. Like the others, he was an impossible man; his doctor recorded in 1862 that 'I can come to no other conclusion than that Dr Livingstone is out of his mind and a most unsafe leader,' and his alcoholic wife Mary didn't make his life any easier. His converts were few; but his contribution to our knowledge of the continent and to the cause of anti-slavery was immense, and it says much for his character that on his death his attendants – having insisted that his heart must be buried in Africa – carried his body over 1,000 miles so that it could be returned to Britain for burial. It now lies in Westminster Abbey.

Henry Morton Stanley is chiefly famous for having correctly identified David Livingstone – a story he very probably invented later. A Welshman by birth, he made his way to America when little more than a boy. There he fought on both sides in the Civil War, deserting from each and finally finding a job with the *New York Herald*, which sent him to Africa. After their meeting, he and Livingstone continued the journey together and eventually established that there was no connection between Lake Tanganyika and the Nile. After Livingstone's death Stanley set off on his most dangerous journey of all, to follow the course of the Congo River to the sea. Out of 356 participants, he was the only European to survive. His later exploits, arranging to take over large tracts of the Congo on behalf of the odious King Leopold II of the Belgians, do nothing for his reputation, any more than does the comment of one of his fellow travellers: 'Stanley shoots Negroes as if they were monkeys.'

Perhaps the most majestic of all these explorers was Samuel White Baker, KCB, FRS, who also held the titles of pasha and major-general in the Ottoman Empire and Egypt. He served as Governor-General of the Equatorial Nile Basin and he discovered Lake Albert. His wife, whom he had met when she was for sale in an Ottoman slave market, spoke German, Hungarian, Romanian and Arabic and accompanied him everywhere, riding camels as easily as horses and never venturing into the wilds without her pistols. He called her Flooey.

But no survey of the British discovery of Africa can be complete without a mention of Mary Kingsley. Dressed from head to foot in black bombazine, she concentrated on West Africa, first Sierra Leone and later Gabon, and had all the right ideas, arguing that 'a black man is no more an undeveloped white man than a rabbit is an undeveloped hare'. She hated missionaries for wanting to change the people of Africa, and for requiring converted men to leave all but one of their wives, thus depriving them of any support for their children. (She was all for polygamy anyway.) She died of typhoid at thirty-seven while nursing Boer prisoners, and was buried at sea.

All the above, except the last, had completed their achievements before the late 1870s, when the 'Struggle for Africa' began, with all the major countries of Europe wanting a slice of the cake. Some, like Leopold, were in it purely for profit; others sought increased trade, protection of other possessions, legitimate extraction of minerals or simply the swagger of imperialism. Burton, Speke, Livingston and Baker all got there before the unsavoury scramble; they all had high motivations, and I wish I could say as much for Stanley. As for Mary, she lived through the first part of the struggle, but I should be surprised if she knew anything about it. It wasn't the sort of thing she cared about.

Twentieth-Century
England

Introduction

With the accession of King Edward VII in January 1901, England was transformed overnight. The King at sixty was no longer young and, thanks to his mother's refusal to allow him any political responsibility – or even to see state papers – during her lifetime he had adopted the life of a royal playboy, racing and gambling and mixing in high (and not-so-high) society. This is perhaps the principal reason why the Edwardian decade tends to be seen as an age of garden parties, dirty weekends and long sunlit summer afternoons, those lucky enough to be enjoying them all oblivious of the oncoming storms. The impression is not altogether false – the First World War was a lot harder to predict than the Second was to be – but it does not of course tell the whole story. There was still abject poverty, and a yawning gap between rich and poor, even though it was very gradually narrowing.

In the field of technology, however, much exciting work was going on. The reign of King Edward saw the transmission of the first radio message; the first tentative steps were taken in the understanding of radioactivity; and at 5.07 a.m. on Sunday, 25 July 1909, Louis Blériot landed his home-made aeroplane on the cliffs above Dover. The age of air travel had begun. But the sands were rapidly running out: five years later the country – together with a good deal of Europe – was at war. Only four years later, from Britain alone, over 900,000 were dead.

King George V and Queen Mary – upright, virtuous, but as unbending and humourless a royal couple as England had ever seen – doubtless disapproved strongly of the vapid and pleasure-loving twenties, and indeed the thirties, though His Majesty saw only half of them. We can only be grateful that he was spared the knowledge of his eldest son's abdication less than a year after his own death; although, with hindsight and in view of King Edward VIII's character and pro-German inclinations, we can now be perfectly certain that this was the best thing that could have happened. King George VI and Queen Elizabeth, by contrast, filled the thankless role to perfection. We could have had no better royal family to see us through the war.

It seems barely credible that the period between the end of the First World War and the beginning of the Second should have been a mere twenty years, and that the entire life of Nazi Germany, from its rise to its fall, lasted just twelve. The war itself, despite the appalling civilian casualties caused by the air raids, resulted in only half the number of British casualties than we suffered in the First – some 450,000. (There were far more in central Europe, quite apart from the 7 million victims of the Holocaust.) But it left England – and the world – a different place. The empire, to begin with, was no longer tenable. Canada, Australia and New Zealand remained the virtually independent dominions they already were; our remaining possessions, or most of them, joined the Commonwealth. India and Pakistan were the first to gain their independence, in 1947; other territories followed suit, throughout the fifties and sixties. Only thirteen former colonies still keep, by their own choice, their British Governors.

The first huge post-war step forward was the establishment

in 1947, by the Labour government of Clement Attlee, of the welfare state and the National Health Service, with the government undertaking to look after every man and woman in the kingdom 'from the cradle to the grave' and health care 'free at the point of use'. It was of course generally accepted that the scheme would be formidably expensive; in fact it proved more so than even the pessimists had expected, and within three years charges were being made for spectacles, dentures and prescriptions. Still, it worked; and, over sixty years later – up to a point – it still does.

What have been the major achievements of the past half-century? One, certainly, has been what we all hope is the final solution of the Irish problem. Another has been our final success, after twelve years and a repeated veto from the French, in joining the European Community. Scotland and Wales have both received a measure of devolution, with their own Parliament and Assembly; and in Margaret Thatcher Britain has had its first female Prime Minister, who soon after taking over the government led us into a victorious war with Argentina in the Falkland Islands.

The two world wars alone make it impossible to describe the twentieth century as a happy one. On the other hand, it witnessed advances in science and technology of which nobody, in 1900, would have dared to dream. At its beginning, most transportation was still based on the horse; only two-thirds through its course, we had not only landed men on the moon, we were able to watch the landings in our own homes. By the time it ended, we could fly to any spot on earth within forty-eight hours, and to most within twenty-four. If this rate of progress continues, one almost fears to speculate on what the twenty-first century will bring.

83

Lizard Marconi Wireless Station
CORNWALL

Till Belvoir's lordly terraces the sign to Lincoln sent,
And Lincoln spread the message on o'er the wide vale of Trent;
Till Skiddaw saw the fire that burned on Gaunt's embattled pile,
And the red glare on Skiddaw roused the burghers of Carlisle . . .

*I*n the old days it was the beacons: the succession of enormous bonfires, each of them within sight of the next, which in times of emergency could be used to pass important news across the country in a matter of hours – perhaps even minutes. Their moment of greatest glory came, as Macaulay describes, on the sighting of the first ships of the Spanish Armada in 1588. But beacons were uncertain things at the best of times; they were, for example, useless after heavy rain, and they could never hope to cross any but the narrowest stretches of sea. It was not until 1866, with the laying of the first successful transatlantic cable by Isambard Kingdom Brunel's *Great Eastern*, that a message could be sent across the ocean in less time than it took a steamship to carry it. For thirty-five years the cable was supreme; then, in an otherwise insignificant corner of Cornwall, it too met its challenge.

It did so at Poldhu, on the west coast of the Lizard peninsula, on 12 December 1901, when the famous Italian inventor and physicist Guglielmo Marconi* – winner of the 1909 Nobel Prize, but then only twenty-seven years old – having set up a 152-metre kite-supported antenna mast, sent a radio message the 3,500 kilometres to Signal Hill in St John's, Newfoundland. A tall granite pillar marks the spot today. It must be admitted that this remarkable scientific achievement was greeted with a degree of scepticism: the signals – which consisted only of the Morse code letter S (---) sent repeatedly – were extremely faint, and barely distinguishable through the atmospheric noise. But Marconi went a long way towards justifying his claim in the following year when, while crossing the Atlantic on SS *Philadelphia*, he picked up daily transmissions from Poldhu at a distance of some 3,400 kilometres. The Lizard Wireless Station, as it is called, has been beautifully restored by the National Trust, and contains several gloriously primitive-looking pieces of original equipment. It set another record in April 1910, when it received the first ever SOS message to be received by a coast station – two years before the *Titanic*. In the same hut there is an amateur radio station (GB2LD), from which radio amateurs are welcome to operate: they receive, I understand, a special certificate for doing so.

In his later years, Marconi rather lost his pre-eminence; others, younger than he, showed more brilliance and inventiveness and cast him rather into the shade. On the other hand, he became a considerable public figure in his native Italy, where he was made first a senator, then a marquis. After 1922 he became a prominent member of the Fascist Party; at his

---

* If I may be allowed a brief personal note: I remember Marconi, who was a friend of my mother's. She had recently bought her first radiogram, which developed a slight fault. He offered to mend it for her. It never worked again.

second wedding in 1927, Mussolini was his best man. When he died in 1937 he was given a state funeral, and all the radio stations across the world observed a two-minute silence.

But we must return to the Lizard. Clearly visible from the Wireless Station a few hundred yards along the coast, is a large white cube. This is the old Lloyd's Signal Station, a fact that is made all too clear – in gigantic and quite unnecessary black lettering – when you approach it. Built in 1900 and the oldest surviving purpose-built wireless communications centre in the world, it served to test and monitor the transmissions from Poldhu. It was there, already on 23 January 1901, that Marconi had received the first signals from the Isle of Wight, 186 miles away. Like the Wireless Station, it has been immaculately restored to its pristine state.

For those who know rather more about wireless telegraphy than I do, the Lizard is a place of pilgrimage. So too is the neighbouring Goonhilly Down, now registered as a Site of Special Scientific Interest. Goonhilly was at one time the largest satellite earth station in the world, possessing no fewer than twenty-five communications dishes in use, with another forty or so held in reserve. On 11 July 1962 the very first of these dishes, Antenna One – known to its intimates as Arthur – received the first live transatlantic television broadcasts from the United States via the Telstar satellite. Arthur is twenty-six metres in diameter; his companion Merlin is even larger – thirty-two metres. Other dishes include Guinevere, Tristan and Isolde: here in west Cornwall the Arthurian legend is still very much alive. Alas, all these great saucers have now assumed the status of ancient monuments: BT closed down Goonhilly in 2008 and moved its operations to Madley Communications Centre in Herefordshire. Until May 2010 there remained an excellent and highly informative Visitor Centre, but now that too has closed, though there are hopes that it may one day reopen. Visitors may – or may not – console themselves with the sight of a nearby wind farm, consisting of fourteen 400-kilowatt turbines, and a neighbouring exhibition of Cornish camels.

The Lizard marks the southernmost tip of England, just as nearby Land's End marks the westernmost. The whole area is absurdly romantic, though many people have complained that the immense satellite dishes, the wind turbines and the radio masts ruin its previously unspoilt beauty. So, in a way, they do – although they are still invisible from large areas of the peninsula. On the other hand, in our twenty-first-century world, in which the whole science of telecommunications has assumed an importance of which Marconi, his colleagues and his many rivals could never have dreamed, surely the monuments of those early pioneering days possess a romance and beauty of their own, to which the superb surroundings provide a magnificent background.

Tomb of Sir Richard Burton, Mortlake, Surrey. Surely the dottiest tomb in England, it was erected in 1890 by his widow to the memory of the great explorer, writer and soldier. Stone is not perhaps the most suitable material with which to build a tent; thanks to the resultant inflexibility, entrance is by ladder at the back.

The Lizard Marconi Wireless Station, Cornwall. I have never been much of a man for radio-communications, but even I can understand the excitement of those first barely audible bleeps. And no one was to know whither they would lead . . .

Tattenham Corner, Epsom Racecourse, Surrey.
Emily Wilding Davison's desperate act marked that dread moment when legitimate campaigning gives way to single-issue fanaticism; the Suffragette Movement was never to be the same again.

The Daily Mirror 24 Pages

THE MORNING JOURNAL WITH THE SECOND LARGEST NET SALE.

No. 3,060.   THURSDAY, JUNE 5, 1913   One Halfpenny.

WOMAN RUSHES ON THE DERBY COURSE AND SNATCHES AT THE BRIDLE OF THE KING'S HORSE, INJURING HERSELF AND THE JOCKEY.

PHIL COOPER

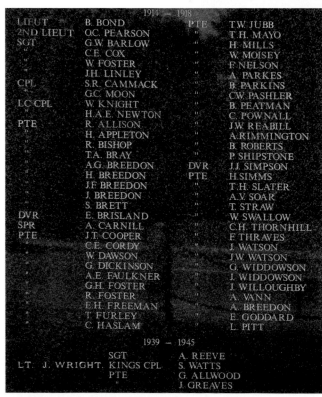

1914 — 1918

LIEUT	B. BOND	PTE	T.W. JUBB	
2ND LIEUT	O.C. PEARSON	"	T.H. MAYO	
SGT	G.W. BARLOW	"	H. MILLS	
"	C.E. COX	"	W. MOISEY	
"	W. FOSTER	"	F. NELSON	
"	J.H. LINLEY	"	A. PARKES	
CPL	S.R. CAMMACK	"	B. PARKINS	
"	G.C. MOON	"	C.W. PASHLER	
LC·CPL	W. KNIGHT	"	B. PEATMAN	
"	H.A.E. NEWTON	"	C. POWNALL	
PTE	R. ALLISON	"	J.W. REABILL	
"	H. APPLETON	"	A. RIMMINGTON	
"	R. BISHOP	"	B. ROBERTS	
"	T.A. BRAY	"	P. SHIPSTONE	
"	A.G. BREEDON	DVR	J.J. SIMPSON	
"	H. BREEDON	PTE	H. SIMMS	
"	J.F. BREEDON	"	T.H. SLATER	
"	J. BREEDON	"	A.V. SOAR	
"	S. BRETT	"	T. STRAW	
DVR	E. BRISLAND	"	W. SWALLOW	
SPR	A. CARNILL	"	C.H. THORNHILL	
PTE	J.T. COOPER	"	F. THRAVES	
"	C.E. CORDY	"	J. WATSON	
"	W. DAWSON	"	J.W. WATSON	
"	G. DICKINSON	"	G. WIDDOWSON	
"	A.E. FAULKNER	"	J. WIDDOWSON	
"	G.H. FOSTER	"	J. WILLOUGHBY	
"	R. FOSTER	"	A. VANN	
"	E.H. FREEMAN	"	A. BREEDON	
"	T. FURLEY	"	E. GODDARD	
"	C. HASLAM	"	L. PITT	

1939 — 1945

	SGT	A. REEVE
LT. J. WRIGHT.	KINGS CPL	S. WATTS
	PTE	G. ALLWOOD
"		J. GREAVES

War Memorial, Loudham, Nottinghamshire.

Jarrow Crusade Memorial, Tyne and Wear. Was Jarrow a damp squib? I fear it may have been; it certainly deserved better. Still, it entered history and produced a fine memorial in the town – whose name, at least, now lives for ever.

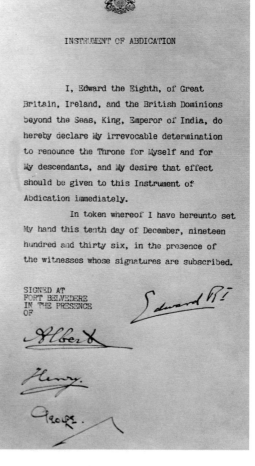

Fort Belvedere, Windsor, Berkshire. Look at Magna Carta, or any of the great legal instruments of English history. Then look at this: a single typed sheet that many of us believe did more than change a King; it saved a nation.

INSTRUMENT OF ABDICATION

I, Edward the Eighth, of Great Britain, Ireland, and the British Dominions beyond the Seas, King, Emperor of India, do hereby declare My irrevocable determination to renounce the Throne for Myself and for My descendants, and My desire that effect should be given to this Instrument of Abdication immediately.

In token whereof I have hereunto set My hand this tenth day of December, nineteen hundred and thirty six, in the presence of the witnesses whose signatures are subscribed.

SIGNED AT
FORT BELVEDERE
IN THE PRESENCE
OF

Coventry Cathedral.
14 November 1940: that is the date etched and burnished into the history of Coventry; this aerial view, taken the following morning, is one of the most moving photographs I know. But of the devastation, Basil Spence's third cathedral was soon to be born, together with two sublime masterpieces: Graham Sutherland's tapestry of *Christ in Glory* and Benjamin Britten's *War Requiem*.

The Hangar at Heston, Middlesex. Flying was still an excitement in itself and all eyes were on Heston, with hundreds driving there almost daily to see the Prime Minister Neville Chamberlain off or to welcome him home during those dark days of 1938. Few of us could even find the place today.

The Churchill War Rooms, London. How different the world was. While Neville Chamberlain was Prime Minister and spent his weekends at Chequers, the house had only one telephone, and that was in the kitchen. These War Rooms, on the other hand, represented the cutting edge of technology, unlike the Transatlantic Telephone Room which could easily have been mistaken for a broom cupboard.

Hut 8, Bletchley Park, Buckinghamshire.
There is strong reason to argue that without the work done in this curiously unlovely mansion the Second World War might have been lost, or at least prolonged by another two or even four years. This was the Government Code and Cipher School, to which the German Enigma signals – the most important in the war – soon revealed their secrets.

Watford Gap Motorway Service Area. Watford Gap – apart from having been for centuries a key location on Britain's road system – symbolizes the opening of our first section of motorway. The Blue Boar Café was opened on the same day in 1959.

The Thatcher Plaque, Grantham. Lincolnshire. The town, I believe, should be feeling a little ashamed of itself. A statue would perhaps have been premature; but for the first woman prime minister, surely a bust would have been appropriate? If a plaque it had to be, on her father's corner shop, then perhaps a date or two, and just a little space around the edges?

Greenham Common, Newbury, Berkshire. For nineteen long years, from 1981 to 2000, a large body of women were part of the Berkshire scenery, inhabiting a sort of gypsy camp just outside the RAF and USAF air base in protest against the decision to install 96 nuclear Cruise missiles.

The National Theatre, London. In my youth, the two British institutions of which I was proudest were the BBC and the National Trust. I have since added a third. The National Theatre seems to me to be the success story of the past half-century; it has enriched our whole theatrical world in a way I should never have believed possible.

Shakespeare Cliff, Kent. Forget about Eurostar, though it has changed all our lives for the better. The point is that England remains an island, and still presents to the returning traveller from across the Channel that unforgettable prospect of the White Cliffs which, particularly during the invasion threat of 1940, became a symbol of resistance and courage.

84

Bateman's
EAST SUSSEX

*B*ateman's is a perfectly nice seventeenth-century house in the Sussex Weald, but it has always struck me as somehow dark and chilly. However, Rudyard Kipling and his American wife Carrie seem to have been as happy there as they ever were – which was, I suspect, not very happy. The Kiplings bought the house in 1902; it came with a mill and thirty-three acres and it cost them £9,300. The price would probably have been a little higher had there been a bathroom, electricity or any running water apart from a cold tap in the kitchen; but they loved it, and that was all that mattered. There had been a mill on that spot since 1196, though Kipling's dated from only about 1750. Nevertheless, he had no compunction about tearing out all the grinding mechanism and installing instead a water turbine that drove a generator. This, we are told, produced enough current to light ten sixty-watt bulbs for about four hours every evening. The house, now owned by the National Trust and open to the public, has barely changed since Kipling's time, and the great man's venerable Phantom I Rolls-Royce still lurks in the garage.

Rudyard Kipling is always thought of in connection with India, the subject of a thousand poems and short stories as well as that of his only great novel, *Kim*. In fact he lived there only for the first six years of his life and then for eight more years, working as a journalist, from the ages to sixteen to twenty-four. It was his happiest time. Already speaking fluent Hindustani, unshackled by army or Indian Civil Service, he could mix in every *milieu*, from that of the hopeful English girls – known locally as 'the fishing fleet' – newly arrived in Delhi or Simla, to the earthiness of the barrack room or the exoticism of the bazaar. Thus it was that by 1886 there suddenly appeared the first writer of real stature that British India had ever produced – an overworked young man of twenty-one, filling the vacant spaces of his newspaper with short stories and satirical verses that quickly made his name a household word. By the time he left, he had produced – not counting two books part-written with other members of his family – no fewer than nine volumes of poetry and prose. Two years later, by the end of 1891, the total had risen to sixteen.

What did he really feel about the empire? Certainly, in his youth Kipling was no dyed-in-the-wool imperialist. Mr Nirad C. Chaudhuri – author of several superb prize-winning books on his native country – once assured me that *Kim* was the best ever written. No one else, he claimed, British or Indian, had succeeded in embracing, in a single vision, all its classes and castes and religions. Moreover Kipling writes with love: there is no suggestion of racial superiority. As in nearly all his Indian stories, the natives are infinitely more sympathetic, and often a good deal wiser, than the British, while Christian missionaries come off worst of all. Of course Kim ultimately joins the Secret Service: he would have known that British rule was the best thing – not necessarily for Britain but for India; that the British were good rulers, the ICS being on the whole kind, competent, selfless and incorruptible; and, finally, that if they were ever to leave there would be bloodshed on a huge and hideous scale. How right he was.

And that brings us to a basic tenet of Kipling's imperialist philosophy: the concept of the empire as a duty, based not on what can be got out of subject peoples but what can be contributed to their education and welfare.

> *Take up the White Man's burden –*
> *Send forth the best ye breed –*
> *Go, bind your sons to exile*
> *To serve your captives' need;*
> *To wait in heavy harness*
> *On fluttered folk and wild –*
> *Your new-caught, sullen peoples,*
> *Half devil and half child.*

Patronizing? Of course it is, to our modern sensibilities; but in 1898 it would have struck people very differently. And note, please, that marvellous word 'fluttered'. Could anyone but Kipling have used it? I don't think so.

The appearance of *Kim* in 1901 coincided with the height of the Boer War, caused by the natural reluctance of the two Boer (originally Dutch) republics to accept the British idea of unifying the whole of South Africa under the imperial flag. In October 1899 the Boers invaded Natal and Cape Province and immediately besieged three towns, Ladysmith, Mafeking and Kimberley. The British thought – not for the last time – that it would all be over by Christmas; in fact it dragged on till May 1902. Kipling flung himself into the cause heart and soul. Not only were the Boers rebels; their attitude to black Africans was precisely what he most deplored. How, he demanded, could we accept a people who crowded no fewer than 20,000 of them into sixty-six different concentration camps, raping vast numbers of the women? He travelled ceaselessly backwards and forwards to South Africa, writing, lecturing, reporting and, incidentally, getting his first and last experience of battle. It was a small, inconclusive engagement to which he was taken by a native driver in a bullock cart – all his life he was terrified of horses – and it is unlikely that his life was seriously at risk; but it thrilled him to the core and enabled him, he felt, to write still more graphically of the army in the field.

It comes even now as something of a surprise to read that Kipling's idea of manliness as immortalized in 'If' – one of the most famous of all his poems – was based on the character of that most pig-headed of men Sir Leander Starr Jameson, whose notorious raid on 29 December 1895, undertaken after six attempts to stop him, resulted in sixty-five of his own men killed and wounded, the Boers losing just one. Jameson was later sentenced to fifteen months' imprisonment in Holloway. No wonder that a friend of mine used to keep above his desk a framed inscription reading: 'If you can keep your head when all around you are losing theirs and blaming it on you – could it be that you have incorrectly appraised the situation?'

Does Rudyard Kipling deserve his reputation? First, just what is that reputation? Few writers in all literature are more loved or loathed: hardly any reader, as C.S. Lewis pointed out, 'likes him a little'. By the age of thirty, his fame had spread all over the world. And yet, although he remained a celebrity till the end of his life and his books continued to sell in huge numbers, his reputation began to decline soon after the Boer War. His award of the Nobel Prize for Literature in 1907 aroused a howl of protest. Yet he remains a giant: frequently vulgar and tasteless – as is the way of giants – and occasionally downright nauseating, but a giant none the less. What is more, he was his own giant. His subject matter, his viewpoint, his opinions, his style both in verse and prose – all were his and his alone. Few writers have owed less to their predecessors, just as few have given more to the language. His values may not be our values, but however firmly we may reject them we cannot deny the brilliance with which they are expressed, a brilliance that has given them – and their author – immortality.

85

British Motor Museum

BEAULIEU, HAMPSHIRE

I f you go to the British Motor Museum at Beaulieu today
you will find, nestling among the 250-odd milestones
in the history of the motor car – Sir Malcolm Campbell's
Sunbeam, Donald Campbell's *Bluebird*, several of James
Bond's Aston Martins (suitably tarted up by Q) and the flying
Ford Anglia from the Harry Potter films – a small but fascinating collection of various versions of *The Spirit of Ecstasy*.
She still graces the front bonnets of Rolls-Royce cars, and she
embodies a secret: the secret passion of the second Lord
Montagu of Beaulieu for his secretary, Miss Eleanor Velasco
Thornton. (Photographs of Miss Thornton strongly suggest
that the statuette was in no sense intended to be a representation of her person; rather the emotions she inspired in His
Lordship.) Their love continued until her death – rather surprisingly by torpedo, when the ship in which the two were
travelling to India in 1915 encountered a German submarine
off Crete.

Other people have, however, over the past two centuries,
made rather more distinguished contributions to the history
of English motoring than Eleanor Velasco Thornton. In 1801
the inhabitants of Camborne in Cornwall had a Yuletide to
remember: it was Christmas Eve when Richard Trevithick
mounted his steam carriage – which he called the Puffing

Devil – and successfully carried several men up Camborne Hill to the nearby village of Beacon. Unfortunately it caught fire four days later, but in 1803 Trevithick had another go. This time he drove his machine – rather more pompously known as the London Steam Carriage – from Holborn to Paddington and back. It was considered a pity that its passengers were literally black and blue by the end; another – and far more serious – drawback was that it practically caused a general stampede of London's horses. Still, a giant step for mankind had been taken: the first working motor vehicle had travelled, however painfully, over an English road.

And Richard Trevithick had started something. Less than sixty years later, in 1861, a panicky Parliament had inaugurated that interminable process of motor vehicle legislation that continues even today to overshadow our lives. In 1865 there had followed the Locomotive Act, which set a speed limit of four miles an hour in the country and two in towns, and required each machine to have a crew of three, one of whom should walk sixty yards in front brandishing a red flag. It wasn't till 1896 that, in a sudden burst of devil-may-care recklessness, our legislators shrugged off the crew and upped the speed limit to 14 m.p.h. In that same year the Daimler chief Harry J. Lawson organized the first London-to-Brighton car run – which still continues – to celebrate Emancipation Day. It began with a breakfast at the Charing Cross Hotel, which included the symbolic tearing in two by Lord Winchelsea of a red flag.

By now things were hotting up. The first British-built car (Daimler again) had been driven from John o'Groats to Land's End; the intrepid Dr E.C. Lehwess had made the first attempt to drive round the world in a Panhard Levassor bus felicitously named 'Passe-Partout' (he made it as far as

Nizhni-Novgorod, where the snow defeated him); and in 1903 we suffered the by now inevitable Motor Car Act, introducing the concept of driving licences and the registration and numbering of cars. (Doubtless to soften the blow, the speed limit simultaneously went up to twenty.) Finally there was another Motor Car Act in 1921. It was not popular, since it taxed cars for the first time – at £1 per RAC horsepower. Fortunately, however, there was an important exemption: no tax of any kind was payable on cars that were used solely for taking one's servants to church.

Who were the heroes of the English motor industry? One of the founding fathers, certainly, was Frederick Richard Simms, who took part in that first London–Brighton run and made a significant contribution to the English language by founding the Royal Automobile Club and inventing two of our most useful and commonly used words: *petrol* and *motor-car*. Though 'of an old Warwickshire family', he was born and brought up in Germany and was bilingual in German, so it was no great surprise when in 1889 he teamed up with Gottlieb Daimler, from whom he bought the rights to use and manufacture Daimler's high-speed petrol engine. For the next forty years he was active – and unfailingly inventive – in the fast-developing industry: there were Simms-Welbeck cars, lorries and marine engines, Simms magnetos, Simms rubber bumpers, Simms dynamos and spark plugs. Such was his serendipity that he even discovered a previously unknown waterfall in Austria, now happily known as the Simmswasserfall.

Simms was obviously a character; William Richard Morris, later Viscount Nuffield, was not. Starting his career at the age of fifteen by repairing bicycles, he worked up steadily through motorcycles to cars, buying up bankrupt car companies and steadily developing the huge works at Cowley,

Oxford. He was a generous philanthropist: having no children of his own, he spent most of his immense fortune on his Nuffield Foundation and on Nuffield College, Oxford; yet somehow, for all his good works, he obstinately fails to come alive. Inspired and industrious as he undoubtedly was, life at nearby Nuffield Place was not, I strongly suspect, a barrel of fun.

It was one of those great historic encounters – the greatest, perhaps, since Stanley ran into Livingstone – when on Wednesday, 4 May 1904, at the Midland Hotel, Manchester, Charles Stewart Rolls and Henry Royce met for lunch. Their backgrounds could hardly have been more different: Rolls was an Old Etonian and aristocrat; Royce, fifteen years older, had started his professional life as a telegraph boy. But Rolls, who had recently opened a business selling luxury cars, was embarrassed by having no British model on his list, and when shown photographs of the ten-horsepower car that Royce had just produced, was instantly struck by its quality. The two men took to each other at once.

The rest is history. The stage was set for Eleanor Velasco Thornton and ultimately the 31 million cars on our roads today.

86

Tattenham Corner
EPSOM DOWNS RACECOURSE, SURREY

*I*t was Derby Day at Epsom, 4 June 1913. King George V's horse, Anmer, was not doing well; he was third from last as he thundered round Tattenham Corner before coming into the straight towards the finishing line and the royal box. Then suddenly a small dark figure pushed her way under the rails and flung herself in front of him, brandishing the purple, white and green banner of the suffragettes, inscribed VOTES FOR WOMEN. Anmer fell, but struggled to his feet again and finished the race, riderless. His jockey, Herbert Jones, wearing the King's colours, was thrown and left on the ground, suffering from broken ribs and concussion. After thirty-eight years during which he claimed to be 'haunted by that woman's face', he committed suicide in 1951. The suffragette was rushed to hospital, where she died four days later of a fractured skull and serious internal injuries.

Her name was Emily Wilding Davison. As head steward of the Women's Social and Political Unit she had already served six or seven prison terms for hurling rocks – some of them labelled 'bomb' – at government ministers' cars, going on repeated hunger strikes and setting fire to pillar-boxes. She had also furiously attacked a man she believed – erroneously – to be David Lloyd George. She had even flung herself off a prison balcony and down a thirty-foot stairwell. Whether on

Derby Day she had deliberately intended to take her own life is uncertain; her handbag contained a return ticket to London and an invitation to a suffragette meeting that night. In any case she was surely justified in hoping that this time she would at least be taken seriously. Alas, she wasn't. She was written off as 'a mentally ill fanatic', and some previous champions of the suffragette movement were so shocked as to withdraw their support. The newspapers showed themselves far more interested in the well-being of the horse and jockey – particularly the horse.

But the movement went on. It is hard to say when it started; perhaps, in a primitive form, immediately after the Reform Bill of 1832, which first excluded women from the electorate. It was drawn into focus, however, by Emmeline Pankhurst, who with her two daughters Christabel and Sylvia founded the Women's Franchise League in 1889 and the WSPU in 1903. The other giants in the suffragette establishment were two other sisters: Millicent Fawcett, who in 1897 formed the National Union of Women's Suffrage Societies, and Elizabeth Garrett Anderson, the first woman in Britain to gain a medical doctorate and the first to be elected mayor of a town (Aldeburgh, Suffolk, in 1908). Nor should we forget the perfectly magnificent Dame Ethel Smyth, whom I remember well as a child. She had been allowed to study music in Leipzig, where she had known Clara Schumann and Brahms. In 1911 she wrote 'The March of the Women', which became the suffragette anthem. After breaking a prodigious number of windows she served two months in Holloway Prison, where Sir Thomas Beecham went to visit her. He found the many suffragette prisoners marching round the prison yard singing, as Ethel Smyth leaned out of a window conducting with her toothbrush. At the age of seventy-one she was to fall passionately in love with Virginia Woolf, who said it was 'like being caught by a giant crab'.

In the previous year, Lady Constance Lytton had gone on hunger strike, the normal punishment for which was known as 'force feeding', in which nutrition was rammed into the body – usually but not invariably down the throat – often with unspeakable brutality. Suspecting that her title would ensure her special treatment, Lady Constance adopted the name and disguise of a working-class seamstress and received the worst the prison authorities could give – to which her tragically early death was later ascribed. Another victim of force feeding was Emmeline Pankhurst, which is why in March 1914 Mary Richardson slashed the 'Rokeby Venus', declaring that she was maiming a beautiful woman just as the government was maiming another. All through those years and months leading up to the First World War the incidents grew worse, to the point where many of them – the bombing of churches and public buildings, for example, including Westminster Abbey – would nowadays be described as terrorism. Those banners of purple, white and green – 'purple stands for the royal blood that flows in the veins of every suffragette, white for purity in private and public life, green is the colour of hope and the emblem of spring' – began to strike terror into the hearts of politicians.

But with the outbreak of the First World War in August 1914 Emmeline and Sylvia, convinced that the defeat of Germany was more important even than women's suffrage, persuaded the WSPU to suspend all operations, while the NUWSS continued its activities by dignified correspondence only. Meanwhile the serious manpower shortage on the home front made it necessary for women to take on many of the traditional male duties, thus showing the world just what they were capable of doing. This led logically enough to the Representation of the People Act, 1918, which, gingerly and with infinite caution, allowed the vote to women over thirty who figured or whose husbands figured on the Local Government Register. It wasn't for another ten years that women received the vote on the same terms as men – over the age of twenty-one. (The age was reduced to eighteen – for both sexes – in 1969.)

At last the cause of women's suffrage had, after the better part of half a century, achieved its object. In doing so, it had shown just how determined women could be in the defence of what they believed to be right. The sweet delusion, so long cherished by men, of the little woman waiting obediently at home and having the dinner hot by the time he returned had to be radically revised. Now, as the old music-hall song ran:

> *Put me on an island where the girls are few,*
> *Put me amongst the most ferocious lions in the zoo,*
> *Put me on a treadmill, and I'll never fret,*
> *But for pity's sake don't put me with a suffragette.*

87

War Memorial

LOWDHAM, NOTTINGHAMSHIRE

*T*here are thousands of town and village war memorials up and down the country, any one of which could be substituted for that of Lowdham. The village today has a population of some 2,000; in 1914 that figure would have been appreciably less – perhaps 1,000 or so. That means 500-odd males, of whom let us say 200 may have been of fighting age. These figures are obviously very approximate; what is all too clear is the list of those men of Lowdham killed during the First World War. It numbers sixty-two. The Breedon family alone contributed five.

So much has been written about that war that it's hard to know where to begin. I was born only eleven years after it ended, and my early childhood was still gently overshadowed by it, for it was even then a topic of daily conversation. My father, who as a member of the Foreign Service had been allowed to join the army only in 1917, had survived; had he gone to France with most of his friends in 1914, it is extremely unlikely that I should be sitting here at my desk today. There was something almost inevitable about the slaughter; I remember my mother telling me that by the end of 1916 every single man she had ever danced with was dead. During the Second World War, thank heaven, this never happened to anything like the same degree: only four more names were added to Lowdham's memorial. For all its horrors, that second war was more fluid, more mobile, and above all more merciful than its predecessor. Soldiers were on the whole spared that nightmarish trench warfare that proved such a torment to body and spirit alike, when a young man of twenty knew that his probable life expectancy was about six weeks.

And why? That was another anguish. In 1939 the image of Hitler and the Nazi Party was clear in our minds; we all knew exactly what we were fighting for. In 1914 we didn't. Why should the killing of an overweight Austrian archduke by an adolescent Serb mean that whole families of Englishmen should be mown down like flies? And who, anyway, were the Serbs when they were at home? We were told that it was something to do with keeping the peace in the Balkans; why couldn't the Balkans keep their own peace? Anyway, most of those men lying in the mud would have been hard put to it to find the bloody Balkans on the map.

Of all warfare, that of the trenches was perhaps, in the long term, the cruellest of all. Not only was there the constant threat of death – on the first day of the Somme we lost 57,000 – often in the messiest and most painful form imaginable. There was the cold, the foot-deep mud, the lice – which caused not only unbearable itching day and night, but also trench fever – and the millions of rats, which gnawed at you as you tried to sleep; the brown variety could grow to the size of a cat. To top all this, at the beginning of the Second Battle of Ypres on 22 April 1915, there appeared a new horror. Around 5 p.m. sentries noticed a curious yellow-green cloud drifting slowly towards their line. It was chlorine gas. Within seconds of inhalation it destroyed a man's lungs, virtually choking him to death. Now the gloves were off; the French and British armies were both to use gas in later battles. Fortunately it was to prove an ultimately unsatisfactory weapon – the wind had only to change a little for it to be blown back in the user's face – but the psychological effect was huge, to the point where simply to use the word 'gas' was a punishable offence; the gas canisters were always delicately known as 'accessories'. None the less, as in so many other wars, the biggest killer was disease. Dysentery, typhus, cholera, trench mouth, trench foot – not to mention exposure in the devastating cold of the winter months. These were just some of the sufferings that were visited on those sixty-two miserable men whose names figure on the Lowdham memorial, and on the many more who were lucky enough to survive, a good many of whom may nevertheless have sustained hideous injuries.

Despite everything, there were moments of exhilaration. On 25 August 1918 my father wrote to my mother:

> [That moment] was followed by the most glorious of my life. A full moon, a star to guide us, a long line of cheering men, an artillery barrage as beautiful as any fireworks creeping on before us, a feeling of wild and savage joy . . . I was the first of my Company in the German trench. I boast like a Gascon, but it was what the old poets said war was, and what the new poets say it isn't.

He was right. The new poets did indeed say it wasn't:

> *What passing-bells for these who die as cattle?*
> *Only the monstrous anger of the guns.*
> *Only the stuttering rifles' rapid rattle*
> *Can patter out their hasty orisons . . .*

So wrote Wilfred Owen, perhaps the most moving of all those whom we have learned to call the war poets: Rupert Brooke, Siegfried Sassoon, Robert Graves, Edward Thomas and the rest. He ends his sonnet:

Their flowers the tenderness of patient minds,
And each slow dusk a drawing-down of blinds.

Benjamin Britten set it magnificently in his *War Requiem*, which I remember hearing soon after it was written in the early sixties, with Dietrich Fischer-Dieskau – most importantly a German – singing the baritone part. When it drew to its close, there was a silence of a good ten seconds before the audience was able to recover sufficiently to applaud – but what applause there was when they did.

Owen was killed exactly one week before the signing of the Armistice. His mother received the dreaded telegram on Armistice Day itself, as the church bells were ringing out in celebration. Sixty-seven years later, on 11 November 1985, her son was one of sixteen Great War poets commemorated in Poets' Corner, Westminster Abbey. The inscription on the stone is this:

MY SUBJECT IS WAR, AND THE PITY OF WAR.
THE POETRY IS IN THE PITY.

The words could have been equally well inscribed on the Lowdham memorial.

88

Jarrow Crusade Memorial
TYNE AND WEAR

J arrow is celebrated in English history for three things: the early medieval monastery that housed the Venerable Bede; the huge shipyards that were the lifeblood of the town; and the Jarrow Crusade, the protest march that took place in October 1936 from the smallish town at the mouth of the River Tyne to the Palace of Westminster in London – a distance of very nearly 300 miles. It was organized after the closure of the shipyards as a result of the Great Depression of the 1930s. The 200-odd marchers were nearly a month on their journey, finally reaching their destination on 31 October. Four days later their local Member of Parliament, Miss (later Dame) Ellen Wilkinson – better known as 'Red Ellen' – who had marched much of the way with them, handed in to Parliament a petition bearing 12,000 signatures, seeking government aid for Jarrow. The town now prominently displays a memorial in the form of a collection of five statues – two of them children – representing the marchers and carrying a banner.

The march itself seems to have been quite a spirited affair, ablaze with blue and white banners, accompanied by a second-hand bus full of cooking equipment and a mouth-organ band. The organizers had insisted that all those participating should have medical certificates that they were fit to do so. (There was a separate march of 200 blind people.) Women and Communists were barred. Many of the twenty-one towns where they stopped overnight gave them enthusiastic welcomes, Barnsley even opening its heated public baths specially for their benefit. (Miss Wilkinson got the Ladies' Foam Bath to herself.) And yet, somehow, it was all a bit of a flop. Stanley Baldwin, the Prime Minister, refused to receive any of the marchers or their representatives, on the typically English grounds that he was too busy and that 'it would set a dangerous precedent'. The demonstration on 1 November at Hyde Park Corner was sparsely attended. The petition itself was accepted by the Speaker with a single sentence of acknowledgement, after which the House returned to the business in hand. There is no indication that anybody ever read it. Polite sympathy was expressed to the exhausted marchers, but virtually nothing was done for them – except that each man was given £1 with which to buy a railway ticket back to Jarrow.

The marchers – or the crusaders, as they described themselves – deserved better. Only thirty years before, at the beginning of the twentieth century, more than a quarter of the world's shipping tonnage was built in north-east England, and theirs had been a boom town. Directly or indirectly, the shipyards had given employment to thousands; now they were gone. Unemployment had reached about 70 per cent. Unemployment benefit lasted for only twenty-six weeks, and many families had been in trouble for very much longer than that. As Ellen Wilkinson herself was to write three years later:

> There was no work. No one had a job except a few railway-men, officials, the workers in the co-operative stores, and a few workmen who went out of the town . . . The plain fact is that if people have to live and bear and bring up their

children in bad houses on too little food, their resistance to disease is lowered and they die before they should.

Much of this distress was of course due to the Great Depression that had been hanging over Europe and America since 1929. But if we are really to understand both the physical and the psychological strains from which working-class England was suffering, we must go back further than that, to the end of the First World War. Had not David Lloyd George promised that his coalition government would make Britain 'a land fit for heroes to live in'? What had gone wrong? On 4 February 1920 a letter appeared in *The Times* signed 'Ex-Battery Commander'. He wrote:

> During the War all those that put on the King's uniform had a great access of friends. We were heroes in those days ... When at last we came home, were demobilised and doffed our uniforms, we realised how much our welcome had depended on the glamour of our clothes ... In mufti we were no longer heroes, we were simply 'unemployed', an unpleasant problem.

And that problem grew steadily worse – culminating in the General Strike of 1926 which, to put it mildly, put the wind up the government far more than the poor Jarrow marchers were able to do ten years later. Whereas the Jarrow men were shipbuilders, the General Strike was rooted in the mines, where prices and productivity alike were falling. And yet the mine owners – still an extremely rich class of men – had announced their intention of reducing their employees' wages and, where necessary, extending their working hours. No wonder the Miners' Federation of Great Britain dug in its toes: 'Not a penny off the pay, not a minute on the day'. Those were its terms, and the Trades Union Congress backed it to the hilt, though wisely deciding to bring out workers in key industries only – railwaymen, dockers, printers and workers in iron and steel. To do more, they felt, might let the strike get seriously out of hand; after all, they had seen what had happened in Russia, less than ten years before.

Even as things were, there seemed to many a distinct possibility that revolution might indeed be on the cards, and there was immense relief throughout the country when on 12 May – the tenth day of the strike – the TUC General Council visited No. 10 Downing Street to announce their decision to call it off, on condition that there would be no victimization of strikers; but even this proviso failed, the government pointing out that it had 'no power to compel employers to take back every man who had been on strike'. Some miners continued the struggle, but before the end of the year they had nearly all returned to work – those who had any. Their bosses had won again. England was back from the brink.

It is not a pretty story; and the depression was to grind on until the outbreak of the Second World War. Finally it lifted – as it had to: we all had new things to think about, new challenges to meet, new tasks to perform. Yet there were those for whom the twenty-one short years that separated the First World War from the Second constituted one huge broken promise: that we had so signally failed to make England a land fit for heroes to live in.

89

Fort Belvedere

WINDSOR, BERKSHIRE

ort Belvedere was constructed as an eye-catcher – a jolly little toy fortress with toy guns, built in the 1750s to amuse the odious Duke of Cumberland, butcher of Culloden. It has, however, caught relatively few eyes, having remained for most of its existence in well-deserved obscurity. The only exception has been the seven years from 1929 to 1936, when it was the favourite residence of Edward, Prince of Wales, soon to become King Edward VIII.

To his parents and to successive British governments, Edward – or David, as the family called him – had always been a problem. In his youth he had left his naval training at Dartmouth before graduation and Oxford University without a degree. His tutors reported that he was 'underprepared intellectually'; what they meant was that he was quite unusually stupid. On his public appearances, his obvious easy charm and film-star good looks, his mastery of the jaunty cap and the naughty wink – qualities so lacking in his brother and successor – told in his favour; but his relentless pursuit of pleasure and his endless affairs with married women were the despair of his father. 'After I am dead,' King George V was heard to mutter, 'the boy will ruin himself in twelve months.' The prince's secretary Sir Alan Lascelles went even further, confiding to a colleague in 1927: 'I can't help thinking that the best thing that could happen to him, and to the country, would be for him to break his neck.' That same year, accompanying him on an official tour of Canada, he noted that he felt 'as a stage manager might feel if his Hamlet persisted in breaking off the play and balancing the furniture on the end of his nose'.

But the prince had a far bigger trick than that up his sleeve. In December 1933 he fell besottedly in love with an American divorcée, Mrs Wallis Simpson, travelling openly with her all over Europe and showering her with the best and brightest – and the most expensive – jewellery that Cartier could offer. Then in January 1936 George V died and, with astonishing accuracy, his prophecy came true. The following summer Edward VIII and Mrs Simpson – now suing for her second divorce – chose to forgo the pleasures of Balmoral in favour of an extended Mediterranean cruise; and on 16 November the King sent for the Prime Minister, Stanley Baldwin, and announced his intention of marrying as soon as the divorce came through.

Instantly, the cat was among the pigeons. Baldwin argued that the idea was impossible. The King, he pointed out, was Defender of the Faith, Supreme Governor of the Church of England. He of all people must uphold Church law. A marriage in Westminster Abbey – or anywhere else – would be out of the question while the bride had even one former husband still alive; Mrs Simpson had two. The British people could never accept such a woman as their queen. He discreetly drew a veil over her alleged liaisons with Mussolini's son-in-law Count Ciano, with the German Ambassador Joachim von Ribbentrop and with a Mayfair car dealer named Trundle. There were also dark rumours – espoused among others by the chaplain to the Archbishop of Canterbury – that her obvious complete domination of the King could be explained only by some mysterious oriental techniques learned and developed in a Shanghai brothel.

So what was to be done? Various options were considered: there could, for example, be a morganatic marriage: Mrs Simpson would not become queen, but would content herself with some lesser title, much as the Duchess of Cornwall does today. This idea was turned down flat by the Prime Ministers of Canada, Australia and South Africa. Leading politicians followed the government's line, with the exception of Winston Churchill (who counselled delay, on the grounds that the King could fall out of love just as quickly as he had fallen in) and Lloyd George (who also supported the King but couldn't do anything about it since he was on holiday in Jamaica with his mistress). Another delicate moment came at the beginning of December, when the press – who had long known about the story but had hitherto loyally suppressed it – suddenly released the brakes. Henceforth, and for as long as the crisis lasted, the British public thought and spoke of little else.

It seemed – as so often in such crises – that everything that could go wrong did go wrong. There was, for example, an embarrassing moment in early December when, Mrs Simpson having wisely fled to the south of France, her lawyer decided that he must see her urgently. He had a weak heart and had never flown before, so asked his doctor to accompany him. The doctor, as it happened, was resident at a maternity hospital, and the press had a field day: 'Gynaecologist rushed to Mrs Simpson: abortion suspected'.

As the days passed, however, the situation became ever clearer. The King had made up his mind; abdication it would have to be. Not since the days of the Anglo-Saxons had a British monarch voluntarily laid aside his crown, and no one was quite sure how it should be done. Effectively, he did it with his famous broadcast on 11 December: 'You must believe me when I tell you that I have found it impossible to carry the heavy burden of responsibility and to discharge my duty as King as I would wish to do, without the help and support of the woman I love.'

It seemed a disaster – especially to his unfortunate brother Bertie and his wife, who had to pick up the pieces. In fact, it was the best thing that could have happened. Whatever the truth about Ribbentrop, there is no doubt that the Duke and Duchess of Windsor – as they now became – were enthusiastic Nazi sympathizers; less than a year after the abdication they were warmly received by Hitler, to whom the duke gave the full Nazi salute. When the Germans occupied France in 1940, he asked them to place guards in front of both his Paris and Riviera homes; they obligingly did so. When the British suffered the first air raids, the duchess laughed to an American journalist, 'I can't say I feel sorry for them.' In August the duke was sent out to govern the Bahamas – where, in Churchill's opinion, he could do the least possible damage. Even then, he managed to blame the civil unrest of 1942 on 'men of Central European Jewish descent'.

Had King Edward remained on the throne – with or without Mrs Simpson – during the Second World War, the consequences are almost too nightmarish to contemplate. She, and she alone, prevented that from happening; and so, for all her faults, do we not owe her a considerable debt of gratitude? We certainly do if, as is generally believed, she also made the best joke of the whole unhappy story. 'Darling,' she is reported to have said to the King at the height of the crisis, 'you must understand – you can't abdicate and eat it.'

The fourth plinth, perhaps, in Trafalgar Square?

90

Hangar

HESTON, MIDDLESEX

Nobody remembers Heston any more. In the 1930s, however, it was London's second airport after Croydon. It boasted the first purpose-built control tower, on which all others have since been modelled; the first flights of several prototype aeroplanes (including my own personal favourite, the Watkinson Dingbat); and the first hangar to be made of reinforced concrete, constructed in 1929 and now listed Grade II. This may still be admired, standing as it does at the end of Aerodrome Way, though not many people take the opportunity to do so. Perhaps they should, because it was from Heston that Prime Minister Neville Chamberlain left on all three of his flights to Nazi Germany during the second half of September 1938.

It had taken successive British governments a long time to wake up to what was happening in Germany. Hitler had been nearly six years in power; and for at least five of those years far-sighted Jewish refugees had been seeking asylum in England and America. In 1936 Hitler had occupied the Rhineland, in flagrant disobedience to the Versailles Treaty; two years later he had annexed Austria (where, let it never be forgotten, he had received a rapturous welcome); now he was making threatening noises about the 3 million Germans in the Sudetenland, since 1919 the northern part of the newly formed republic of Czechoslovakia. It was when these noises turned into tub-thumping demands for the annexation by force of the whole region that on 15 September 1938 (my ninth birthday) Neville Chamberlain – who had never flown before – clambered into a British Airways Lockheed Electra at Heston and took off for Munich, where he caught a train for Hitler's mountain retreat at Berchtesgaden.

Since he immediately promised the Führer that he would persuade the Czechs to yield to his demands without further ado, that first conversation went well enough; but when Chamberlain returned to Germany on the 22nd – it was Bad Godesberg this time – with the intention of presenting his peace plan, Hitler suddenly turned nasty. He now produced a completely new series of demands. The entire Sudetenland, he insisted, must be given up unconditionally by the 28th; there could be no international commission to supervise the transfer; and Germany would not renounce war as an option until all the territory containing Polish and Hungarian minorities had also been surrendered. Almost unbelievably, the Prime Minister seemed prepared to go along with this; but his Foreign Secretary Lord Halifax put his foot down and the terms were rejected. Hitler was icily informed that Britain would accept the Berchtesgaden terms or nothing, and that Britain and France would consider any German attack on Czechoslovakia as an attack on themselves. For Neville Chamberlain it was a bitter pill: 'How horrible, fantastic it is,' he said in a radio broadcast a day or two after his return, 'that we should be digging trenches and trying on gas masks here because of a quarrel in a far-away country between people of whom we know nothing.'

Trenches were in fact being dug in Hyde Park in preparation for the expected German invasion, and British spirits were low indeed when on 28 September Chamberlain announced that Hitler had invited him back to Munich, for a conference to be attended also by Mussolini and the French Prime Minister, Edouard Daladier. Once again, the Führer was informed that everything he wanted was his for the taking. Chamberlain flew back to Heston, proudly brandishing a piece of paper, bearing Hitler's signature as well as his own and undertaking that the two countries would never go to war again. He appeared to place much confidence in this paper; for Hitler, it had obviously been just another autograph. Yet England went mad. That evening the Prime Minister stood on the balcony of Buckingham Palace, flanked by the King and Queen. He had brought back, he proclaimed, peace with honour. Of course he had done nothing of the kind. As my father pointed out when he resigned from the government on the following day, war with honour or peace with dishonour he might possibly have been persuaded to accept; but war with dishonour – that was too much.

The three ill-starred meetings had served only to delay the inevitable. On 14 March 1939 the German tanks thundered into an utterly defenceless Prague. Then, on the last day of that month, Neville Chamberlain showed, for the first time, a little gumption. The British and French governments, he told the House of Commons, were offering a guarantee to Poland, the last item (for the moment) on Hitler's shopping list. Should Poland be attacked, the two allies would come to its aid. If, however, the Prime Minister believed – which he probably did – that this threat would frighten Hitler into abandoning his plans, he was as usual wrong: in August the Führer announced the Nazi-Soviet Non-Aggression Pact, which overnight reduced the impact, such as it was, of Chamberlain's words to mere sabre-rattling.

At dawn on Friday, 1 September 1939, the full might of the German army was hurled against Poland. 'Our enemies,'

Hitler told his generals, 'are little worms – I saw them at Munich.' Parliament met the next morning, fully expecting to hear that war had been declared – but no, the Prime Minister was at it again. If, he argued, through Italian mediation, the German advance could be suspended, there could be another conference along the lines of Munich and the whole issue could still be peacefully settled. But by now the patience of the House was at an end. Threatened by revolt among his own ranks, Chamberlain consented to send the German government an 'ultimatum' that would expire at 11 a.m. on 3 September. From Germany, predictably, there came only a deafening silence; and therefore, at 11.05 that Sunday morning, the Prime Minister made a short broadcast to the nation, informing it – the words sounded more like a confession – that 'this country is at war with Germany.' On such occasions he could never resist a reference to his own feelings. 'You may imagine,' he continued, 'what a bitter blow it is for me.' There's a marvellous moment in Noël Coward's film *In Which We Serve*, in which Able Seaman Blake, played by John Mills, listens to his words and murmurs, 'It ain't no bleedin' bank holiday for us either.'

Eight months later Neville Chamberlain resigned, to be succeeded by Winston Churchill; six months after that he was dead. He continued to believe that he had been right: 'without Munich the war would have been lost and the Empire destroyed'. It is on this point, and this point only, that his reputation stands or falls. To expect otherwise, in the words of the historian David Dutton, 'is rather like hoping that Pontius Pilate will one day be judged as a successful provincial administrator of the Roman Empire'.

91

Churchill War Rooms
LONDON

*T*he Churchill War Rooms – or the Cabinet War Rooms, as they used to be called – are London's only true time capsule. Down you go, through that poky, unassuming little entrance at the foot of the Clive Steps, and instantly seventy years fall away; there's a war on, and we're in the thick of it. It's not for claustrophobes, this rambling rabbit-warren of winding passages and corridors, but it leads to the two great strategic nerve centres of the whole complex: the Cabinet Room and the Map Room. Neither of these was used very much at first; while Neville Chamberlain remained Prime Minister, he presided in the Cabinet Room only once, in October 1939. But when Churchill took over in May 1940 he had no doubts. 'This,' he said – and we can almost hear him saying it – 'is the room from which I shall direct the War.' Altogether there were to be 115 Cabinet meetings there over the following five years, the last being held on 28 March 1945, six weeks before VE Day.

And, inevitably, it is the spirit of Winston Churchill that still fills the War Rooms. Here is his office/bedroom, used more in the former capacity than in the latter, since he always preferred to sleep either at No. 10 or in the Annexe to the War Rooms, a flat directly above; the office had a telephone line connected straight to the BBC, by means of which he made four of his broadcasts to the nation. Here, too, is his Transatlantic Telephone Room, by which he was able, at least in theory, to speak to President Roosevelt on a scrambled line – though we know that he often had a terrible time doing so. It seems now that his relationship with the President was nowhere near as close as he later claimed; still, there is no question that in the early years of the war he successfully influenced many of Roosevelt's decisions, including the critical one in 1942 to delay the attack on France that his top military advisers had been urging – which would have been hopelessly premature and almost certainly calamitous – in favour of the invasion of North Africa. Other rooms were used, as one might imagine, as office-bedrooms for ministers and senior members of the armed forces; yet others for typists, telegraphists and switchboard operators, and as dormitories for the junior staff. Individually they may be of limited interest; it is the ensemble that impresses, this astonishing microcosm of the world outside, ugly, cramped and deeply uncomfortable, yet for five years the most powerful and historically significant area of its size in the western world.

In the high summer of 1940, the chips were down. France, our only major ally apart from the dominions, was lying in the dust. America was mildly benevolent perhaps, but still firmly neutral. Nazi Germany, by contrast, was racing ahead on all fronts, apparently invincible. Invasion seemed almost inevitable – an invasion of the kind our island hadn't suffered for nearly 1,000 years and for which we were hopelessly unprepared; the Battle of Britain was raging above our heads; German U-boats swarmed in the Atlantic. Few outside observers would have given us a snowball's chance in hell. That we finally won through was due, I firmly believe, to Winston Churchill alone. No other British political figure – certainly not Anthony Eden or, heaven forbid, Lord Halifax

– had the imagination, the dogged determination, the persistence, the inspiring oratory or the sheer dazzling charisma that
he possessed in such abundance, all of which qualities were
essential if the war was to be won.

To the health-and-safety-minded nannies who rule our
lives today he would have been anathema: smoking like a
chimney, drinking like a fish (though less than is generally
believed; he was a sipper rather than a swallower, and a single
whisky and soda could last him two hours or more), abhorring
all physical exercise, working most mornings from his bed but
frequently dictating until 3 or 4 a.m. the following day. He
was, as we know, subject to terrible 'black dog' depressions; he
could be petulant, unreasonable, impossibly demanding; he
frequently drove his staff raving wild. And yet, one and all,
they loved him. When the black dog loped away and his eyes
began to twinkle, no one was kinder, funnier, wittier or more
sparkling company. And he had an extraordinary power of
directing his concentration. Whatever he was doing – arguing
with his generals, painting a picture, singing old music-hall
songs, talking to his dog, building a brick wall or feeding his
beloved goldfish – took up his entire concentration for as long
as it lasted; nothing else mattered; indeed, nothing else
existed. There was a child-like innocence about him. He
adored the cinema, following the story with rapt attention
and maintaining a ceaseless running commentary; he and his
wife and my parents and I used regularly to attend the Venice
Film Festival, and I remember one particularly depressing
film about Irish gypsies: 'Oh, poor people!', 'Oh, poor, *poor*
people!' and on one occasion 'Oh, poor horse!' Finally, as the
story moved to its hideous climax: 'Oh, jealousy, jealousy –
most *barren* of all vices!' Everyone who ever met him has their
own stock of 'Winston' stories, and they are all important,
because each helps to fill out the picture of one of the most

memorable and colourful figures in our long history. No other man has, so swiftly and so single-handedly, changed the mood of the nation and focused its courage.

How was it, then, that on 26 July 1945, less than three weeks before our final victory over Japan, the general election resulted in a Labour landslide and Winston Churchill was voted out of office? The truth was, it seems, that for nearly six years he had concentrated entirely on the war; military victory was the only thing that counted; party politics he had largely ignored. With the war in Europe over and the war in the east as good as won, he found himself without any clear sense of direction. Meanwhile the Labour Party was holding the pre-war Conservatives responsible for Chamberlain's appeasement policy and the failure to rearm, while promising a new social order that would ensure free medical services and full employ-ment. To many, none the less, it seemed like an act of contemptible ingratitude – as indeed it did to the man him-self. 'Perhaps,' said his wife consolingly, 'it's a blessing in disguise.' 'In that case,' he grumbled, 'it's very well disguised.'

In fact, as we know, he soon bounced back and returned to power. But by now he was getting old, and he had outstayed his welcome. We all prefer to remember him during the dark days, marching through the ruins of the Blitz in those strangely old-fashioned clothes – blue spotted bow tie, heavy watch-chain and that extraordinary headgear, halfway between a top hat and a bowler – his very presence inspiring the bombed-out victims with a new determination, defiance and hope. That was the Churchill magic. An anonymous London woman put it as well as anyone. 'Gradually,' she said, 'his stature grew larger and larger, until it filled our sky.'

92

Coventry Cathedral
WEST MIDLANDS

C oventry is the only city in England with three cathedrals. The oldest, St Mary's, started life as a modest Benedictine monastery – originally endowed in the eleventh century by Coventry's heroine, Lady Godiva – but failed to survive Henry VIII's disastrous Dissolution in 1539. There are only a few ruins left. The second, originally one of the country's largest parish churches, was a late medieval building which was promoted to cathedral status when Coventry was given its own diocese in 1918. Alas, it fell victim to the great air raid of 1940; only the tower, the spire and an outer wall survived. The third is a contemporary building by the architect Sir Basil Spence, built alongside the bombed-out ruins so that the two parts effectively form a single church. Its consecration in 1962 was celebrated by the first performance of Benjamin Britten's *War Requiem* (see **Lowdham War Memorial**).

This was not the first raid that the city had suffered; there had been several previous ones in the high summer of 1940, but nothing yet on the scale of the devastation already inflicted on London or Birmingham. Then, on the night of 14 November, there came an operation on an utterly different scale to anything that had been experienced before. Codenamed Mondscheinsonate – Moonlight Sonata – it was carried out by 515 German bombers and was designed

[431]

principally to destroy all the city's heavy industry and arma-ments factories. It began at 7.20 p.m., with an initial wave of aircraft dropping marker flares; then the heavy bombers moved in. Within an hour their high-explosive loads had knocked out the water, electricity and gas supplies; they had also filled the main roads with deep craters, making the move-ment of ambulances and fire brigades almost impossible. (In fact there had already been a direct hit on the Fire Brigade Headquarters.)

It was at about eight o'clock that the cathedral burst into flames. The volunteer firefighters did their best but, as more and more incendiaries rained down, their task was soon seen to be hopeless. With the water mains already out of action, most of the fires proved impossible to put out anyway. The raid reached its climax at around midnight, but it was only at six fifteen the next morning that the sirens sounded the final all-clear. The precise death toll has never been established; it was certainly no fewer than 600, with more than 1,000 ser-iously injured. About three-quarters of the city's industrial plants and factories were put out of action, and more than 4,000 homes utterly destroyed. Such was the overall effect that Joseph Goebbels, the Nazi propaganda chief, began using the term *coventriert* – 'coventrated' – to describe the similar fate of other towns and cities – not that there were many of them.

Here, in a single city on a single night, we see the full power of the Blitz, the sustained campaign of aerial bombing of Britain by Nazi Germany during the eight months between 7 September 1940 and 10 May 1941. By the time the long nightmare was over, more than 43,000 civilians had been killed, about half of them in London, which was bombed for seventy-six consecutive nights and where more than a million houses were destroyed or damaged. In other circumstances it might have continued for much longer; fortunately by May Hitler's attention had shifted to Operation Barbarossa, his disastrous adventure in the east. He was to return to the attack in 1944, with the development of the V-1 pilotless flying bombs and the V-2 rockets, which killed another 9,000; but by that time British morale was high again.

For all its horror, the Blitz was merely the sequel to – and perhaps the consequence of – another, very different engagement: the Battle of Britain. This was the first major campaign in world history to be fought exclusively in the air. It had as its origin Hitler's decision 'to eliminate the English home country as a base for the continuation of the war against Germany' – in other words, to invade us. For an invasion to be successful, however, 'the English air force must have been beaten down to such an extent morally and in fact that it can no longer master any power of attack worth mentioning against the German crossing.' His total failure to achieve this objective – thanks to the heroism of Fighter Command and the speed and firepower of its Spitfires and Hurricanes – has passed into legend.

In fact, when the battle first became intense in mid-August 1940, Britain and Germany were fairly evenly matched, each side possessing just over 1,000 fighter planes; but the British had several important advantages. The German fighters were hamstrung by having to protect their bombers; their distance from base meant that their operational time was limited; British pilots who bailed out could be back in the air the same day, while Germans were taken prisoner. But such considerations in no way diminish the splendour of the achievement or the courage of the young men, whose casualty rate that August was 22 per cent. In early September we lost no fewer than 133 pilots; but the survivors' sense of humour remained intact. When, on 20 August, Churchill made his great statement to the Commons that 'never in the field of human conflict had so much been owed by so many to so few', the general opinion voiced by the airmen concerned was that he must have been talking about mess bills.

By May 1941, after the Battle of Britain and the Blitz, the British had good reason to feel proud of themselves; but the danger was by no means past. It would be at least another year, after our successes in North Africa, before there was any real break in the cloud. Henceforth, however, despite all the hideous wartime privations, life for most people would be at least a degree more bearable. For our enemies, on the other hand, it would grow steadily worse, culminating in our utterly indefensible bombing of Dresden in February 1945, when the war was as good as won. Dresden and Coventry: through their sufferings, those two cities have gained iconic status; to know that groups of young Germans helped in the building of the new cathedral, while similar groups from England worked on the Frauenkirche, can only give one hope that such barbarities will never be seen again.

93

Hut 8, Bletchley Park
BUCKINGHAMSHIRE

*W*ith the possible exceptions of No. 10 Downing Street and the Cabinet War Rooms, there is no building in all England that made a greater contribution to our victory in the Second World War than a large, rambling and perfectly hideous house on the edge of Milton Keynes known as Bletchley Park. It was the nerve centre of British intelligence, the wartime home of many of the most fearsomely intellectual men and women alive, its very air loud with the sound of cracking as one enemy code after another surrendered its mystery. The super-top-secret information that it provided, codenamed Ultra, is said by the official historian of the subject, Harry Hinsley, to have shortened the war by not less than two years and probably four; indeed, it may have won it.

The story really began with the Poles when, five weeks before the beginning of the war, their *Biuro Szyfrów* (Cipher Department) revealed its early code-breaking successes with the German Enigma ciphers to British and French intelligence. On 15 August 1939 the Government Code and Cipher School moved to Bletchley, taking over the ground floor and leaving the top to MI6. Inevitably, however, the whole place proved far too small and, as the volume of enemy transmissions increased, more and more huts were erected around the house, first in wood and later in concrete – and, of course, more and more staff had to be recruited.

But how was this to be done? Not everyone could be a cipher-buster. Mathematicians were of course in heavy demand, and we were lucky indeed to have the benefit of at least one genius, Dr Alan Turing FRS, whose statue in Sackville Park, Manchester, describes him as 'The Father of Computer Science'. Working from the celebrated Hut 8, it was he who invented what was known as the Bombe, an electromechanical gizmo the workings of which I could not begin to explain; suffice it to say that it tackled the German Enigma-encrypted signals with exemplary success. Turing was, like all geniuses, a bit dotty: every June, a martyr to hay fever, he would cycle to his office in a gas mask, and he kept his mug chained to the radiator to prevent its being stolen; but his contribution to Bletchley's work was incalculable, even by him. Apart from Turing there were chess champions such as the great Harry Golombek, crossword puzzlers – those who could sink a special *Daily Telegraph* crossword in less than twelve minutes – top Morse code telegraphists, and of course a number of Jewish refugees from central Europe, whose perfect fluency in their native languages was of enormous value.

As the war continued and the threat from Germany gradually faded, Bletchley was faced with the even more intractable problem of Japanese. Early in 1942 the government instituted a series of six-month crash courses in the language, each to be attended by twenty undergraduates from Oxford and Cambridge; special trains reserved for them ran twice daily between Cambridge and Bletchley. At the end of the course the successful ones – by no means all who attended, Japanese being a fearsomely difficult language – settled down to breaking the naval codes issuing from Tokyo. By mid-1945 over 100 people were fully engaged on this operation; thanks to them, by VJ Day in August 1945 the Japanese merchant navy was losing 90 per cent of its tonnage.

Over 12,000 people worked at Bletchley Park at some time or other during the war, more than 80 per cent of them women. After the United States had joined the war and Churchill and Roosevelt had agreed to pool resources, there was also a considerable number of American cryptographers. Much to the fury of General de Gaulle, we did not share our secrets with the Free French; for all their heroism, their security was hopeless, and once the Germans even suspected that we had access to their Enigma ciphers, Bletchley was finished. Nor, thank God, did we reveal anything to the Russians. Looking back, it is little short of astonishing that not a word of what was going on ever leaked out, not just during the war, but for about thirty years afterwards. Some time before his death Churchill praised the staff as only he could, referring to them as 'my geese, that laid the golden eggs and never cackled'. It was only in the 1970s that the truth was publicly revealed.

It was possibly this long silence that contributed to the near-downfall of Bletchley Park. By 1990 one of the greatest monuments of the Second World War was lying derelict, at risk of demolition for redevelopment. Salvation came in the nick of time. In 1992, most of the park was declared a Conservation Area; the Bletchley Park Trust was established to create a museum; and two years later the museum was officially inaugurated. It is now up and running, and open to the public, endeavouring to explain – so far as this is possible to the layman – not only the secrets of cryptanalysis but of computer development over the last half-century, from the huge, humming wartime machines the size of a garden shed to the iPads of today.

It remains to trace the rest of the life of Alan Turing. In 1952, I am ashamed to report, the British government saw fit to prosecute him for his homosexuality, of which he had never made any particular secret; and if that were not bad enough, he was given the choice between imprisonment and chemical castration. He chose the latter. His security clearance was removed, which meant the end of his cryptographic work; he was denied entry to the United States. On 8 June 1954 he was found dead of cyanide poisoning; a half-eaten apple was by his side. He was very nearly forty-two. Our immense debt to him was ill repaid.

94

Watford Gap Motorway Service Area
NORTHAMPTONSHIRE

*T*he Watford Gap Service Area ('Watford Gap, Watford Gap, A plate of grease and a load of crap,' sang Roy Harper) is not perhaps the most throbbingly romantic of our 100 sites; but it represents, none the less, a milestone in the long history of English roads. It was opened, together with the first stretch of the M1 motorway, with much fanfare on 2 November 1959, its restaurant a few weeks later. In those early, innocent days, the restaurant had some pretensions to what the owners believed would be a 'fine dining experience', with a corps of ladies best described as maîtresses d' as well as the table staff; the truth soon became clear, however, that modern motorists were in far too much of a hurry to wish to toy with their *filets de sole bonne femme*, particularly as – not surprisingly – there was no wine to go with them. Before long it was just another cafeteria, and foreign travellers, who had always been brought up to believe that English food was uneatable, found their worst suspicions confirmed.

The Gap itself isn't much to look at – it is simply a fairly level corridor between two small Northamptonshire hills – but, since nobody likes a gradient if it can be avoided, it has attracted road-builders for the past 2,000 years. One of the most important of the Roman thoroughfares, Watling Street, passed through it; and so, more recently, have a railway and a canal. It was also one of the key stopping-points on the old east–west stagecoach road across England, and the site of one of the country's major coaching inns, called, somehow inevitably, the Watford Gap. Today, alas, not one brick of it is left on another.

A rudimentary road network was Rome's greatest gift to Britain. The roads radiated out from London: eastward through Canterbury to the Channel ports; westward through Silchester to the Fosse Way; north-east to Colchester, where there was a connection with the prehistoric Peddars Way across East Anglia. Another road headed south to Chichester. Finally there were the two great highways to the north, Watling Street and Ermine Street. Their principal function was to allow the rapid movement of troops and military supplies. Being paved, they were passable in all weathers – a Roman legion could march a steady thirty miles a day, carrying full equipment – and they also provided a vital infrastructure for merchants and the heavy ox-wagons that they so often needed for the transportation of their merchandise.

But by the beginning of the fifth century the Romans were gone, the roads fell further and further into disrepair, and those who simply had to travel round the country found themselves increasingly reliant on the rivers. It was not until the Middle Ages that anything at all was done, and even then it wasn't much – just a few roads made by the religious orders, or by rich landowners for convenience in visiting their more far-flung estates. One of the busiest was of course the road to Canterbury which was, after the murder of Thomas Becket in 1175, a hugely popular pilgrimage shrine; it was also regularly used by the archbishop and his suite on their regular progresses to and from London. With these few exceptions, the condition of the paved or metalled highways continued to be little short of disgraceful until towards the middle of the eighteenth century, with the popularization of Turnpike Trusts. In these the trustees were given the responsibility for the upkeep of given sections of a road, with the right to exact tolls from those using it. In the years between 1750 and 1772, no fewer than 389 of these trusts were established – each by a separate Act of Parliament – and the state of the roads was transformed. For the first time, too, rough timekeeping became possible.

The next important moment occurred in 1784, when John Palmer of Bath inaugurated a transport revolution with his plans for carrying mail by coach. By 1800 four-horse mail coaches – each protected by a guard with a blunderbuss – had become the principal form of transport. Between twenty and thirty coaches a day would be changing horses in inn yards the length and breadth of the country. But the blunderbusses were necessary: highwaymen had long been a scourge, and these new mail coaches promised rich rewards. The interesting thing about highwaymen is how often they were seen as romantic heroes in the Robin Hood mould. There was, for example, an outstandingly handsome Frenchman called Claude du Vall. He was hanged at Tyburn at the age of twenty-seven, but was then given a slap-up funeral at St Paul's Covent Garden, with a tombstone reading:

HERE LIES DU VALL: READER, IF MALE THOU ART
LOOK TO THY PURSE; IF FEMALE, TO THY HEART.
MUCH HAVOC HAS HE MADE OF BOTH; FOR ALL
MEN HE MADE STAND, AND WOMEN HE MADE FALL.
THE SECOND CONQUEROR OF THE NORMAN RACE,
KNIGHTS TO HIS ARMS DID YIELD, AND LADIES TO HIS FACE.
OLD TYBURN'S GLORY; ENGLAND'S ILLUSTRIOUS THIEF,
DU VALL, THE LADIES' JOY; DU VALL, THE LADIES' GRIEF.

The unrivalled hero of the Turnpike Trusts was John Loudon McAdam, who in his heyday had 300 sub-surveyors to assist him and who gave a new word to the language. But this great Pickwickian age of the turnpike, though still commemorated on a million Christmas cards, lasted little more than a single generation: the railways were coming – faster, safer and infinitely more economical. Once more the road network seemed doomed. But no one had foreseen the advent and the subsequent impact of the motor car. Already by the beginning of the twentieth century the countryside was changing again. Road building was resumed on an unprecedented scale, and continues to this day. And the quality of the provender available in the Watford Gap Service Area is, I am reliably informed, much improved.

95

20 Forthlin Road and Mendips, 251 Menlove Avenue

LIVERPOOL

Not many people live to see their childhood homes opened to the public as a shrine. Sir Paul McCartney has, and John Lennon would have as well had he not been assassinated before it could happen. Their two Liverpool houses, 20 Forthlin Road and Mendips, both essentially unchanged, are now accessible to pilgrims on National Trust minibuses. Book early to avoid disappointment. Special arrangements may be made for wheelchairs.

Lord Byron recorded, after the publication (by John Murray, of course) of *Childe Harold's Pilgrimage*, that 'he woke up and found himself famous'; but his fame was nothing compared to that of the Beatles. Indeed, one is tempted to wonder whether anyone else in history has ever enjoyed such wild and instant celebrity, coming as a direct result of their own enormous talents, as did John Lennon (rhythm guitar), Paul McCartney (bass guitar, played left-handedly), George Harrison (lead guitar) and Ringo Starr (drums). They all of them came in on the vocals. The group – already containing the first three, with Ringo joining them in 1962 – had started in 1960 in Liverpool and Hamburg; but the big breakthrough came early in 1963, when I remember seeing them at the Hammersmith Apollo. 'Seeing' is the word, rather than 'hearing', since the whole enormous theatre was a cacophony of shrieking, howling teenage girls who completely drowned them out.

No matter. The Beatles single-handedly caused a revolution in English popular music. Before them, the level had never risen far above the standard set in 1946 with 'Cruising Down the River on a Sunday Afternoon'; now, suddenly, there was real imagination, with exciting breakthroughs in melody and harmony, and occasional shafts of genuine poetry. It certainly caught the attention of the chief music critic of *The Times*, William Mann, who suggested that Lennon and McCartney were 'the outstanding English composers of 1963'. The following year they hit New York. There had apparently been a degree of misgiving over their probable reception, but they needn't have worried: 4,000 hysterical fans had gathered to see them off at Heathrow; 3,000 more awaited them at Kennedy. Two days later, their first live performance on US television was watched by 74 million people – over 40 per cent of the American population.

But by this time they weren't *just* the Beatles; more than anyone or anything else, they seemed to stand for the whole counterculture of the sixties. In the early days they were innocent and fresh-faced, wearing neat, clean identical suits and ties; then as time went on and hippiedom took hold, their ties disappeared, their hair grew longer, their clothes wilder, their habits more outlandish. They took to marijuana and LSD; they worshipped at the feet of the Maharishi; they went, to a greater or lesser degree, psychedelic. (And when did we last hear *that* word?) Finally and inevitably, with everyone doing his own thing, the group's solidarity came under strain; and on the last day of 1970 McCartney filed a suit for the dissolution of the partnership, though legal disputes were to continue until 1975 or even later. Then in 1980 John Lennon was shot dead by a lunatic in New York, and in

2001 George Harrison died of cancer. Only Paul – now *Sir* Paul – and Ringo remain.

What, ultimately, was the Beatles' achievement? First of all, their arrival marked the beginning of a new era. They broke through all the constraints of their time to revolutionize popular music, leaving it permanently transformed, never to be the same again. Second, they successfully challenged the United

States, which for the past forty years – through Hollywood, New Orleans, Nashville, Memphis and Broadway – had dominated the light entertainment industry; now, thanks to them, it was Britain's turn. The concert in New York's Shea Stadium with which they opened their 1965 North American tour attracted over 55,000 people and grossed £304,000 – both these figures being all-time records in the history of show business. Finally, they inspired the entire younger generation. England by 1965 was a completely different place to what it had been even five years earlier. They gave it youth, colour, energy and imagination. Above all, they made it fun.

And they were in no way an isolated phenomenon. They exemplified what was in effect a cultural revolution, when for the first time in history members of the working class had an equal opportunity to rise to celebrity and stardom. They did so not only in the world of popular music but in many other fields as well: in the theatre and cinema, with actors like Michael Caine, Albert Finney and Tom Courtenay; in film, with directors such as Ken Loach; in photography, above all with David Bailey; or in fashion, with models like Twiggy. And this, it should be noted, was no passing fashion: the road to fame remains open to all, and we are all enriched. No wonder those two humble houses in Liverpool have become places of pilgrimage. So they should be.

96

Thatcher Plaque

GRANTHAM, LINCOLNSHIRE

*I*t's not a very nice plaque, on the wall of her father's corner shop; she deserves a far better one, which will doubtless come in time. The inscription, too, is simple enough: *Birthplace of the Rt. Hon. Margaret Thatcher, M.P. First Woman Prime Minister of Great Britain and Northern Ireland*. Well, yes: but there's somehow rather more to it than that.

Margaret Thatcher is, at the time of writing, still with us; but she has recently been living in quiet retirement and has now become part – and a very important part – of history, which is why I feel entitled to speak of her in the past tense. She was a phenomenon – the greatest political phenomenon that this country has produced since Winston Churchill. She aroused violent emotions: loved by some, detested by others, held in vast admiration or icy contempt. Pitiless, humourless and hard as nails, she was also totally self-confident and, as she proved again and again, utterly without fear. She slept four hours a night. Not for nothing was she known as the 'Iron Lady'. No British Prime Minister ever showed greater toughness with those who crossed her, whether the leaders of the Soviet Union, the miners or the Argentines. She survived the bombing by the Provisional IRA of the Grand Hotel, Brighton, during the Conservative Party Conference in October 1984. The bomb exploded at 2.54 a.m., while she was still working on her speech for the next day, completely destroying her bathroom; she presided at the conference at nine thirty the next morning, immaculate as ever, with not a hair out of place.

That hair was an essential part of her persona. A hairdresser came at seven thirty every morning and travelled with her on all her trips abroad; she would emerge in Tokyo after a twenty-four-hour flight, looking fresh as a daisy and clearly longing for her first engagement of the day. And she was intensely feminine: nobody ever saw Margaret Thatcher in trousers, or without a hat (until hats went out of fashion), a spotless pair of gloves and gleaming leather handbag. She loved to talk cooking, clothes and interior decoration, and would always make it perfectly clear that she knew far more about the subject than her interlocutor. The patronizing note in her voice drove many people mad.

And yet she possessed undoubted greatness. Mrs Thatcher came to power in 1979 and when on 2 April 1982 the military junta in Argentina invaded South Georgia and the Falkland Islands, would any other post-war Prime Minister have instantly launched a major task force to win them back? Certainly the Argentines did not expect it: the islands were 8,000 miles from England, less than 500 from Argentina, which possessed 122 active fighter planes as against our 34. No wonder the US Navy considered a successful counter-invasion to be 'a military impossibility'. Yet just ten weeks later Argentina surrendered. It was largely this victory – 'the Falklands Factor' – that ensured Mrs Thatcher's re-election in the following year.

Just in time, as it happened, to deal with the miners' strike. The miners had been largely instrumental in bringing down the previous Conservative government of Edward Heath; Mrs Thatcher had watched them carefully, and was determined to succeed where Heath had failed. From early 1983 her government had been quietly stockpiling coal, converting several power stations to burn petroleum and recruiting a regiment of road hauliers to move the coal in case the railways came out in a sympathetic strike with the miners. It was thus fully prepared when in March 1984 the National Coal Board announced the closure of no fewer than twenty of the 174 state-owned mines. Some 20,000 jobs would be lost, and many villages in the north of England, Scotland and Wales would be effectively devastated. Two-thirds of the country's miners, led by the National Union of Mineworkers under its firebrand leader Arthur Scargill, downed tools; but once again Mrs Thatcher showed her steel. For her this was just such another Falklands War. 'In the Falklands,' she said in a speech at the time, 'we had to fight the enemy without. We always have to be aware of the enemy within, which is much more difficult to fight and more dangerous to liberty.'

The strike lasted nearly a year. There were several violent confrontations between the miners and the police, with casualties on both sides – fortunately the Prime Minister had ensured that the police had received special training and had been equipped with riot gear – but the government refused all the NUM's demands. At last, in March 1985, the strikers conceded without a deal. The cost to the economy was estimated at over £1.5 billion. More than 27 million working days had been lost. Nor was this the end. Over the next ten years 150 collieries were closed down. Unemployment figures soared. But Margaret Thatcher, rightly or wrongly, had brought the unions to heel.

Then, suddenly, it all began to unwind. Her great mistake was to introduce the 'poll tax' in 1990, perhaps the most unpopular policy of her premiership; more than 100,000 protesters filled Trafalgar Square; over 400 were arrested. She remained confident – but this time she was wrong. By 1990 the Conservatives were trailing badly in the polls, and her behaviour to her colleagues was becoming more and more overbearing and dictatorial. On 1 November Sir Geoffrey Howe resigned as Deputy Prime Minister, and on the following day Michael Heseltine mounted a challenge for the party leadership. Finally, and with much difficulty, she was persuaded to resign. She never forgave what she saw as an indefensible betrayal, and – feminine to the last – left Downing Street in tears.

97

Greenham Common
NEWBURY, BERKSHIRE

On 5 September 1981 a bunch of determined Welsh ladies arrived outside the RAF Greenham Common Air Base near Newbury, having marched from Cardiff. Their concern was the recent decision to install ninety-six nuclear Cruise missiles on the base, a decision on which they demanded a public debate. When this was refused they set up a sort of gypsy camp on an adjacent stretch of waste ground. Gradually others came to join them; the movement grew and grew, and they and their successors and supporters remained there for the next nineteen years. Their living conditions were primitive in the extreme, but their publicity was inspired: in December 1982, about 30,000 women joined hands to 'embrace the base'; four months later roughly 70,000 formed a fourteen-mile human chain from Greenham to the Atomic Weapons Establishment at Aldermaston and to the ordnance factory at Burghfield. Several times they were evicted; they were usually back by nightfall, and eventually Newbury Council gave up. Then, in 1991, the last missiles left the air base and it seemed to many as though the Greenham ladies had lost their *raison d'être*. But no: by now their cause had been absorbed into the Campaign for Nuclear Disarmament, and they stayed put.

CND, as it was universally known, was the original nuclear protest movement from which all the others sprang. Founded in 1958 to promote unilateral nuclear disarmament and non-proliferation, it achieved an impressive following, with Bertrand Russell as its president and supporters who included scientists, religious leaders, composers, actors, authors, journalists and academics. At Easter 1958 it organized a fifty-two-mile march from London to Aldermaston; thenceforth the march – though now in the reverse direction – became an annual event; in 1962 and 1963, when it probably reached its highest point of popularity, the marchers numbered some 150,000. It demanded the unconditional renunciation of the use, production or dependence upon nuclear weapons and a worldwide disarmament convention. Meanwhile, Britain must no longer fly aircraft carrying nuclear weapons, must end nuclear testing and must refuse to provide nuclear weapons to any other country.

During these early years of the campaign, the moment when the world came nearest to catastrophe was probably the Cuban missile crisis in the autumn of 1962, when the United States blocked a Soviet attempt to establish a nuclear missile site in Cuba. CND had high hopes that this crisis would hugely increase its following, but oddly enough it was the opposite that occurred: six months after President Kennedy's success in facing down Nikita Khrushchev, Gallup polls found that public anxieties about a nuclear war were at their lowest level since 1957. This mood continued through the rest of the sixties and throughout the seventies; it was only in the early eighties that support for CND revived – owing largely to America's decision to deploy Pershing missiles in western Europe and in 1982 Britain's decision to replace the Polaris submarine fleet with the highly controversial Trident.

But in a quarter of a century the political – and, one might almost say, the philosophical – climate in the country had changed. So far, at least, the movement had failed in all its objectives. Apart from South Africa, which voluntarily decommissioned its nuclear weapons in 1989, there had been no nuclear disarmament. Atomic weapons were still being manufactured. The bomb had not been banned, for the simple reason that it was unbannable: many people were beginning to realize that something once invented could not be disinvented; somehow it had to be lived with. Non-proliferation, apart from the five 'Nuclear Weapon States' (USA, Russia, Britain, France and China), was indeed devoutly to be wished; but it too would prove a pipe dream. (After another thirty-odd years we must now add India, Pakistan and probably Israel and North Korea to the list. Iran too is being very carefully watched.) And – let us not deceive ourselves – there will be more. In such a world, no responsible government will dream of giving up its weaponry, though it may, for economic reasons, agree to reduce its arsenal. With all these unpleasant truths (and several others as well) CND has had to come to terms.

It was inevitable, sooner or later, that the movement should attract the attention of MI5. From the late sixties to the mid-seventies it was actually designated as 'subversive' and 'communist-controlled'. It was of course nothing of the kind, although it had doubtless been infiltrated by Soviet agents – how could it not have been? Anyway, the spooks seem to have realized that they had exaggerated: in the late seventies CND was downgraded to the rank of 'communist penetrated'. (They had, incidentally, also penetrated it themselves, by placing an agent of their own, one Harry Newton, in the CND office.)

With the collapse of the Soviet Union in 1989 and the consequent end of the Cold War, the threat rapidly declined and support for CND predictably fell. Not only had CND failed to persuade any national government to accept its way of thinking, but it had been equally unsuccessful with the British public itself. The majority continued to favour the nuclear option; after half a century the movement still had not a single major success to its credit. In recent years CND has turned its attention to the whole nuclear power industry, which it wishes to close down entirely. Since Britain's nineteen nuclear reactors are already producing 20 per cent of our power this plan, if suddenly imposed, would plunge one household in five into total darkness.

But let us return to where we began, Greenham Common. The last protesters – after nine years without a single missile to protest against, they must surely have been feeling a trifle *désoeuvrées* – left in the year 2000, and the plot of ground that was for so long their home is now designated as a Commemorative and Historic Site. The monument consists of a circle of seven standing stones from Wales surrounding a sculpture symbolizing a campfire, and a separate sculpture in a vaguely spiral design bearing the inscription 'Women's Peace Camp 1981–2000 – You Can't Kill the Spirit'. Next to it is a small garden laid out in memory of Greenham's only casualty: a young lady who was run over by a passing horsebox.

98

National Theatre

LONDON

*H*eaven knows it was a long time coming; there were moments – I remember that dreadful day in 1961, already ten years after the laying of the foundation stone, when Harold Macmillan's government categorically announced that the nation could not afford one after all – when we found ourselves very close to despair. But eventually the go-ahead came, and now that it is here at last the National Theatre has proved one of our major success stories. To many people Sir Denys Lasdun's vast blocks of solid, uncompromising, undressed concrete at first seemed brutal and overbearing; Prince Charles described them in 1988 as 'a clever way of building a nuclear power station in the middle of London without anyone objecting'; but Sir John Betjeman admired the building from the start, and many of us have since grown to love it, particularly at night, when the superb floodlighting transforms the daytime grey into huge bursts of glorious colour. And what a triumph it has been: with its three separate and widely differing theatres, each capable of handling three plays in repertory, it can keep nine plays simultaneously on the go – and that doesn't begin to take into account the activities that take place during the summer on the riverside forecourt and the terraces.

Why did we need a National Theatre anyway? The simple

answer is because the English dramatic tradition is so immeasurably rich; no other country can hold a candle to it. If the whole of that tradition is to be kept alive, including the best that contemporary playwrights have to offer, some sort of government structure represents the only way of doing so. You can't rely on professional theatre managers, even the most enlightened – and some are very enlightened indeed – to put on plays employing very large casts or demanding expensive stage effects if they have little hope of recouping their outlay. The National, on the other hand, can stage productions of this kind, knowing that it can cover the costs with others that are pulling in the crowds. The only golden rule, of course, is that it must remain completely free of politics; imagine only what a Nazi National Theatre or a Soviet National Theatre would have done with such an opportunity.

The repertoire covers an enormous range. Shakespeare, of course, is always catered for. Indeed, in the Royal Shakespeare Company he has a publicly funded theatre of his own, though this doesn't stop the National from featuring him as well. And even Shakespeare isn't the beginning; we have had classical Greek theatre before now, and plays by several of Shakespeare's contemporaries, including that majestic Spaniard Lope de Vega. After him there's the rich seam of Jacobean tragedy, best represented by Webster's *The Duchess of Malfi*, before we come to those splendid Restoration dramas like Dryden's *All for Love* and – a particular favourite of mine – Otway's *Venice Preserved*, to be followed by a spate of rumbustious comedies like Vanbrugh's *The Relapse, or Virtue in Danger* or Congreve's *The Way of the World*.

The eighteenth century is dominated for me by Richard Brinsley Sheridan, whose *School for Scandal* and *The Critic* are surely among the funniest comedies ever written. After that there seems to me to be rather a long gap, in which the

Irishman Dion Boucicault's *London Assurance* rattles around almost painfully until that astonishing and mutually antipathetic pair Sir William Gilbert and Sir Arthur Sullivan sweep all before them. Then at last we come to the genius of Oscar Wilde, soon alas to be ostracized from polite society, but not before he had given us *Lady Windermere's Fan*, *A Woman of No Importance*, *An Ideal Husband* and *The Importance of Being Earnest* – all of them dazzling, the last a masterpiece.

The years following the First World War saw the appearance of another genius – Noël Coward. Coward, it seemed, could do anything: he could play the piano, sing and dance; he could write any number of wonderful songs, some of them the funniest in the language; and he could write comedies such as *Private Lives*, *Hay Fever* and *Blithe Spirit* – each of them tossed off in under a week – that easily stand comparison with Sheridan and Wilde. His contemporary Terence Rattigan was content simply to write plays, and very good plays they were too – *The Deep Blue Sea*, *The Browning Version*, *The Winslow Boy* – always beautifully constructed, and written with deep understanding and compassion.

But then, suddenly out of a clear sky in 1956, came John Osborne's *Look Back in Anger*. It was everything Coward and Rattigan weren't: aggressive, bitter, ill-mannered, symptomatic of a new and distinctly unpleasant post-war spirit. This was the world of the 'Angry Young Man', and it took England and the world by storm, condemning Coward and Rattigan to a humiliating series of flops. The 'Kitchen Sink' School, with Arnold Wesker and the extraordinary magic of Harold Pinter followed, and a new genius, Tom Stoppard, who carried all before him with *Rosencrantz and Guildenstern are Dead* – to this day, perhaps, my favourite play.

Now the pendulum has swung back again; Coward and Rattigan have returned to fashion and, according to the recently published figures for 2010, more people are flocking to the theatres than ever before. Recent years have seen the growth of many outstanding small ones in London – the Almeida, the Tricycle, the Donmar to name but three – not to mention the many superb provincial centres like the Crucible in Sheffield, the Royal Exchange in Manchester and the Bristol Old Vic. Even if rather too much of the West End seems flooded with blockbuster musicals, I cannot remember a time when a richer or more varied spread has been laid out before the theatre-goer. How much of this is due to the impact of the National? It's impossible to say; but I never go there, or even see it from a distance, without a thrill of pride.

99

The Mouth of the Channel Tunnel
FOLKESTONE, KENT

*I*n the summer of 1993 Sir Christopher Mallaby, the newly appointed British Ambassador to France, travelled to his new posting on foot. The Channel Tunnel was not yet quite completed, and he didn't actually walk *all* the way; after all, it's nearly thirty-two miles long. Part of the time he went in a little buggy along the line, but I have it on his own authority that he did walk *most* of it. And in doing so he made history.

People had been talking about the possibility of such a tunnel for nearly 200 years. The first serious proposal was made as early as 1802 – a remarkably bad idea at a time when Napoleon was already seriously considering the possibility of invasion – but there was, thank heaven, staunch opposition, led by the Duke of Wellington, who wrote at about this time to his friend Lady Wilton: 'We always have been, we are, and I hope that we always shall be, detested in France.' And, let's face it, even among Francophiles the idea did not seem to be universally popular. There were many who argued that England's whole strength lay in its insularity:

> *This precious stone set in the silver sea*
> *That serves it in the office of a wall*
> *Or as a moat defensive to a house*
> *Against the envy of less happier lands . . .*

Why throw it all away? they asked; think how many invasions we have been spared by that narrow strip of water. Nostalgically, they quoted the famous (if apocryphal) headline: 'Heavy Storms in Channel: Continent Isolated'. As for the French, they didn't particularly seem to want a closer connection either; most of them were not remotely interested in England; and anyway, the food was uneatable.

Still, the idea refused to go away. In 1881 experimental tunnels, each just over a mile long, were actually dug from the opposite coasts. Technically, it was a success: the compressed-air boring machines worked perfectly, and the much-feared flooding was so slight that the pumps were switched on for only half a day every fortnight. Within five years the two sides hoped to have a pilot tunnel, seven feet in diameter, from one country to the other. Then, as so often happens in Anglo-French affairs, the friendship cooled. The two governments squabbled mightily over the Suez Canal and their rival colonies in Africa, and called the whole thing off. Nearly a century passed; two world wars didn't help, though it was calculated that if we had had a tunnel in 1914 to supply the trenches and get the wounded home, the first of them might have been shortened by two years. Finally in 1974 it looked as if we were all set at last, but the following January the newly elected Labour government pulled out again, and cries of '*Perfide Albion!*' were clearly audible from across the Channel. Soon after this, it seems that both governments lost interest in the idea of financing a tunnel themselves.

It took, I need hardly say, Margaret Thatcher finally to get things going. In 1981 she and President Mitterrand set up a working group to look into a privately funded project. Interestingly, not all the proposals submitted to this group were for tunnels. One was for a 'Eurobridge': a suspension bridge carrying a roadway in an enclosed tube; another was for a 'Euroroute': a thirteen-mile tunnel between artificial islands approached by bridges. There was also the idea of a 'Channel Expressway', which was to consist of large-diameter road tunnels, with ventilation towers sticking up at intervals out of the water. Most of these proved to be non-starters: their champions ignored the fact that the Channel was not only by far the busiest waterway anywhere in or around Europe, but that it was also subject to appalling weather for at least several months a year, when visibility was often minimal. It was the rail proposal, presented by the Channel Tunnel Group/France-Manche, that was finally selected, and there can be no doubt that it was the right choice. Much disappointment was expressed by motorists that they would not be able to drive through the thing; but this would have raised serious problems of ventilation, and of the ever-present danger of drivers becoming hypnotized over such a distance. The difficulties of dealing with the inevitable accidents 250 feet under water and sixteen miles from the nearest land hardly bear thinking about.

And so – in June 1988 on the French side, in December on the English – the tunnelling dinosaurs swung into action. Typically, the six English ones were simply numbered; the French were called Brigitte, Europa, Catherine, Virginie, Pascaline and Séverine, which somehow made all the difference. On 30 October 1990 the two trains working on the service tunnel – the first to be bored – met in the middle, to the relief of both sides: however meticulous the calculations, it was good to be assured that they had not somehow missed each other. On 6 May 1994, the Queen travelled through the tunnel to Calais on a Eurostar train, stopping – just in time – nose to nose with President Mitterrand who had arrived from Paris. After the opening ceremony there, the two of them rattled back together on the car-carrying Le

Shuttle – one of my favourite pieces of *Franglais* – to a similar celebration (only in English) at Folkestone. On 14 November of that same year Eurostar opened as a regular passenger service and the rest, as they say, is history. There have been several improvements since, the principal ones being the high-speed rail links at both ends, and the transfer of the London terminus from Waterloo – a station of which the French were never particularly fond – to St Pancras, a vast improvement since nobody has ever heard of him.

And so for me – if I may end on a personal note – the wheel has come full circle. Once again I arrive in Paris no longer as I have done for the past half-century, through a grisly and comfortless suburbia, but the way I did on my first visits as a child, emerging from the Gare du Nord in the heart of the city. There is my old friend the Hôtel Grand Terminus du Nord just as it was in 1936, and there next to it is the Grande Brasserie du Nord, still dishing up the same icy piles of *fruits de mer* that I remember from seventy-odd years ago. And the years fall away, and I fall in love with France all over again.

100

The Gherkin
LONDON

*T*he Gherkin – less delicately known as the Crystal Phallus – has in the seven years of its existence been thought to symbolize a number of different things; here it must stand for the City of London, of which, whatever we may think of it architecturally, we have to agree that it constitutes an unforgettable feature, second only to St Paul's Cathedral itself. It is the work of Sir Norman Foster & Partners, and is principally occupied by the Swiss Re Bank. The only pleasantly old-fashioned thing about it is its address: 30 St Mary Axe.

In my lifetime, the Square Mile has changed out of all recognition. I remember it as a child as a vast pincushion of church spires and steeples, all clustering around the great dome of St Paul's, which towered over them all. Then came the Blitz, and devastation; then many years of apparent neglect, with gaping, weed-ridden spaces between the few buildings that had survived; and now, finally, the glittering glass forest that we see today. What has not changed in the City is its *raison d'être*; for the past 300 years it has been a financial, banking and insurance centre – first of Britain, then of Europe, and now of the world.

The heart of this huge throbbing organism is the Bank of England – in fact, of the whole United Kingdom. It dates from 1694 when, as a result of a series of crushing defeats in the Channel by the French, King William III and his advisers decided that the only hope of recovery was to build a powerful navy. As there were no public funds available the bank was established in order to provide them. It raised £1.2 million in twelve days and, figuratively speaking, has never looked back. It moved to its present home in Threadneedle Street (another nice address) in 1734. It has the exclusive right to the issue of banknotes in England and Wales (though Scotland, Northern Ireland and the Isle of Man issue their own), which still bear the signature of its Chief Cashier.

Several of the other leading banks can also trace their histories back to the eighteenth century or earlier: Barclays (no apostrophe) was founded in 1690, though it did not acquire its name for another half-century; Rothschild's, which still belongs to the family and which by 1800 was already one of the richest and most powerful banks in Europe, opened its London branch in 1811, just in time to provide funds to the Duke of Wellington's armies in the Peninsular War. Later it funded Cecil Rhodes in the development of the British South Africa Company, setting up the Rhodes Scholarships which continue to this day. Its headquarters have been at the same address in St Swithin's Lane – though not in the same building – for the past 200 years. The saddest story of all is that of Barings, another family firm founded as early as 1762; it was they, in 1802, who organized the Louisiana Purchase, still today the largest land transaction in history. (The deal also had the effect of largely financing Napoleon, but that couldn't be helped.) In 1845–6 they supplied immense quantities of maize ('Indian Corn') to Ireland as famine relief after the failure of the potato crop, refusing their normal commission. And so they went on, from strength to strength, until 1994. Then disaster struck. They were brought down by one of their staff in

Singapore. By a combination of wild risk-taking and criminal fraud this man lost his employers a total of £827 million, twice their available trading capital. The collapse cost another £100 million. On 26 February 1995, after well over two centuries, Barings was declared insolvent.

In the very shadow of St Paul's in Paternoster Square stands the present London Stock Exchange. It is not, I understand, the largest of its kind in the world – New York and Tokyo pip it to the post – but at the end of 2010 it had a market capitalization of US$3.6 trillion, which sounds an awful lot of money to me. The idea of share trading began with the financing of long voyages – very much the sort of thing that goes on in *The Merchant of Venice*. Two in particular needed vast backing: that of the Muscovy Company, which tried to reach China via the White Sea and the north coast of Russia, and the first major voyage of the East India Company to the Indies in 1688. Seven years later there were some 140 joint-stock companies, in those days centred around two coffee-houses, Garraway's and Jonathan's, which produced a regular publication called, rather charmingly, *The Course of the Exchange and Other Things*. The first real Exchange was built in Threadneedle Street after Jonathan's burned down in 1748, moving to its present home as recently as 2004.

The most important day in its recent history, however, was Monday, 27 October 1986, when, overnight, the Stock Exchange became a different place. This was the day of the so-called 'Big Bang', the deregulation that Margaret Thatcher had made one of the cornerstones of her financial policy. Fixed-commission charges were abolished, the distinction between stockbrokers and stockjobbers came to an end; most important of all was the change to electronic, screen-based trading. The consequences were dramatic: the resultant boom expanded beyond the City and was largely responsible for the appearance of London's second financial centre, Canary Wharf.

The celebrated Lloyd's of London also had its origins, as everyone knows, in a coffee-house; the date was again 1688. (The last quarter of the seventeenth century must have been an exciting time indeed for Londoners.) It began with marine insurance, and shipping is still its primary concern; through the eighteenth and early nineteenth centuries, much of its business came from the insurance of the slave ships, slaves at that time being one of the most important – and most profit-able – commodities on the market. But it has long since branched out into every other field including, some eighty years ago, Marlene Dietrich's legs. The great crisis came in the late eighties and early nineties, when Lloyd's found itself on the brink of catastrophe. Swingeing damages awarded by American courts for APH – asbestos, pollution and health hazard policies – some going back as far as the 1940s, led to enormous claims being made by clients, and many underwriters found themselves ruined. Now, thank God, order has been restored, though the casual passer-by, gazing up at the wild ramifications of Richard Rogers's astonishing building at No. 1 Lime Street, may well find themselves wondering exactly how this could have been achieved.

Epilogue

In writing this book, I have been struck once again by how unlike the English are to any of their neighbours. We are a hybrid people, speaking a hybrid language; perhaps that has something to do with it. The traditional John Bullish sort of Englishman in fact has Celtic, Roman, Anglo-Saxon, Viking and Norman blood running through his veins – and, in all probability, a good many other varieties as well. We are, in short, a pretty unique mixture; and the immense good fortune we have in inhabiting an island has, in a sense, forced the mixture to set and sealed it in.

We are lucky in other ways too. Our land is for the most part amazingly fertile; our climate is benign, seldom subjecting us to those extremes suffered by some of our less fortunate brethren on the Continent; and our temperament is, on the whole, equable. We also have a remarkable talent for self-government, having managed to create for ourselves a workable constitutional monarchy which – admittedly with the occasional hiccup – has endured for the past eight centuries. We have developed a parliamentary system unlike, and infinitely superior to, any other. We have known brief periods of persecution, but we have avoided being torn apart by religious wars like those which have ravaged much of northern Europe.

We are surprisingly artistic. We do not – or did not – paint as well as the Italians, nor did we compose music as well as the Germans and Austrians; but our poets, playwrights and novelists can hold their own with those of any race on earth, as could our architects. No nation in the world possesses such a variety of superb country houses, nor so many thousands of exquisite medieval parish churches, nor any cathedrals of the quality of Durham, Lincoln or Canterbury.

It seems, too, that we are of a scientific bent. Certainly it was with the Age of Enlightenment that we really came into our own. The fact that Sir Isaac Newton was an Englishman got us off to a splendid start; the Royal Observatory consolidated it; Harrison's chronometers made possible the establishment of longitude; it was not long before English nautical charts were being used all over Europe. The decision to fix the Prime Meridian at Greenwich became a matter of course. And this new interest in physics and the natural sciences led inevitably to the Industrial Revolution. James Watt, George Stephenson and their colleagues provided the scientific knowhow; Abraham Darby, Richard Arkwright and their friends built the mills and factories. The climax came with the Great Exhibition of 1851, when millions flocked to Joseph Paxton's dazzling Crystal Palace to admire, gathered together for the first time, the greatest manufactures of which the world – but particularly England – was capable.

A lot has happened since 1851. We have gained and lost an Empire, have survived the two most fearsome wars in history, have wedded ourselves to the European Union and have at last physically linked our island to the Continent. One of the consequences of Empire has been immigration from our former colonies and from within Europe: it would be a brave man who would prophesy what England will be like in ten years, let alone fifty. Our past, on the other hand, is immutable;

it can never be taken away. And it is of our past, in its modest and distinctly quirky way, that this book is a celebration.

Some fifteen years ago, while writing a book about Shakespeare's history plays, I asked myself a question. If a would-be student of the fourteenth and fifteenth centuries had no other authority but the plays to go on, how accurate a picture would he receive? I decided that despite all the liberties that Shakespeare took with chronology – he was, after all, first and foremost a dramatist, whose principal purpose was to produce as good a play as he could – he was nearly always right where and when it really mattered. That student might consequently draw a number of wrong conclusions; but the overall picture – including that of the reign of Richard III – that he carried away with him would not, in its essentials, be very far wrong.

I am not, heaven knows, comparing myself with Shakespeare. He was writing some of the greatest plays ever written: I have set my sights no higher than a modest history book.

Kings and Queens of England

✤ HOUSE OF MERCIA

757–796   Offa

✤ HOUSE OF WESSEX

802–839	Egbert
839–856	Aethelwulf
856–860	Aethelbald
860–866	Aethelbert
866–871	Aethelred I
871–899	Alfred the Great
899–925	Edward the Elder
925–940	Athelstan
940–946	Edmund
946–955	Edred
955–959	Edwy
959–975	Edgar
975–978	Edward the Martyr
978–1016	Ethelred II the Unready
1016	Edmund Ironside

✤ House of Denmark

1016–1035	Cnut (Canute)
1035–1040	Harold I Harefoot
1040–1042	Harthacanut

✤ House of Wessex

1042–1066	Edward the Confessor
1066	Harold II

✤ House of Normandy

1066–1087	William I
1087–1100	William II
1100–1135	Henry I

✤ House of Blois

1135–1154	Stephen

✤ House of Angevin

1154–1189	Henry II
1189–1199	Richard I
1199–1216	John

✤ House of Plantagenet

1216–1272	Henry III
1272–1307	Edward I
1307–1327	Edward II
1327–1377	Edward III
1377–1399	Richard II

✤ House of Lancaster

1399–1413	Henry IV
1413–1422	Henry V
1422–1461	Henry V

✤ House of York

1461–1483	Edward IV
1483	Edward V
1483–1485	Richard III

✤ House of Tudor

1485–1509	Henry VII
1509–1547	Henry VIII
1547–1553	Edward VI
1553–1558	Mary I
1558–1603	Elizabeth I

✤ House of Stuart

1603–1625	James I (King of Scotland as James VI 1567–1625)
1625–1649	Charles I

✤ Commonwealth

1649–1653	Commonwealth
1653–1658	Oliver Cromwell (Lord Protector)
1658–1659	Richard Cromwell (Lord Protector)

✤ House of Stuart

1660–1685	Charles II
1685–1688	James II

✤ House of Orange

1689–1694	William III of Orange and Mary II (jointly)
1694–1702	William III (alone)

✤ House of Stuart

1702–1714	Anne

✤ House of Hanover

1714–1727	George I
1727–1760	George II
1760–1820	George III (Elector, 1760–1815, and King, 1815–20, of Hanover)
1820–1830	George IV
1830–1837	William IV (King of Hanover 1830–7)
1837–1901	Victoria (Empress of India 1876–1901)

✤ House of Saxe-Coburg-Gotha

1901–1910	Edward VII

✤ House of Windsor

1910–1936	George V
1936	Edward VIII
1936–1952	George VI
1952–	Elizabeth II (Queen of Great Britain and Northern Ireland, Head of the Commonwealth of Nations)

Acknowledgements

I am more than grateful to Kate Parkin of John Murray and to my wife Mollie, who have put every bit as much work into this book as I have myself.

Illustration Credits

BAL: Bridgeman Art Library London
NTPL: National Trust Picture Library

Section 1, pages 1–8
© English Heritage Photo Library/James Davies: 1. © NTPL/Howard Phillips: 2 above. © NTPL/Ian Shaw: 2 below. © The Trustees of the British Museum: 3. © The British Library Board (Cott.Nero D.IV.f95): 4. © D. Gascoyne/Getty Images: 5 above. © The Photo Library Wales/Alamy: 5 below. © Ancient Art & Architecture Collection/Alamy: 6 above. © Julia Hedgecoe: 6 below. © Holmes Garden Photos/Alamy: 7 above. © Robert Harding World Imagery/Getty Images: 7 below. © NTPL/Andrew Butler: 8 above. © The British Library Board (Cott.Nero.II. f.177)/BAL: 8 below.

Section 2, pages 9–16
© Michael Jenner/Alamy: 9. © The British Library Board (Add.42130.f.172r): 10 above. © NTPL/Robert Morris: 10 below. © NTPL/Andrew Butler: 11 above. © The British Library Board (Roy.18E.I.f.175): 11 below. Reproduced by permission of the Provost and Fellows of Eton College: 12 above. © NTPL/David Sellman: 12 below. © The British Library Board (Roy.16F.II.f.73): 13 above. © NTPL/John Blake: 13 below. © Belvoir Castle, Leicestershire/BAL: 14. © NTPL/Andrew Butler: 15 above. Private Collection/BAL: 15 right. © Victoria & Albert Museum London/BAL: 15 below left. © National Gallery of Ireland, Dublin/BAL: 16 above. © Woburn Abbey, Bedfordshire/BAL: 16 below.

Section 3, pages 17–24
© NTPL/James Kerr: 17 above. © The British Library Board (G.11429.40): 17 below. Private Collection/BAL: 18 above. © William Robinson Derbyshire/Alamy: 18 below.

Index